DATE DUE

LANGUAGE, RACE, AND SOCIAL CLASS
IN
HOWELLS'S AMERICA

LANGUAGE, RACE, AND SOCIAL CLASS
IN
HOWELLS'S AMERICA

Elsa Nettels

THE UNIVERSITY PRESS OF KENTUCKY

Scholarly publisher for the Commonwealth
serving Bellarmine College, Berea College, Centre
College of Kentucky, Eastern Kentucky University,
The Filson Club, Georgetown College, Kentucky
Historical Society, Kentucky State University,
Morehead State University, Murray State University,
Northern Kentucky University, Transylvania University,
University of Kentucky, University of Louisville,
and Western Kentucky University.

Editorial and Sales Offices: Lexington, Kentucky 40506-0024

Library of Congress Cataloging-in-Publication Data

Nettels, Elsa.
    Language, race, and social class in Howells's
America

    Bibliography: p.
    Includes index.
    1. Howells, William Dean, 1837-1920—Knowledge—
Language and languages.   2. Howells, William Dean,
1837-1920—Language.   3. Howells, William Dean, 1837-
1920—Characters.   4. English language—United States—
19th century.   5. American fiction—19th century—
History and criticism.   6. Dialect literature,
American—History and criticism.   7. Race awareness
in literature.   8. Language and languages in
literature.   9. Characters and characteristics in
literature.   10. Sociolinguistics—United States.
I. Title.
PS2037.L33N4   1988   818'.409   87-18895
ISBN 0-8131-1629-5

To my Mother

Contents

Preface

This study centers on William Dean Howells as a writer about language. To read his fiction, criticism, and letters is to realize that no other American novelist before or since has written so fully about so many aspects of language; no other has commented so often on the habits of speech of characters or placed such importance on speech as an index of their culture and social class. A study of his novels substantiates the statement of William M. Gibson in his *William D. Howells* (Minneapolis, 1967): "Mark Twain created a revolution in the language of fiction; Howells was the architect of the revolution" (p. 40).

The first three chapters in this study present the ideas of Howells and his contemporaries about a number of subjects important to Howells the novelist and critic: e.g., the nature of language, the importance of "correct English" and the standards by which it is defined, the implications of slang, euphemism, and exaggeration. The first chapter surveys prevailing ideas about language in the post–Civil War period to provide background for Howells's views, set forth in Chapter 2. The third chapter deals with one of the central issues of the period, the relation of British and American English. Howells's emphasis on the uniqueness of American conditions and the integrity of American English forms the ground of his philosophy of realism, set forth in Chapter 4.

The second part of the study examines the implications in fiction of one aspect of Howells's realism: his defense of dialect and the vernacular as a means of rooting characters in their environment and conveying the reality of their conditions. Chapters 5 and 6 examine the effects of dialect by which characters of certain races and nationalities are identified in the fiction of Howells and his contemporaries. Chapter 7, 8, 9, and 10 analyze the connections between speech, social class, and moral character in Howells's novels from *Their Wedding Journey* (1872) to *The Leatherwood God* (1916).

In this book I have used the words *dialect* and *vernacular* as Howells used them: *dialect* to denote speech identified with a particular region or race; *vernacular* to denote speech that departs from standard English in grammar and idiom, usually speech of characters of rural origins. My purpose is not to determine the accuracy of Howells's representation of different habits of speech but to analyze the effects of dialect and the vernacular in his fiction and to identify the attitudes implicit in his rendering of the speech of his characters.

I am grateful to the College of William and Mary and its Faculty Research Committee for the award of a summer grant and a semester's research leave during 1982-83. My work on this study was also substantially aided by a year's Fellowship for College Teachers, awarded by the National Endowment for the Humanities, for 1984.

For permission to quote from unpublished materials, I am grateful to William White Howells, for the heirs of the Howells estate, for letters, diaries, and other manuscripts of Howells; to the Houghton Library, Harvard University, for letters and other manuscripts of Higginson, Howells, Henry James, William James, and Lowell; and to the following holders of unpublished letters of Howells: the American Antiquarian Society; Olin Library, Cornell University; Ripley Hitchcock Papers, Rare Book and Manuscript Library, Columbia University; and the William Dean Howells Collection (#5651), Manuscripts Department, University of Virginia Library. Republication requires these permissions.

The following copyright holders have granted permission to reprint material originally published in their journals: *New England Quarterly* for parts of "William Dean Howells and the

American Language," *New England Quarterly* 53, no. 3 (1980): 308-28; and the Department of English, the University of Texas at Arlington, for parts of "One and Many: Howells's Treatment of Race," *American Literary Realism* 18, nos. 1 and 2 (1986): 72-91.

In preparing this study I have been aided by colleagues, former students, and friends: Lynn Z. Bloom, Catherine Clark, Margaret W. Freeman, Irene Goldman, Elizabeth Jacoby, Donald C. Johnson, Terry Meyers, Erika Monson, Elsie P. Nettels, and Robert J. Scholnick. I thank them all.

Introduction

In a letter for the celebration of William Dean Howells's seventy-fifth birthday, Henry James praised his friend for revealing more finely than any other novelist the nature of American life: "Stroke by stroke and book by book your work was to become, for this exquisite notation of our whole democratic light and shade and give and take, in the highest degree *documentary*; so that none other, through all your fine long season, could approach it in value and amplitude."[1]

Many others—contemporaries of Howells and later critics—have granted Howells the same preeminence. As early as 1879, Thomas Wentworth Higginson, never an uncritical reader of Howells, declared the novelist's importance: "To trace American 'society' in its formative process you must go to Howells; he alone shows you the essential forces in action." English as well as American contemporaries acclaimed Howells the foremost analyst of American society. A writer in the *Saturday Review* advised readers: "Any one who wishes to gain an insight into the conditions of life in America, and to peer into its social complexities, cannot do better than to give his days and nights to the study of Mr. Howells's stories in general and of *The Rise of Silas Lapham* in particular." According to James Fullarton Muirhead, "Novels like 'Silas Lapham' and 'A Modern Instance' will give a clearer idea of American character and tendencies than any other contemporary works of fiction."[2]

At a meeting of the American Academy in honor of Howells

in 1922, two years after his death, the novelist Robert Grant paid tribute to Howells as "the chronicler incarnate of our manners and customs, of our intimate thoughts and involuntary class reactions," the one American writer whose work must be read by all "who would know everyday Americans as they really were, set down with sympathy but without extenuation." More succinctly, F.O. Matthiessen made the same claim for Howells: "Social historians will discover nowhere else such a complete picture of everyday American existence in the last half of the nineteenth century."[3]

No aspect of "everyday American existence" was of more enduring interest to Howells than the speech of his countrymen; no subject fascinated him more than the nature of language. All his life he listened to people talking and recorded what they said—in drawing rooms, offices, churches, courtrooms, boarding houses, ships, trains, and hotels. For more than fifty years he filled his letters and notebooks with remembered fragments of conversation, oddities of idiom and pronunciation, and words that revealed the speaker's culture. In his travel diaries one meets people of the Ohio River country remembered for their "rhythmical sweetness of speech," two Englishmen praying in a Cambridge chapel "with a rapt indifference to their h's," gondoliers with "windy voices," Capriates whose accent "has something of German harshness and heaviness," a boy guide in Alameda speaking a "strange dialect shorn of all final sibilants," a young Englishman from Sweden "who remakes his *a*'s, *i*'s," Henry Irving playing Romeo in a voice "flat, metallic, leaden, which he lifts and lets fall." In a letter to his wife, he described a sexton in Marion, Kansas, who rang the church bells before Howells's lecture "so's to kind of rouse folks up," and a twenty-year-old Kansas farmer who addressed the sixty-year-old Howells as "my friend" and referred to hilly farm land as "them *upright* farms." When T.S. Perry said that Howells "describes what he sees, and his eyes are exceedingly sharp," he could also have said that Howells recorded what he heard, and his ear was exceedingly keen. Howells himself, surprised by how much he remembered of his childhood when he began to write *A Boy's Town*, wondered whether "my strongest faculty, after all, may have been an art of seeing and hearing everything."[4]

In novel after novel Howells showed how characters reveal themselves and their social conditions by their speech. "The most vigilant of writers" as one reader called him, he recorded in his fiction the habits of speech of New England provincials, upper-class Bostonians, middle-class westerners, transplanted southerners, and German and Irish immigrants. Convinced that "the smallest particular is of value," he made the single word the index of a character's culture; characters identified themselves not only by their habitats but by whether they "lived" or "resided" there. Howells's novels are not only "mines of American idiom," as H.L. Mencken observed; they are filled with the narrator's observations about language, his descriptions of voices and pronunciations, and judgments made by characters about each other on the basis of their speech.[5]

In his criticism as well as his fiction, Howells testified to his absorbing interest in the American language. More than twenty of his essays and reviews are devoted to the differences between American and British English, points of grammar, spelling reform, the pronunciation of the letter *r* in the United States, and the values of dialect in literature. His first essays on American life, written weekly for the *Nation* from November 2, 1865, through April 26, 1866, include discussions of euphemisms, the word *Negro*, American fondness for titles, the dangers of overstatement, and sensational journalism. His first "Editor's Study" in *Harper's Magazine* (January 1886), contains an eloquent tribute to the vitality of American English. He was not a trained linguist, but his reviews and essays show him familiar with the important works on language and with basic linguistic principles.

Howells was also a loyal supporter of the movement for spelling reform; he noted in a letter to Higginson that he had gone to the Simplified Spelling Convention in New York "for three successive years." He thought English spelling "chaotic," "an offense to reason," and "a witless impertinence," and he now and then wrote phonetic forms in letters. "I so detest al idl and unecesary leters in riting," he wrote to E.C. Stedman, "that I wud willingly banish them from print, and I think that by going over the various English spellings of the past, one cud realy arive at something lik a sens of uniformity strugling with the pedantry of the lexicografer, and cud construct a tru orthografy from the authors of the midle period."[6]

Although he detested dictionary spelling, he delighted in dictionaries. He found in the Fifth Edition of Bartlett's *Familiar Quotations* (1868) "much of the strange fascination belonging to unabridged dictionaries, which, we maintain, are more agreeable reading than most romances and poems constructed from them." He thanked Frederick Duneka of Harper's for the gift of a dictionary: "I never had a Valentine more to my mind. I may now indulge my passion for strange words almost riotously." The desire to master foreign languages, which drove him in his adolescence to teach himself German, Spanish, French, and Latin, remained with him all his life. On his travels he bought grammars of different tongues and compared the dialects of different regions. His diaries, essays, novels, and letters show that he was, as Oscar Firkins has said, "astonishingly sensitive to languages, to pronunciations, to intonations, to every property and aspect of human speech." Among the tributes paid to Howells after his death was that of Robert Frost, who wrote to Hamlin Garland on February 4, 1921, to acknowledge his "great debt" to Howells: "I learned from him a long time ago that the loveliest theme of poetry was the voices of people. No one ever had a more observing ear or clearer imagination for the tones of those voices. No one ever brought them more freshly to book. He recorded them equally with actions, indeed as if they were actions (and I think they are)."[7]

In his preface to the First Part of *Democracy in America*, Alexis de Tocqueville identified "equality of conditions" in the United States as "the fundamental fact from which all others seem to be derived and the central point at which all my observations constantly terminated." He analyzed the effect of equal conditions upon language by comparing the language of a democracy like the United States with that of an aristocracy, where the separation of people in castes or classes produces not a common tongue but "a language of the poor and a language of the rich—a language of the citizen and a language of the nobility—a learned language and a vulgar one." The effect of equal conditions, he observed, is to erase distinctions, to produce a common store of words upon which everyone draws. When people are no longer bound by rank or class barriers, words likewise lose their power to fix the social status of the speaker. "Persons springing from different ranks of society carry the terms and expressions they are accustomed to use with them, into whatever circumstances they may pass; thus the origin of words is lost like the origin of individuals, and there is as much confusion in language as there is in society."[8]

Measured by Tocqueville's definition, the language of the Americans that Howells portrayed is closer to the democratic pole than to the aristocratic. But their language is not uniform, as their conditions are not equal. A lawyer educated at Harvard, a country squire, farmers in an isolated village, Irish servants, boarding house keepers, and Boston Brahmins do not all speak alike; some use words and expressions that others never use. Those who care about origins and who fear confusion seek to preserve distinctions; others never perceive the existence of a standard or despair of achieving it.

In rendering the different habits of speech of his characters, Howells dramatized the divisive effects of language, the power of speech to reinforce the barriers that divide the social classes, the races, and the sexes. Indeed, in fiction, if not in life, speech, more powerfully than anything else, creates the reader's impression of a character's culture and distinguishes him or her from persons of a different culture. To study the language of Howells's characters is thus to see the contradiction at the heart of a society that proclaimed itself democratic; it is also to see the contradiction at the heart of Howells's conception of the American realist, whose office was to unite people in recognition of their common humanity, but also faithfully to reveal a society in which language elevates some people above others and so belies the ideal of equality.

When Howells's views on language are juxtaposed with those of his contemporaries, one sees which of the prevailing assumptions he embraced and which he rejected. How he defined "good English," what he said about slang, euphemisms, American and British English, and dialect in literature, help to place him in relation to the major and minor writers of his age—to the genteel essayists, to the journalists, to the humorists, to the professors of English in the universities, and to his greatest contemporaries—Henry James, Walt Whitman, and Mark Twain. By the way he distinguished in his fiction between different speakers—blacks and whites, native-born Americans and immigrants, the crude and the well-bred, the provincial and the cosmopolitan, the unlettered and the well-educated—Howells revealed the divided sympathies within his own mind and the divisions within the American world it was his life's work to portray.

Chapter One

Language in
Howells's America

In his lifelong fascination with language, Howells was a man of his age. With his contemporaries in America and Europe he followed the developments in the new science of philology, which evolved in the early nineteenth century. He wrote about language during the years when linguistic study in America issued in publications such as the successive editions of Webster's *American Dictionary* and Bartlett's *Dictionary of Americanisms,* and in the founding of organizations—the American Philological Association (1869), the Modern Language Association (1883), and the American Dialect Society (1890). Reflected in these endeavors was the widespread interest of American readers in the ways the transformations wrought by westward expansion, immigration, industrial growth, and social change were mirrored in their language.

Americans' interest in language can most easily be studied in the national magazines, those creators and reflectors of taste and opinion acknowledged by one observer to be "the recognized gateway to the literary public."[1] During the decades of Howells's long career, beginning before the Civil War and ending some seventy years later with his death in 1920, the leading magazines, such as the *Atlantic, Harper's, Scribner's,* the *Century,* and the *North American Review,* in which most of Howells's work first appeared, published scores of articles on language. These magazines regularly reviewed dictionaries,

rhetorics, grammars, histories of the language, and other philological studies by the foremost American and European
scholars. The most learned essays appeared in the *North American Review*. In one decade, the 1870s, that journal published
studies by William Wetmore Story on "The Origin of the Italian Language" and by Karl Hillebrand on Herder's theory of
language, as well as a twenty-page criticism by Fitzedward
Hall of T.L.K. Oliphant's *The Sources of Standard English*.
Particularly controversial was one of three essays by William
Dwight Whitney of Yale, "Darwinism and Language" (1874), a
refutation of the theories of the Oxford linguist Max Müller,
who thereupon savagely attacked Whitney in his book of essays
Chips from a German Workshop (1876), which the *North American Review* in turn denounced for its misrepresentation of
Whitney's views. Controversies over theories of language and
points of usage generated as much heat as any subject did.

During the postwar years, the more popular magazines—
Harper's, Lippincott's, Scribner's, and *Appleton's*—published articles for the general reader on a wide range of subjects including Noah Webster, Americanisms, uses of dialect in literature,
the teaching of English in the schools, errors in dictionaries,
Pidgin English, puns, place names, and studies of the English
language in Germany. *Harper's Magazine* later engaged three
leading American scholars, Thomas R. Lounsbury of Yale,
Brander Matthews of Columbia, and George L. Kittredge of
Harvard, to write series of articles supporting or refuting
current theories and opinions about usage, spelling reform,
and British and American English. The confidence of *Harper's*
in the appeal of scholarly treatment of these subjects is indicated by publication of Lounsbury's series of twenty-two articles, which appeared every few months from July 1903
through June 1909. Most controversial of the widely read writers on language was Richard Grant White, a critic of music and
art as well as literature, whose twenty-one papers, later published as *Words and Their Uses*, appeared in the *Galaxy* from
February 1867 through June 1869. White's strictures and pro-
nouncements provoked an extended attack by Fitzedward Hall

in the *Nation* as well as agreement and objection by less heated critics. Defending himself in the pages of the *Galaxy* and the *Atlantic*, White roused his critics to further response which in turn moved him on one occasion (after receiving thirteen letters on his discussion of *Whiskers*) to marvel at "the interest taken by people generally...in discussion about words."[2]

The *Atlantic* under Howells's editorship (1871-81) published its share of articles, notices, and notes about language. Among the books Howells chose to be reviewed were philological studies by Whitney, Lounsbury, Oliphant, and Maetzner and the latest edition of Webster's dictionary. Howells himself reviewed several works including Richard Grant White's *Words and Their Uses*, to be valued, Howells believed, not as an instrument of reform, but as "the best and most intelligent comment upon the English of our times." Howells's knowledge of the principles of modern philology prompted his criticism of John Weisse's history of the English language for being "thoroughly unscientific" in its failure to examine the syntax of the language, "which is the sure way to learn the truth about it." Likewise, he dismissed George Crabbe's dictionary of synonyms as a disgrace to modern scholarship: "The etymological information is a relic of the old-fashioned ignorance which should be as much forgotten nowadays as the navigation of triremes." Howells published eight essays on "Americanisms" by White, from April 1878 through May 1879. Then, undeterred by a testy letter from James Russell Lowell, who confessed himself "tired to death of Grant White's laborious demonstrations that we have a right to our mother tongue," Howells in the next year published four more essays by White on American and British English.[3]

In January 1877, Howells began a new department in the *Atlantic*, the Contributor's Club, to which readers sent observations and questions about current topics. No topic was more popular than language. Contributors wrote to identify the origin of place names, to protest "the deplorable condition of the hyphen," to advocate spelling reform, to attack and defend the accenting of *Parnell* on the last syllable, to object to Henry

James's calling a cottage in the Boston suburbs a *chalet*, to deplore the use of *gents* and the misuse of *likely* and *then*. Several readers stressed the need of a pronoun of common gender. One called for a new word; a second proposed a conflation: *hesh, hizer, himer*; a third suggested that *they* and *them* be made both singular and plural, like *you*.[4]

The range of subjects indicates the diversity of interests. Writers in the *North American Review* addressed readers who wished to know something about current developments in the study of philology. Writers of articles for the general reader stressed the knowledge of history and culture to be gained from the study of grammars and dictionaries from which, according to John Fiske, "a trustworthy picture of the long-forgotten past may be reconstructed."[5] Readers of the *Galaxy* who liked word games and word puzzles could read George Wakeman's articles on acrostics, palindromes, macaronics, puns, conundrums, and verbal anomalies. The importance of language as an instrument of thought was stressed by White, Price Collier, and others, who in warning of the power of words to distort or conceal the truth anticipated by decades George Orwell's attack on insincerity in "Politics and the English Language."

Widespread among Americans was concern with the implications of language in social intercourse. Repeatedly, writers told readers that it was not enough to make themselves clear; to appear well bred they must speak correctly, enunciate clearly, and avoid vulgarisms. "Ignorance of elementary rules stamps a man as illiterate," Adam S. Hill of Harvard instructed his readers in *Harper's*: "illiteracy seriously injures the influence even of a powerful writer with educated men, and impairs it with the uneducated." "Who is not ambitious to make a good impression?" asked a second writer in *Harper's*. "No one thing...goes further in making one appear to advantage than does a correct, clean-cut pronunciation." "It is undoubtedly true," said Thomas Wentworth Higginson, "that we classify a new-comer, without delay, by his language." Some fifty years earlier, James Fenimore Cooper had defined the standard: "A just, clear and simple expression of our ideas is a necessary accomplishment for all who aspire to be classed with gentle-men and ladies."[6]

Because Americans were not bound by birth to a particular social class and its usages, they enjoyed the prospect of climb-ing the social ladder by acquiring certain tastes and manners, above all those habits of speech widely regarded as "the surest test of a gentleman." As Dennis Baron has observed, pious maxims in the grammars of the eighteenth and nineteenth centuries had converted correct usage into a moral duty. In post–Civil War America, the emphasis was on language as a means of social advancement and a test of social fitness. Al-though, as scholars noted, Americans resisted authority, in-cluding "pedagogical restraints,"[7] that would curb their freedom, and although some Americans indulged in slovenly speech to appear tough and invincible, those who sought to better their position in society, to be persons of "the highest cultivation," studied to pass the linguistic tests. They read books of etiquette that typically contained chapters on "Proper Speech" and "The Art of Conversation." They consulted dic-tionaries and manuals of usage, which Howells compared to books of etiquette, observing that all such works were rarely seen in the homes of Englishmen, who were "contented in the station to which God is pleased to call them" and know by instinct what the social occasion required. "We poor republi-cans," on the other hand, must seek help in the guides to proper speech and behavior. So vital was proper speech to polite behavior that writers made analogies between the rules of etiquette and the rules of grammar. According to one guide, the "formalities of refined society" which "prevent too great famil-iarity" are as necessary as the "hyphen-marks of grammar, which unite without confusing."[8]

The value Americans placed on such instruction is indicated in a number of ways in *Harper's Magazine,* which from its first issue in 1850 aimed to stimulate and satisfy the desire of its readers for standards of correct usage. Mindful that the pur-pose of the magazine was to instruct as well as to entertain, the reviewers of grammars, rhetorics, and dictionaries com-mended those works that helped students acquire "a correct knowledge of English," instructed them in "the canons of good taste," and promoted in their writing "accuracy of thought" and "correctness of diction."[9]

Noting the absence in America of a court or an academy to establish a standard of correct usage, the editors of *Harper's* stressed the importance of teachers, ministers, and the press in shaping the language of Americans. Newspapers, perhaps the most potent force in "fixing the vocabulary of the people," should be models of simplicity, precision, and clarity, not purveyors of extravagance, inaccuracy, and vulgarity. Ministers, the only models of diction and pronunciation that many of their parishioners had, should abjure "artificial mannerisms" and "stereotyped godly drawl" and "take a lead in settling the question now so important to the whole nation: what language is to be spoken and written in America?" Attainment of this ideal—"the inauguration and reign of a pure national speech"— depended above all upon instruction in the schools and universities, for "our popular education is our national academy."[10] Writers in *Harper's* debated the value of knowledge of Greek and Latin to the student learning to write English, emphasized the importance of English literature and the history of the English language in the teaching of composition, questioned whether teaching grammar in the schools did more harm than good, deplored the inability of college students to write well, and proposed ways of reorganizing instruction in languages in the high schools and colleges.

Writers in the magazines proposed various signs by which the cultivated speaker could be identified. To Henry James, the enunciation of words like *due, suit,* and *new* was particularly important. An English writer, Alice Meynall, informed *Harper's* readers of the "educated pronunciation" of *girl, were,* and *Lewis.* A writer in *Scribner's Monthly* offered "I don't know *as*" and "I walked *some*" as "our nearest approach to the English *h*, as marking the line where culture is clearly deficient." Higginson acknowledged that "inelegances" such as "cute," "don't know as," and "a great ways" do not classify the speakers of them as immoral or stupid; "they simply classify such persons

as having reached a certain grade of cultivation, and no further."[11]

For Richard Grant White, a "test of high culture" was the
pronunciation of *a* as in *last* and *father*. The proper use of
certain words and idioms was his chief concern in his *Galaxy*
articles on "Words and Their Uses" (1867-69), which he was
moved to write, he said, after many correspondents had
sought his opinion on disputed points of usage. Proposing to
set forth the "right use" of commonly misused words, he cited
scores of words perverted from their proper use, including
transpire, allude, and *decimate,* about which the writers of
handbooks would be instructing students a hundred years
later. He deplored "hideous hybrids" such as *equestrienne* and
cablegram (an "utterly superfluous monster") and fought more
losing battles against *militate, jeopardize, resurrect, necessitate,*
and other "not words" which offended him, as *finalize* and
prioritize would offend later generations.[12]

White's work was continued two years later, in *Godey's
Lady's Book,* in the ten-part series "Hints on Language," in-
forming readers of errors and vices which "should not be
allowed to corrupt the language." Observing that the "fusion of
classes" in America increases the importance of correct English, *Godey's* writers instructed readers in the proper use of
aggravate, demean, expect, like and *as, lie* and *lay,* and *fully
better,* explained why "promise faithfully" was illogical, and
warned against "Who did you meet?" and other constructions
condemned by "the great body of grammarians."[13]

Those who agreed that good usage was important differed
over the propriety of certain words and constructions. *En-
thused, gents,* and *pants* were generally condemned, as were
inventions such as *priorly, parallic, forlornity,* and *unitize* that
did not survive. *Harper's* denounced *to champion* and *to voice*
("marauders who are always prowling about the newspaper").
Reliable was attacked by White but defended by *Godey's,* which
also defended the stigmatized *talented* and *to progress.* Adam S.
Hill objected to *mentality, burglarize,* and *faddish* as well as to
the short-lived coinages *flirtees, lackness,* and *grotesqued.*

Brander Matthews believed that need would eventually sanction *reliable*, but questioned the fate of *photo* and *phone*.[14]

The battles over *is being done* and *had better* were fought in the pages of the magazines. In the *Galaxy*, White denounced *is being* as an "incongruous and ridiculous form of speech," "the monstrous product of the pedantry of half-knowledge." The *North American Review* seconded White, but Fitzedward Hall defended *is being* in *Scribner's Monthly*, where he accused White, Francis Marsh, Archbishop Whately, and other opponents of *is being* of "sheer prejudice" and "tremulous dread" of change. *Godey's* advised readers to say *would better* rather than *had better*, but Howells rejected *would better* as a priggish affectation, and Lounsbury gave most of one article in *Harper's* to a defense of *had better*, declaring *would better* "so distinctly repugnant to our idiom [as to] provoke a cry of pain from him who has been nurtured upon the great classics of our literature."[15]

Disputes over grammar and usage raised the question of authority: Who should determine what is good usage and provide the standard? Who should control the development of the language, if indeed it could or should be controlled? To define what was correct was to invoke the sanction of authority. For the majority of Americans, the authorities were undoubtedly their school grammars and "the dictionary." As Dennis Baron has shown, the grammarians, such as Lindley Murray, Edward S. Gould, W.C. Fowler, Samuel S. Greene, and Samuel Kirkham, whose texts were studied by thousands of American children in the nineteenth century, regarded themselves as lawgivers authorized to prescribe and proscribe, to set forth the rules which produced good English. In Greene's words, "English Grammar...teaches us to speak and write [the language] correctly." Writers quoted in grammar texts as exemplars of the best English were those like Macaulay, regarded as scrupulous observers of the rules of grammar and rhetoric.[16]

An index of the power of the grammarians' authority is the vehemence with which their position was attacked by the leading writers and scholars of literature and language. In the opinion of Joel Chandler Harris, "The worst English is written by those who call themselves grammarians. An article or a book may be grammatically perfect and at the same time be written in vile English." Repeatedly in their essays in *Harper's*, Matthews and Lounsbury identified as the greatest enemies to good English the pedants and purists, half-educated authors of "little manuals" which impose artificial rules and "pretend to regulate our use of our own language," "often in ignorance of what good usage is." Slaves, not masters of the language, grammarians "sacrifice sense to any method of expression which they fancy to be consistent with grammar"; they "reject with their ignorant formalism" the "high-honored idioms of our tongue."[17]

Rejecting the grammarians as the arbiters of language, Lounsbury identified "the whole body of the cultivated users of speech" as the final authority. "The standard of speech is...the usage of the cultivated. Such men are the absolute dictators of language. They are the lawgivers whose edicts it is the duty of the grammarian to record." For Lounsbury, the supreme law-givers are the great writers, who may occasionally break the grammarian's rules (use *lay* for *lie,* for instance) but who do not thereby negate "the right to rule which inheres in the collective body of great authors."[18]

In his attack upon pedants and "half-educated censors," Matthews goes beyond Lounsbury, placing authority not in the example of great writers and cultivated speakers alone, but in the usage of the people as a whole, who are "better judges of their own needs than any specialist can be." Whereas Louns-bury would reject such forms as *some better* and *illy* if shunned by "all authors of excellence," although "thousands of a lower class" might use them, Matthews takes a "what will be will be" attitude and is prepared to accept whatever "the mass of the people," guided by "sturdy common sense" in preferring the "least roundabout and the most direct," may dictate—whether it be the abandoning of the subjunctive or the use of *don't* for *doesn't,* "which is certain to sustain itself in the future, because it calls for less effort." Matthews agrees with Lounsbury that it is not the province of the grammarian to prescribe rules, and both writers seek occasions to defend what the grammarians condemn. Matthews supports the masses who say *come and see*, split their infinitives, and use the comparative and superlative of *unique*. Lounsbury invokes the authority of past writers for splitting the infinitive and using *none* as the subject of a plural verb, *whose* in reference to an object, *scarce* as an adverb, and *have got* (condemned by White as redundant).[19]

Those who opposed the rule of the grammarians likewise rejected the dictionaries as final authorities. Lounsbury argued that every dictionary reflects the prejudices of its compilers and is "never a final authority." C.W. Ernst in *Lippincott's Magazine* cited numerous errors, particularly definitions of diplomatic terms, perpetrated by two centuries of dictionaries. White dismissed dictionaries as "mere drag-nets of language...of little or no authority except to the ignorant."[20]

Like Lounsbury and Matthews, White rejected the authority claimed by grammarians. Arguing that "formal grammar" is a "fiction" in English, which is an "almost grammarless language," White insisted that most rules in the guides and manuals are superfluous if not absurd. But White also rejected common usage and the usage of great writers as authorities. Reason and logic, not usage, must determine the standard, he declared. Constructions which are "wrong" (i.e., illogical) must be condemned no matter who uses them. "There is a misuse of language which no authority, however great, and which no usage, however general, can justify." Whereas Lounsbury dismissed as "ridiculous and absurd" the idea that propriety in usage depends upon the derivation of words (he noted that we use many words, such as *December, journal,* and *anecdote* in "actual defiance" of their derivation), White appealed to "etymological and logical tests" in accepting and rejecting words.[21]

White was the most articulate, vehement, provocative spokesman for those who believed that English was degenerating in post–Civil War America. He believed that never before the last half century had English been so "tampered with, and violated, and perverted....there have been forced into it monstrous, absurd, and pestilent words and phrases."[22] Although

Matthews and Lounsbury abjured the use of certain words (e.g., *enthuse*), they saw the creation of new words as a sign not of degeneration but of health and intellectual vitality. "By such hardy growths the language will be refreshed and invigorated," Matthews wrote in defense of new words. "If a language should cease to grow, its decay would soon begin." He believed that English was the most fortunate of all the modern languages in drawing its substance from so many sources—from the United States, England, and all the British colonies where English was spoken. He and Lounsbury repeatedly called attention to words such as *audacious, compatible, clumsy, defunct,* and *spurious,* once denounced as barbarisms and corruptions, now accepted as good English. White dwelt upon the need to "purge" the language of errors and vices; Matthews and Lounsbury dwelt upon their fear that grammarians' efforts to regulate language would vitiate it. All three writers agreed, however, that in its power to assimilate new words, English was the most expressive of all languages, in White's words, "the grandest, the richest, and the most varied the world has known."[23]

Whether or not they defended *had better* and *is being done,* scholars were united in their view of language as dynamic, constantly changing, responsive to the spirit of its users. In W.D. Whitney's words, language "is what it is becoming." They contrasted Latin, a "dead language" with fixed rules, no longer subject to change, with English, which as Kittredge observed is "constantly changing, in sounds, in syntax, in vocabulary, and in the meanings conventionally attached to words." Thus, there exists no "absolute, unalterable standard of correctness."[24]

Writers in the magazines also agreed that language was a human creation, shaped by people for their purposes. They denied that language was a natural organism with its own principle of growth independent of the human will. Matthews acknowledged that "language grows...like any other organism," but, he added, "its growth is not spontaneous; it is ever the result of human effort." He endorsed Lounsbury's view: "The English language has been made, is being made, and will be made by those who use it." Whitney denied that languages illustrate Darwin's theory of natural selection and insisted that "languages are not organisms except by a figure of speech." To Fitzedward Hall, language was shaped not only by "uncontrolled tendencies" but by "the conscious effort" represented by "observant scholarship," and "the weight of personal example." All these writers insisted that language must be allowed to develop according to its own laws of growth, "to follow its own bent, and to supply its own needs," but they believed that speakers of the language should guide this growth; they did not want grammarians to "strait jacket the language," but they believed with Brander Matthews that "we can all of us contribute to the healthy development of our mother tongue."[25]

To define language, writers used metaphors that transformed words into human beings or objects subject to human will. Writers acknowledged the importance of language as an indicator of social class by comparing language itself to a social order in which accepted words were the established members of "good English society"; new words of uncertain status were outsiders, on probation, waiting for admission, who might have to enter "the sacred precincts" through "the postern-gate of slang or vulgarism"; condemned words were prowlers, interlopers, usurpers, sneak-thieves, tramps, and marauders, "living a precarious life on the outskirts of society," to be kept out by the "sentries" of good taste and good sense "at the door of the sanctum." Everyday words, respectable but inappropriate in poetry, were useful members of society who knew that they did not belong "in the most select circles." Writers should consider the connotations of their words, for a word, like a person, "is known by the company it has kept." Henry James put his distinctive mark on the analogy, exalting the arts both of speaking and of dining in placing "the parts of our speech"—enunciation, tone of voice, intonation—"among the most precious of our familiar tools." Rather than eat on a "lumpish block" with rough utensils, "let us," he urged, "so far as possible, for properly and habitually entertaining each other, have ivory and silver, smooth clean damask, and the bowl of flowers."[26]

Aware of the entrance each year of thousands of immigrants to the United States, writers in the post–Civil War period often compared new words to aliens seeking admission and citizenship. As America for decades had admitted foreigners without restriction, so, according to Matthews, "from the very beginning our language has held open the door to immigrants of every degree, glad to naturalize them and admit them to citizenship, if only they were worthy of acceptance." Less approvingly, S.S. Cox observed that "we naturalize outlandish words with more speed than we naturalize aliens." Those like White and Joseph Fitzgerald who feared corruption in the infusion of new words "clamoring for the right of Anglic citizenship" urged America to "treat them as aliens, and to agitate for an exclusion act against them." Others urged that only the undesirable words—"the criminals and paupers"—be excluded and that applicants still lingering on the border who have "taken out their papers" and shown themselves to be "useful members of society" be granted full citizenship.[27]

The power of language to reinforce class differences is also seen in the countless metaphors of language as money, indicative of the commercial base of American society. Words are coined and put into circulation; language is "verbal currency" inflated by the "popular demand for an increased *per capita*" and so "ever in danger of debasement." Speakers careless of the standard keep "counterfeit coin" in circulation but in time "usage may stamp it current" and make it "legal tender." Americans who are ready talkers never lack "small counters of conversation," whatever may be the state of their gold reserve. If, however, all one's fortune consisted of "light social conversation"—"small change that passes from hand to hand"—"we should soon be bankrupt." Theodore Roosevelt attested to the binding force of the analogy when he identified the foremost qualities essential to good citizenship in a democracy: "the gift of money-making and the gift of oratory."[28]

Writers in the late nineteenth century continued to use the

analogies of language to natural processes that appear so often in the pages of Emerson and Thoreau. W.W. Story compared the Italian language to a "living tree" which in developing new forms retains its "vital structure." To Matthews, English-speaking nations and colonies were "nurseries for the seedlings of speech" which might survive only in "the local conditions of soil and climate." Henry Sienkiewicz predicted that the Polish language in America, "torn from the maternal stem," would be transformed, "like a plant transplanted to a strange soil." But such analogies were far outnumbered by metaphors expressive of human creation and control. According to Professor Frank E. Bryant of the University of Kansas, "language is no more alive than the steam engine, or the silk-loom, or than any other artfully constructed instrument. Language is a tool. It can do nothing—not even to reproduce itself or maintain itself—except through the agency of man." Writers could marshal words like armies and give them "the force of daggers." The best writers had "the greatest retinue of words at their command," but writers should not "put a fence of words" around their ideas. Writers should choose and place their words as carefully "as the worker in mosaic selects and fits each tiny bit of stone." A writer is like a mechanic; when confronted with a new word he should ask, "have we need of this tool?"[29]

Many Victorian writers dwelt upon the perils of speech, the inadequacy of words, and the virtue of silence, "most noble till the end." These themes were sounded in such works as Tennyson's *In Memoriam*, Browning's *Pauline*, Swinburne's "Atalanta in Calydon," and Carlyle's *Sartor Resartus*, but the pessismistic view of language did not prevail in Howells's America. Howells, for instance, devoted an "Editor's Study" to attacking the contentions of E.J. Phelps, who in "The Age of Words" invoked Carlyle and exalted thought and silence over the spoken word. "When was thought mightier than speech," Howells demanded, "and how did the fact become known? ...We have ourselves the belief that it is the age of words because it is also the age of thoughts." John Hay wrote to Howells at once to applaud him for "that delightful dressing down you gave our silently-vocal word-mongering friend in your last study."[30]

Howells's contemporaries knew that words could be used to deceive, but they believed that words could convey meaning clearly and precisely. They realized that English was rich in words of multiple meanings and connotative power, but they believed with Kittredge that words are signs which can convey the same meaning to all who use them, that there exists an "unspoken consensus of all who speak the language" which determines what words mean.[31] When Mark Twain drew up his list of words misused by James Fenimore Cooper, he was acting on the assumption that words can be used with precision, that a word fits its referent as a hook fits its eye. The ideas that words are "the great foes of reality" or "mere sounds to be bandied about until they were dead" were ideas of a later age. Howells and his contemporaries believed with Lounsbury that language "is an instrument which will be just what those who use it choose to make it."[32] They valued language as the instrument with which to do business, regulate society, and write books, and they saw themselves as masters, not victims, of that instrument.

Chapter Two

"Good Natural English"

Probably the best known fact about Howells and language is his deleting profanity from the manuscripts Mark Twain asked him to edit. But to take this fact alone as representative of Howells's practice is to disregard the complexity of his view and to imply that because he advised Mark Twain to remove Huck Finn's complaint "They comb me all to hell" from *The Adventures of Tom Sawyer*[1] he was therefore a prudish slave to genteel conventions and a hidebound stickler for rules. Almost the opposite is true. Twenty years before Matthews and Lounsbury attacked the grammarians in *Harper's Magazine,* Howells insisted on the futility of attempts to enforce rules and control the development of the language.

Underlying Howells's statements about language are his basic premises: language is the creation of living speakers; its forms are never fixed. "It has always been supposed by grammarians and purists that a language can be kept as they find it; but languages, while they live, are perpetually changing." Although he praised Richard Grant White's *Words and Their Uses* as a valuable record of the language at the time, he doubted whether such guides would effect reforms; he condemned as "a very deadly thing" the attemps of White and others to preserve archaic forms. He anticipated Matthews and Lounsbury in observing that prescribers of rules who prided themselves on writing more correctly than such "notoriously incorrect writers" as Shakespeare, Addison, and Thackeray, were usually barren of ideas and destitute of the power to express memorably what little they did have to say. As James Russell Lowell, Howells's friend and mentor, urged writers to seek language, not in "the grammar and dictionary" but "at its living sources," so Howells insisted that "the English language is primarily in the mouths of living men; it has no transmissible life but what comes thence, and there we must seek it if we would say anything clearly or stoutly to our own generation."[2]

The New England writers—notably Emerson, Thoreau, and Lowell—extolled the speech of unlettered people as more forceful than that of the well educated. Howells stressed a different kind of distinction in a letter dated May 20, 1894, to Thomas Wentworth Higginson: "To my mind there is good literary English, and there is good natural English. This distinction established, I will confess that I prefer the good natural English....it is better to write as...simply as we speak, unless indeed we speak as formally as we write." He declared in an interview of the same year: "The colloquial style is best for a writer beyond question. We should write in the simple, direct manner that we talk."[3]

In urging "good natural English" as the standard for both speaking and writing, Howells embraced Lowell's desire to close the "gap between the speech of books and that of life" and opposed those who held that written and spoken English are essentially different, that what is acceptable in conversation may be inappropriate in writing. In an essay on "English Literature and the Vernacular," Mark H. Liddell warned against creating a "special language" for literature, but insisted on the "distinction between the language of literature and the vernacular" and advised that such usages as contractions, colloquialisms, and repetitions of words and phrases, acceptable in speaking, be avoided in writing. Lounsbury stressed not only the existence of two languages created by the difference between the spelling and pronunciation of words, but also the "distinctly different styles" of "colloquial speech" and "grave discourse." In warning against "elevat[ing] the literary diction too far above the speech of the plain people," Brander Matthews assumed the existence of two kinds of people and two kinds of discourse. According to Kittredge, "Every educated man has at least two dialects,—unless, indeed, he is so unfortunate as always to 'talk like a book.'" Howells desired that "we write as simply as we speak"; Kittredge distinguished "the untrammelled dialogue of everyday" from the "studied diction of the printed word."[4]

In *The Development of the Colloquial Style in America*, Richard Bridgman documents the separation of "spoken language" and literary language in pre–Civil War America and analyzes the process by which the vernacular was transformed into the language of literature during the postwar years.[5] In this period, Howells, more than any other American writer, established as a critical principle the value of common speech in the work of literature. He regarded Defoe's *Roxana*, written in "the spoken tongue of that day," as one of "the best-written novels in the language." He praised Bjornson for writing of the life of the people in language renewed by "the never-failing springs of the common speech." He valued Heine, one of his earliest "literary passions," above all for showing him that "the life of literature was from the springs of the best common speech." (The modifier *best* should be noted.) He liked "the absence of literosity" in Mary Wilkins's stories, which were as "unrhetorical" as the works of Turgenev and Bjornson.[6]

In the introduction to a 1918 edition of *Pride and Prejudice* Howells noted that in Jane Austen's time even the most observant writers had yet to learn to render a character's words "as they really saw or heard them."[7] He made their failure the theme of an episode in *The Vacation of the Kelwyns* in which Emerance, the young teacher and student of life, listens to school boys declaiming lines from Sheridan's *Pizarro*, an adaptation of Kotzebue's play *The Spaniards in Peru*, then asks them to express the characters' feelings in natural English. "I want you to think how you would have spoken and acted if you had really been the friend of a man who was going to be put to death to-morrow morning, and the guard of his prison, who respected and pitied him." When the boys say they can't "put it in common talk," he replies: "The fault is in the man who wrote the piece. He had a bit of nature to express, but he couldn't do it naturally" (pp. 116-17).*

Howells had surprisingly little to say about the poetic language of Walt Whitman, who like Howells sought to fuse literary English and the vernacular. Because Howells was unable to appreciate the form of Whitman's poetry, which seemed to him lawless, shapeless, "intolerant of all bonds and bounds," he never included Whitman among his "literary passions." But he credited Whitman with "[making] it possible for poetry hereafter to be more direct and natural than hitherto." Among the "great and fruitful" elements he recognized in *Leaves of Grass*, he counted as most important the results of that "aesthetic revolt" which brought Whitman's poetry "nearer to the language and the carriage of life." As Howells preferred "spoken English" to "book English," so he preferred the "over-vernacular" to the "pedantic" and the "formless beauty" of Whitman's poetry to the stilted rhetoric of *Pizarro*. But his ideal of "good natural English" was not Whitmen's idiosyncratic melding of standard English, slang, technical, and foreign words, but the language of Henry James, exemplified in the story "Louisa Pallant" by the narrator's English, "to the last degree informal and to the last degree refined."[8]

In identifying the forms of "good natural English," Howells proposed to break some of the grammarians' rules but insisted upon keeping others; he welcomed the new and the colloquial but condemned certain words and forms and cared to preserve certain distinctions. His guiding principle was that there should be one language, not two, that one should neither write what one would not say nor say what one would not write. He repeatedly urged writers to allow themselves and their characters to make "full use of spoken forms," avoiding such stilted, artificial constructions as "am I not," "will you not," and "can we not," which "nobody but a half-bred prig ever dreams of using...in actual parlance." He believed contractions such as

*Full bibliographical information on the works of Howells cited will be found on pages 227-28.

isn't, wouldn't, didn't "infinitely more graceful and vigorous" than the "*is not, would not,* and *did not* demanded by convention in written English. He imagined writing, but did not write, an essay with all the contractions used in speaking.[9]

He warned against the temptation to use "store words," to write "he made the necessary purchases" instead of "he bought what he wanted." He cited as "one of the most common errors" the use of the participle: e.g., "seeing you in the window, I stopped to call." The advocate of "good natural English" would write and say "I saw you and stopped." He objected to inversions such as "protested the man" as "ungainly" and "not modern" and criticized himself for using them in *The Rise of Silas Lapham*. He also objected to the practice of forcing together the "idiomatically divided" conjunction and verb as in "do as do the Romans," which no one would say but many write "in fancied refinement." He dismissed other rules that resulted in a stiffly artificial style. To Higginson, a purist who occasionally criticized Howells's violation of rules, he argued for placing a preposition at the end of the sentence because "it makes a lighter and pleasanter movement in the prose, and is more conformable to good colloquial usage, to do so. I have studied much upon it, and the effect is not the effect of haste with me."[10] Howells's novels are filled with sentences ending with a preposition. Typical examples are these from *Indian Summer:* "He dressed and waited for the mature hour which he had ordered his breakfast for." "They were going about to eke out their salaries with the gifts of people whose windows the festival season privileged them to play under" (pp. 42,82).

At the same time, Howells upheld certain rules of grammar and usage. He objected not only to the "odious" *would better* for *had better,* but also to *gotten* for *got,* and *different than* for *different from.* For him, as for his contemporaries, speech indicated the place of people on the scale of refinement and cultivation. The "semi-cultured" identified themselves by *different than;* "half-bred prigs" said *will you not;* the "pseudo-cultured" joined "the ignorant" in using *over* instead of *about.*[11] Aspirants to gentility, like Mrs. Makely in *A Traveller from Altruria,* were careful to say *drawing room* instead of *parlor.*

Early and late Howells observed the futility of correcting people's errors, but he continued, as he said, "to cry out against the abuses," to urge upon his readers, including members of his own family, the importance of good usage. In 1867, in a letter to his father, he praised his sister Annie's "first literary triumph," but deplored the ignorance that "should not know a tense from a mood, or an adverb from an adjective" and stressed the need of "very severe training" and "very earnest studying." In expressing pleasure in his father's reminiscences published in the *Sentinel*, he advised revising one sentence "containing five relatives...where the meaning was quite obscured." Years later, in a letter to his brother Joseph, who was applying to the State Department for an appointment on Turk's Island, he exclaimed, "And for heaven's sake look out for your grammar!" scolded him for writing "our expenses averages" and warned him that "such schoolboy blunders...would damage you irretrivably with the department." A year later he again called attention to his brother's grammatical errors and again instructed him to "learn the parts of speech and the very few very simple rules that govern them."[12]

For William Dean Howells, however, "good natural English" involved more than the "few very simple rules" set forth in the "simple school grammar" he recommended to his brother. In defining a standard of literary propriety he was also defining his relation to the New England literary world, represented by such figures as Lowell, Longfellow, Holmes, and Norton, whose approval he had sought at the beginning of his career. That he continued to defer to them even after he became editor of the *Atlantic Monthly* is most clearly revealed in his replies to Lowell's letters of praise and correction.

The third installment of Howells's "Private Theatricals" in the *Atlantic* of January 1876 brought forth Lowell's most detailed criticism of Howells's grammar. After praising as "masterly" the "discrimination of characters by what they say and do" and declaring himself "one of the chorus of your admirers and one of the first who began to sing in it," Lowell advised certain changes in the text: "Before you print in a book take your pencil and on page 8 line 9 correct 'if there *was* a bell' to 'if there had been.' Also you have too many 'wants' as a wise father would say to his son. E.G. p. 9 1st col. line 18, 'get away if he wanted,' 'wished' were better. P. 10, 'Don't you want to stop and help,' to read 'Wouldn't you like..."[13]

As James L. Woodress notes, the novel, not reprinted until published posthumously as *Mrs. Farrell* (1921), does not contain Lowell's corrections.[14] But judging by his reply to Lowell, Howells would have made the corrections if he could have. Howells's letter, dated two days after Lowell's, is notable for its mixture of defiance and submissiveness. Evidently moved by the impulse to assert himself even as he deferred to Lowell, to confess his "linguistic uncertainty" while professing to violate the rules willfully, he wrote to Lowell that his criticism was

> perfectly just, and is none the less deserved because the sins were committed as much from perversity as ignorance. Having no proofreader over me, and having so long bowed down to correctness, I did take a wicked pleasure in writing "if there was a bell," but I know that it was foolish, and that I wouldn't have borne it from another. It's too late to bother you with the proof of No IV, but I shall...send you V, when it's in print. What mostly 'stumps' me in this English tongue (it's [sic] elegance seems a thing of negatives, like the bearing of a gentleman), is the wills and shalls, and woulds and shouldn'ts. Their true use comes only from being born in one or other of the Englands, I'm quite convinced—though I would see H-gg-ns-n dead before I'd own it.[15]

Howells's "wicked pleasure" in knowingly violating rules upheld by arbiters like Lowell may have been shared by Mark Twain when he wrote words he knew Howells would delete.

Four years later, Howells was still promising Lowell to "do my best for the *wills* and *shalls*," and confessing that "I am not native to the right use of them." When Lowell in praising an installment of *The Minister's Charge* observed that Howells had said "brings us in closer relation" when he should have said *into*, Howells replied, "I will even try to have the right use of

prepositions and the signs of the future and the conditional."[16]
How skillfully Howells exploited the distinction between
should and *would* is seen in a late novel, *The Kentons*. When
Breckon, the minister from New England, says to Ellen Kenton
and her mother that "he *should* like the pleasure of introducing
them," the Kentons, Midwesterners, "declared that they *would*
be delighted" (p. 112, emphasis added). (Oscar Firkins, who
cites these passages, sees the use of both *should* and *would* in
one sentence as inadvertent.)[17]

Twenty-five years after Howells wrote "Private Theatricals,"
the memory of Lowell's strictures and corrections was still
potent enough to warrant several paragraphs in Howells's
Literary Friends and Acquaintance. After recalling his unsuc-
cessful defense of the word *silvern*, to which Lowell objected,
Howells continued: "He was...such a stickler for the best diction that he would not have had me use slovenly vernacular
even in the dialogue in my stories; my characters must not say
they *wanted* to do so and so, but *wished*, and the like. In a copy
of one of my books which I found him reading, I saw he had
corrected my erring Western *woulds* and *shoulds*; as he grew
old he was less and less able to restrain himself from setting
people right to their faces."[18]

It might have comforted Howells to know that about the
time Lowell was suggesting revisions in "Private Theatricals"
he was also correcting syntax in Henry James's *French Poets
and Novelists*.[19] James made several of the changes that Lowell
recommended, but judging by his essay on Lowell, published
in 1892, shortly after Lowell's death, James felt in no sense
subordinate to him. Howells wrote of Lowell from the point of
view of the friend who never forgot that he had once been a
suppliant and a disciple. James wrote of Lowell with the authority of the artist in full possession of the power to present
his subject in whatever light he chose. In describing his relations with the New England writers, Howells referred to "my
good fortune to be among them as I never could be of them."[20]
James was "of" the New England writers as much as he chose
to be and he was "among them" as often as he cared to be. He
praised Lowell as "an infallible master" of the English lan-

guage, but in his essay he made no reference to Lowell's corrections of his work, and there is no evidence that he ever offered
to send Lowell his proofs.

Today, teachers and writers of handbooks warn students
against wordiness and clichés. In the nineteenth century, the
word *cliché* did not appear in discussions of language, and
brevity was not extolled. Indeed, Lounsbury questioned the
merits of the "gospel of conciseness," and argued that circumlocutions and expletives such as *it is* and *there are* are natural to
the language and should not be resisted.[21] Nor did he and his
contemporaries strive for a taut style, as the reader of their
essays quickly sees.

In the nineteenth century, the stylistic fault most often condemned was verbal inflation—the indulgence in exaggeration
and extravagance, which was not limited to one class or group
but appeared in many places: in polite society, in political
oratory, in newspapers, in sermons. Nineteenth-century critics
identified many kinds of verbal inflation: the overuse of modi-
fiers such as *wonderful, lovely, horrible, superb;* the overuse of
italics and exclamation points; the use by politicians and
newspapers of "Billingsgate epithets" (e.g., muck-worm,
pitiful whelp) to attack opponents; and, at the other extreme,
the fondness of newspapers for flowery circumlocutions such
as "pecuniary compensation" and "votaries of Terpsichore."
Such verbal inflation was denounced as pretentious and affected, as were the use of foreign words and phrases and the
"vice of unexpectedness," i.e., the effort to startle and surprise
by fanciful metaphors and "forced conceits."[22]

Although nineteenth-century writers of the literary estab-
lishment did not preach the virtue of brevity, they did praise
simplicity as the mark of the cultivated person. "The higher the
culture, the simpler the style and the plainer the speech,"
White wrote, echoing the dictum of James Fenimore Cooper:
"One of the most certain evidences of a man of high breeding, is
his simplicity of speech, a simplicity that is equally removed
from vulgarity and exaggeration." To try to animate lifeless
prose by verbal superlatives, Henry James said in an early

review, was "like painting the cheeks and pencilling the eye-brows of a corpse." Repeatedly writers in the *Galaxy, Harper's,* and the *Atlantic* condemned verbal inflation as the sign of feebleness and lack of feeling. When they described writing as "florid," "magnificent," and "grandiloquent" they were dismissing it as hollow, shallow, and trivial. The best writers were distinguished by restraint and moderation. Extravagance of statement marks James's failed artists, such as Roderick Hudson and Theobold of "The Madonna of the Future," who dissipates all his energy in talk, exhibiting "all our native mistrust for intellectual discretion and our native relish for sonorous superlatives....his mildest terms of approbation were 'glorious,' 'superb,' and 'magnificent.' The small change of admiration seemed to him no coin for a gentleman to handle."[23]

Now and then an essayist found merit in Americans' love of extravagance and exaggeration. Higginson observed that the public, if forced to choose, would take heartiness and energy before "good writing," that the extravagances of the "absurdest spread-eagle orator" are often more to be valued than the "neat Londonism of the city editor who dissects him." S.S. Cox, in an essay on "American Humor" in *Harper's,* bestowed some dignity upon the "rhetorical gasconade" of newspapers and political oratory by seeing it as expressive of American energy and inventiveness and by showing that Americans shared their love of exaggeration with the Norsemen and the Celts. But both Higginson and Cox belonged to the tradition that valued restraint, dignity, decorum, and moderation. Higginson advised American writers to observe the forms of polite usage, to "perfect the finer graces without sacrificing things more vital." Although Cox accepted extravagance as endemic to American humor, he observed that extravagance had "emasculated" many of "our old English words" such as *powerful, mighty,* and *magnificent,* while producing "the wildest perversions" of others, and he asked for more refinement in American humor.[24]

Howells criticized the American penchant for exaggeration and "fine writing" in his first essays on language, written for the "Minor Topics" department of the *Nation* in 1866, just before he became assistant editor of the *Atlantic.* In one issue he condemned exaggeration as a falsification of truth which violates the standard of "good natural English." Taking as his starting point an article on Proudhon which declared that the Socialist in indulging in violent statements puts "too high a price on his thought," Howells observed that American journalists and politicians who assail opponents as *liars*, *cheats*, and *idiots* resemble the shopkeeper who exorbitantly prices his goods because he expects to be "beaten down." Therefore, "a large discount has always to be made in their language."[25]

"Nothing can be said simply," he complained in the next week's article, and proposed creating a new office, "commissioners of philology," who should restore all inflated words to their proper meanings. Teachers should be the commissioners, Howells said, but unfortunately they too preferred the grand to the simple, thereby assisting in the debasement of the language. As costermongers have elevated themselves to grocers and their shops to stores, so schoolmasters call themselves professors, a title which itself is "losing caste rapidly" as professors of chiropody and palmistry multiply.[26]

Politicians resort to exaggeration to gain attention and make an impression; teachers and practioners call themselves professors and doctors to dignify themselves and their words; people also use circumlocutions or inflated words when they shrink from referring directly to unpleasant or disturbing facts. Captain Frederick Marryat observed that the desire of Americans to be "excessively refined" in their langauge led them to use "absurd substitutes" for certain words, just as they covered nude statues with drapery. Americans as well as British observers ridiculed the "absurd substitutes," the prudish designation of *legs* as *limbs*, for instance, and *cocks* as *roosters*. All animals that roost are roosters, including hens and canary birds, White pointed out. As for parts and functions of the human body, if one is to speak of them "it is immodest not to call them by their proper names." Cooper instructed his countrymen that when they "have retained the *things* of their ancestors, such as servants, they should not be ashamed to keep the *names*." Kittredge regarded euphemisms as "inevitable—a resistless tendency of language, inherent in its nature," no more to be deplored or reversed than "any other law of the universe." But euphemisms or genteelisms—"squeamish cant"—were generally condemned by writers of the so-called genteel tradition. They scoffed at the vulgar affection that turned a debt into a "pecuniary embarrassment," a drummer into a "commercial gentleman," and a coffin into a "casket for the remains of the departed," and they called for plain simple words.[27]

In his essays in the *Nation,* Howells likewise urged his readers to preserve the integrity of words and adhere to truth by avoiding euphemisms. He cited some twenty words debased by euphemisms, such as *Negro,* "a perfectly proper term," which had been compromised by the genteelism *colored.* When "magnificence of phraseology" is joined to "meanness of fact," he wrote, the result is a "violation of truth" which does not elevate the fact. "A servant is none the less a servant when he is called a 'help'; neither his wages nor his social position is higher." He underscored the economic implications of euphemism when he compared the debasement of inflated words to the depreciation of currency. "In time the new words sink down to the real state of things: then, as with paper money when it depreciates, a new issue is required to purchase the same amount of consideration." Perhaps the words *help* and *colored* had sunk to the level of "the real state of things" by the time Howells published *Suburban Sketches,* for he uses both words repeatedly, at one point referring to "colored help."[28]

Years later, in a discussion of euphemisms for acts of torture and punishment, Howells took a position like Kittredge's, accepting as inevitable and universal the impulse to soften or disguise certain facts: "There has always and everywhere been a tendency to euphemize the names of punishments."[29] He noted that the euphemism may reflect the wish for "scientific precision" (e.g., *exoculate* for *put out the eyes*). More often, the euphemism makes the fact tolerable to the imagination by either masking or burlesquing it. The need to make death tolerable by joking about it Howells believed common to all peoples.

Like euphemism, slang is an indirect or metaphorical way

of saying something, and many euphemisms are also slang—
e.g., certain phrases for *to die, to go mad, to be intoxicated.* In
the late nineteenth century, attitudes toward slang ranged
from unqualified disapproval to enthusiastic acceptance. At
one extreme were the advocates of "pure speech," both men
and women, who believed slang to have vulgarized society and
who advised readers to abjure all slang, characterized by one
writer as "a note of savagery on our hearths and in our draw-
ing-rooms" which violates "the noblest ideal of woman-
hood."[30] At the other extreme was the writer in *Galaxy* who, in
defining slang as "live metaphor," "an intensified language of
the senses," and "ready coined wit" produced by the "strong,
rude, unconscious mind of the crowd," anticipated by some
twenty years Whitman's definition of slang in "November
Boughs." For Whitman, slang was the "lawless germinal element" from which literature sprang; expressive of the life of
the people, slang animated that "vast living body" that is
language, "breathing into its nostrils the breath of life." Representing the people's efforts to "escape from bald literalism,"
slang at its highest reach was poetry "of an appropriateness
and originality unsurpassable."[31]

Scholars and men of letters expressed similar ideas in
blander, more subdued prose. Like Whitman, Brander Matthews defined slang as the "feeder" of language, "the source
from which the decaying energies of speech are constantly
refreshed." He and Lounsbury and Kittredge followed Whitman in defining slang as expressive of people's constant impulse toward the vivid and the concrete and in noting that
many accepted words originated as slang. Kittredge observed
that slang undergoes more rapidly the same changes that
gradually alter the "lawful language" and advised the student
of language to study the processes of slang.[32]

Writers distinguished between different kinds of slang: the
"worthy" and the "unworthy," the ephemeral and the enduring. Matthews defended words such as *mossback, slump, crank,
fad,* and *henchman,* which either replaced worn-out words or
named what had not been named before. He found western
slang more vigorous than eastern and welcomed the western

boom, cinch, jumped on and *sand* (grit). He accepted as part of popular speech technical terms such as those from poker (*call, go it blind*), the Stock Exchange (*corner, margin*), the theater (*mascot, hoodoo*). Writers of polite literature generally disapproved of the racy slang of sports and political compaigns, and condemned the "base jargon" used by thieves and con men to disguise or conceal their evil-doing. The British observer James Muirhead wondered at the "startling contrasts" in the typical American newspapers, which on one page might print restrained and dignified editorials and on another an account of a prize fight in which "the most pointless and disgusting slang, such as 'tapping his claret' and 'bunging his peepers' is used with blood-curdling frequency."[33]

Slang might be praised for being imaginative, poetic, picturesque, expressive, pithy, vigorous, vivid, and pungent, or it might be condemned as grotesque, meaningless, pointless, foolish, vulgar, coarse, low, rank, disgusting, offensive, and base. Writers in the *Atlantic*'s Contributor's Club compared slang words to "unsavory missiles caught up from the gutter," to placers from which the gold of new words is mined, to irredeemable paper money, or to the gold dust eventually minted into sovereigns.[34] The dictionaries of slang, where thousands of obsolete terms are buried, attest to the ephemeral character of much slang.

Howells was hospitable to slang when the ideas expressed were not vulgar. He admired George Ade's creation of his character Artie, "full to the lips of the most graphic and satisfying slang" but possessed of "generous instincts, and a certain invulnerable right-mindedness in the midst of adverse experiences." Although Artie was a "fountain of slang," his thought was "as pure as any that flows from wells of English undefiled." Howells liked the "fortunate mixture" of slang and passion in Clarence King's portrayal of the California painter in *Mountaineering in the Sierra Nevada*. Although Howells questioned the taste of some phrases drawn from "our slang-poisoned vernacular," he did not endorse the view of Lowell, who declared that "slang is always vulgar, because it is not a natural but an affected way of talking." Howells defended slang as "sometimes delightful and forcible beyond the reach of the dictionary. We would not have any one go about for new words, but if one of them came aptly, not to reject its help."[35]

Howells's characters, particularly his refined, well-educated upper-class Bostonians, sometimes use slang, which their social confidence and linguistic security allow them to enjoy without fear of seeming vulgar. Bromfield Corey in *The Minister's Charge* delights in using "a bit of the new slang" (p. 320). The Altrurian traveller, as well-bred as any Bostonian, enjoys the "vulgar vigor" of slang. When, in *Dr. Breen's Practice*, Grace Breen repeats the slang word *bobbish* (in good spirits) used by her suiter, the impeccable Mr. Libby, Howells notes that the woman's respect for the man's word gives rise to slang (p. 126). Howells's "fountain of slang," however, is the midwestern Fulkerson, the brash ebullient promotor of his magazine in *A Hazard of New Fortunes*. In his first appearance, when he urges Basil March to leave Boston and come to New York to edit the magazine, he observes that March fears that he can't "muse worth a cent," but has "always had a hankering for the ink-pots," says he doesn't want "literary hangers-on" on his staff but promises that together he and March will "have the pull" on the syndicate writers, who "won't be able to work the thing," tells March "I do cotton to a Western man" and observes, "the poison's beginning to work in you," admits that he can't offer him "such swell quarters" in New York, but predicts that Mrs. March will "tell you to go in and win," cries "What are you giving me...*Come* off!" when March asks if the magazine will have illustrations, and assures him, perhaps deliberately punning on March's name, that "It's going to be a triumphal march from the word go" (pp. 8-15).

Howells's prose is more like the "good natural English" of Basil March than like the breezy slang of Fulkerson. But throughout his career Howells used colloquialisms, new words, and slang terms in his literary criticism as well as in his fiction. He praised the "fine manly *go*" of E.A. Robinson's "The Klondike" and the "proud unheed" of Emily Dickinson's poetry. He referred to Hawthorne's fear that he was "bamboozling himself" when he admired an old master. He observed that the United States would no longer "stomach" a diet of "humble-pie," wondered whether English critics had not been "barking up the wrong tree," disliked the "wink-tipping" and "cockahoop" in Kipling's sketches, and rejected the idea that a novel must have a "round-up" of characters in the last chapter. He described writers who "skulked," "swapped," "muddled," "grovelled," "bandied words," "whitewashed," "swaggered," wrote "rot," and were "great fellows for virility." He declared that literature was never "indifferent to the butcher's bill," and that "capable critics are always rather rare birds."[36]

Both Richard Bridgman and Alfred Habegger have observed that Howells often signalled by quotation marks or italics his awareness of using colloquialisms and his recognition of another, presumably higher, standard. But often Howells did not bracket colloquialisms or new words. Brander Matthews noted approvingly that in *The Quality of Mercy* Howells used the new words *fake* and *electrics* (for electric lights) "without the stigma of italics or quotation marks."[37] Howells used other neologisms and slang terms without quotation marks: e.g., *fogies*, *jam in the kisses*, *mad* (angry).

Howells had a strong aversion to certain words and expressions. He lamented the use of *pick*, "a very offensive word," in place of "the gentle verb *choose*." He objected to the modern vernacular in describing venerated relics, such as the clothes of George Washington, designated on a placard at the Centennial in Philadelphia as "Coat, Vest, and Pants." "Pantaloons were then unknown," Howells observed, "and 'pants' were undreamt-of by a generation which had time to be decent and comely in its speech." He criticized Barrett Wendell for saying that Emerson's representative men were "of a different stripe," when *stripe* in the sense of *kind* "has remained hopelessly rustic, plebian, common." He condemned neologisms derived from both Greek and Latin roots, such as *automobile* and *electrocute*—"mongrel" words "hateful to the philological sense." He thought *ad* "a loathly little word," admitted that "we must come to it. It's as legitimate as lunch," but mocked the creations of the "adsmith" by proposing *wofsmith* for the writer of a work of fiction.[38]

No writer of the period, however, not even Mark Twain or Whitman, coined more words than Howells did. He called himself a *wordist* and in his literary criticism coined *facetiation, hippopotamic, insight and outspeech, inlook and outlook, under dog and upper dog.* The vocabulary of *Suburban Sketches,* praised by Lowell for the "fastidious purity" of language, includes *cloggist, densified, embrowning, fantasticality, infinitesimality, neighbored, populatory, saplinghood, scarified, suburbanly, unthrift, wharfish,* and *Yankeefied.* In later years he often converted nouns into verbs and participles: he referred to John Fiske's "inability to language his thoughts of infinity"; he praised the stories Jonathan Sturges had "so limpidly Englished" from the French of Maupassant; he wrote to friends of the family's *dentisting, hotelling,* and *occulisting.* His characters *daughter, sister,* and *matronise* each other; one *tempests out* of a house; another *fellowships* his friend; ships *wood* the shore with their masts.[39]

Anything suggestive of the risqué or off-color he unfailingly avoided, acknowledging late in life that "I am still very Victorian in my tastes." On occasion he yielded to his wife, who held up an even higher standard of propriety; he confessed to his brother that when she objected to his saying "eggs fresh from the hen," he submitted and "tamely" wrote "fresh from the coop."[40] Profanity, of course, had no place in "decent comely speech." Although he greatly admired Crane's *Maggie,* in which the title character is the only one who does not vent a stream of *damns* and *hells,* he feared that the language of the novel would shock and lose readers. Possibly Howells's inventiveness and energy, inhibited by genteel conventions which he himself embraced, found its outlet in using colloquialisms, coining words, and breaking the purist's rules.

Occasionally Howells's contemporaries objected to his colloquialisms or coinages. After praising the last installment of *The Lady of the Aroostook* in the March 1879 issue of the *Atlantic,* Lowell added, "You wouldn't know me without one little jab of criticism. No Bostonian ever said 'Was his wife along'. Tis barbarous." Higginson liked the explanation of the origin of slang in *Dr. Breen's Practice,* but thought "she fluted" was "a pretty daring phrase." In praising *Annie Kilburn* he observed that "so essentially a local type" as the New England lawyer Putney would never use *fool* as an adjective. Howells agreed, admitting that "I couldn't resist the color it promised to give; it's a tint of my native Southern Ohio parlance." A correspondent in the *Critic* condemned as "lapses from correct English" in *Indian Summer* the locutions "going to come," "drew him a cup of tea," and "whom the things happened to." Another reader, however, judged the offending sentences "perfectly grammatical according to the best English usage."[41]

Criticisms of Howells's English were few compared to the number of reviews and essays that praised his style for its ease, precision, purity, and grace. His first long narrative, *Their Wedding Journey,* was praised in the *Nation* for truthfulness of language; in *Harper's* for the charm of the style which "prevents his book from being in any sense commonplace"; in *Lippincott's* for the perfection with which conversations and "little shreds of remark" were recorded. E.P. Whipple observed the "singular felicity" of Howells's style. Mark Twain extolled its "clearness, compression, verbal exactness, and unforced and seemingly unconscious felicity of phrasing."[42] Hamlin Garland recalled that on first meeting Howells, he was at once struck by Howells's "exquisite yet simple English" and by his discrimination in the choice of words. Lowell, who kept the most watchful eye over Howells's prose, awarded him, on the publication of *Suburban Sketches,* the accolade of his highest praise. Seeing in Howells the guardian "of those conventions which are the safeguard of letters, and the best legacy of culture," he judged Howells an artist "worthy to be ranked with Hawthorne in sensitiveness of observation, with Longfellow in perfection of style."[43]

In arguing that Whitman alone was not representative of all America, Howells defined two tendencies in American literature: one toward "an elegance refined and polished, both in thought and phrase," the other toward "grotesqueness, wild and extravagant."[44] Howells valued both strains and would not have sacrificed one for the other or have identified one as more "American" than the other. But clearly his contemporaries, like Lowell and Holmes, who compared him to Haw-thorne and Longfellow but not to Whitman or Mark Twain, placed Howells in the school of "the refined and polished," to which they themselves belonged. In particular, Lowell wished to claim Howells as his protégé and disciple. Howells in turn wished to be so claimed but he also resisted the claim. He wished to be a guardian but he also wished to be a creator and an innovator. He would preserve decorum yet remain free to break rules. As he was drawn to both poles in literature—to the "refined and polished" and to the "wild and extravagent"—so he was drawn in opposite directions in his treatment of other issues: the relation of American and British English, the effects of dialect in literature, and the role of language in defining the race and social class of characters in fiction.

Chapter Three

American and British English

Of all the issues pertaining to language discussed in the latter half of the nineteenth century, none was more vigorously debated than the relation of American and British English. More than any other, this issue raised questions of far-reaching political and cultural importance: Were American English and British English one language or two? If one language, was British English the standard? Did an American literature exist or was the literature written by Americans merely a branch of English literature? Implicit in these questions was the fundamental question: What should be the political relation of the United States and Great Britain?

In any event, these questions would have engaged the attention of Americans during the century after the United States became an independent nation. But the need to answer them was intensified by British attacks upon the speech of Americans. Dickens and Mrs. Trollope were but the most famous of the English travelers who criticized American voices, American pronunciation, and American vocabulary. Indeed, Howells believed that the chief source of American hostility to England was not the memory of political conflict but the "sores from the slings and arrows of English tourists and other authors."[1]

Even the British observers most sympathetic to Americans, most ready to appreciate their character and admire their achievements, made unfavorable comments. After visiting America in 1837, Captain Frederick Marryat wondered at "how very debased the language has become in a short period in America." He admired in American metaphors "an energy which is very remarkable," and he admitted that the lower classes in America spoke more clearly than their counterparts in England, but he asserted that "the higher classes do not speak the language so purely or so classically as it is spoken among the well-educated English." Indeed, Americans appeared to have no standard at all: "everyone appears to be independent and pronounces just as he pleases."[2] Some fifty years later, the British writer James Fullarton Muirhead made a similar observation, noting that even well-educated Americans often impaired the force of their speech by the misquoting of foreign words and by errors like saying "as" for "that" and "acrost" for "across," such as an Englishman of equal education and culture would not make. He attributed the extraordinary delicacy and fastidiousness of the foremost American writers, which Howells also noted, to their reaction against "the general tendency to the careless and the slipshod."[3]

Americans particularly resented the criticism made by Dickens, whom they had fêted and lionized when he came to America in 1847. But other English critics of American speech made attacks more savage than those Dickens made in *Martin Chuzzlewit.* To illustrate the violence of the assault, Brander Matthews quoted its most sanctified leader, Henry Alford, Dean of Canterbury, who, in the first edition of *The Queen's English* (1863), denounced the speech and writing of Americans for "reckless exaggeration and contempt for congruity," reflective, he believed, of "the character and history of the nation—its blunted sense of moral obligation and duty to man, its open disregard of conventional right where aggrandizement is to be obtained...its reckless and fruitless maintenance of the most cruel and unprincipled war in the history of the world."[4]

Years later, when time had diminished the resentment generated in America by British attacks on the Union cause in the

Civil War, Americans continued to chafe in knowing that English writers and travelers judged Americans their inferiors in speaking and writing, that the English used "Americanism" as a term of censure. Even an urbane writer like Brander Matthews resented in British attacks on American speech the assumption that "we Americans are outer barbarians, mere strangers, wickedly tampering with something which belongs to the British exclusively."[5] Although the editors of *Harper's* repeatedly reminded readers that critics of Americans, such as Dickens, Mrs. Trollope, and Matthew Arnold, had criticized conditions in England even more vigorously, and that Americans were "substantially benefited" in being shown their imperfections,[6] Americans continued to defend themselves in a variety of ways.

A favorite line of argument was to demonstrate that words and phrases stigmatized as "Americanisms" actually originated in England. Lowell devoted two-thirds of his defense of the dialect in *The Biglow Papers* to showing that "the Yankee often has antiquity and very respectable literary authority on his side." Henry Cabot Lodge observed that many words condemned as Americanisms, such as *guess* (think), the interjection *well*, *flapjack*, and *deck of cards*, appear in Shakespeare's plays. Matthews cited the use by British writers of so-called Americanisms, including *metropolis*, *reliable*, and *scientist*. George Wakeman traced to old English dialects such slang words as *bash*, *go to pot*, *bully*, and *nuts*, and noted that *guess*, *reckoned*, *gumption*, and *passel* are English as well as American provincialisms. A writer to the Contributor's Club discovered that *skedaddle*, a favorite example of an American coinage, was a provincial English word. In his *Atlantic* articles, Richard Grant White pointed out scores of words and phrases, including *folks*, *guess*, *notion*, *go it*, and *give out*, cited as Americanisms in Bartlett's dictionary but actually used by British writers.[7] Other writers defended Americans' creation of new words in response to new conditions. A correspondent to the *Atlantic* insisted that Americans should have "equal property rights" with the English in contributing new words to the language. According to Brander Matthews, Americans had inherited, not borrowed, their language and therefore need not justify the existence of American words.[8]

Believing that the best defense is a vigorous offense, Americans often criticized the way the English spoke and claimed that Americans spoke better. Matthews and White located outside the "pale of good English" a number of "Briticisms," such as *different to*, *directly* for *as soon as*, and *stop* for *stay*. Matthews asserted that English speakers, no less than Americans, said *very pleased*, *like* for *as*, and *without* for *unless* in violation of the "best usage." White regretted that the British use of *awfully* for *very* was spreading rapidly in America, and gave pages to proving that British writers such as Addison, Froude, and Goldwin Smith, held up as models to Americans, perpetuated the very errors in grammar and syntax that Americans were accused of making. Gilbert M. Tucker devoted seven pages of *Our Common Speech* (1895) to quotations of passages with grammatical errors by English writers. Correspondents in the Contributor's Club in the *Atlantic Monthly* deplored as "inelegant" the British pronunciation of *house* and *round*, claimed that erroneous use of the grave accent in *a priori* and *a posteriori* was "almost universal among English writers," and argued that the English had no cause to laugh at queer American names when some of their own were queerer. In defense of Americans' use of *sick* for any disordered state, Lodge, White, and Matthews claimed that the British sometimes perverted the word *ill* when they used it instead of *sick*, and observed that the British retained *sick* in *sick-leave*, *sickroom*, and *sickbed*.[9]

To rebut English criticism of American spelling, Matthews argued that British spelling was even more illogical than American: (e.g., the British dropped the *u* from *emperor* and *error* but retained it in *color* and *honor*). He observed that American spellings deplored by the English, such as *almanac*, *wagon*, and *honor*, were "labor-saving improvements" of the kind favored by the foremost philologists in England and America. He noted that certain American spellings denounced in England (e.g., *center* and *scepter*) were once current in England. Lounsbury defended *honor* on the grounds that the word derived from the Latin *honor* and was spelled *honor* in

England even after Samuel Johnson, who authorized *error* and *mirror*, insisted upon *honour*.[10]

Americans as well as British observers complained of the nasal twang and the harsh tones by which American speakers betrayed their nationality. Charles Dudley Warner, for instance, characteried the "American voice" as "shrill, strident, high-pitched, unmodulated," and complained that "no care is taken about the voice in speech."[11] In his letters, travel diaries, and fiction, Howells repeatedly identified Americans by their loud, grinding voices and their "flat, wooden tones." He argued that the "English ideal"—conformity to a standard in speaking and writing—was to be preferred to the "American ideal"— adherence to no standard at all. Henry James agreed. Measuring the degree to which a society has "achieved civilization" by its "vocal form" and "vocal tone," James informed the graduating class at Byrn Mawr College in 1905 that "our civilization remains strikingly *un*achieved," lacking even the awareness of failure, subjected to influences that "make for the confused, the ugly, the flat, the thin, the mean, the helpless, that reduce articulation to an easy and ignoble minimum, and so keep it as little distinct as possible from the grunting, the squealing, the barking or the roaring of animals."[12]

The "American voice" had its defenders, who asserted that English pronunciation and quality of voice were worse than the American. White remarked the "thick, throaty utterance" of lower-class English speakers and noted that "incapacities of speech" such as lisping and sounding *r* as *w* were much oftener heard in England than in America. Americans asserted the superiority of American voices by their choice of adjectives. Differing from Warner, White found the British voice to be "higher and sharper" than the American, who "speaks from the chest with a graver tone." A writer in *Godey's* attributed to the moist climate of England the "thick, wheezy" pronunciation of British speakers, which when corrected becomes a pleasing "softness and smoothness of utterance." The American voice at its best produces "a resonant and often a melodious clearness."[13]

Americans also defended their speech by criticizing their

countrymen who affected British idioms and pronunciation. From the "Editor's Easy Chair" in *Harper's*, George William Curtis urged Americans not to deny their own country by imitating British speech and noted approvingly that the *New York Times* had recently satirized "American ladies" who returned from England saying *weally* for *really*, *coals* for *coal*, and *cut up* for *grieved*. Although Warner criticized American speech, he ridiculed those culture-seekers who in one city tried to hide their American origins by forming a club to cultivate the broad *a*.[14]

Despite the vehement defense of American speech against the attack of British critics, the prominent writers of the late nineteenth century rejected the idea of an American or Federal language, promoted by Noah Webster in the late eighteenth century and a half century later by James P. Herron, author of *American Grammar: Adapted to the National Language of the United States*.[15] Writers in the magazines insisted that the creation of new words in America neither debased the English language nor created a new language. As one writer in the Contributor's Club put it, "It is not at all likely that the great English language will ever get subdivided into an English and an American language. National intercommunication is too strong for that." A writer in *Lippincott's* observed the British readiness to adopt certain American words and predicted that "amalgamation of dialect will continue to proceed, and at an increased rate." Mark Liddell asserted that "so long as Americans speak English, our words will always be English words. ...we cannot make a new language that will be American, as German speech is German, any more than we could make for ourselves sixfingered right hands." White derided the idea of a Federal language, and insisted that differences between American and British speech were decreasing, that well-bred people in both countries "use exactly the same vocabulary and the same idioms," and that the standard for all speakers of English is the British standard: "that which is accepted as the best by people of the best education and social standing in England."[16]

Brander Matthews and Henry Cabot Lodge likewise affirmed that the English and the Americans spoke one language. According to Matthews, the differences in their English "are really very few—and they are of trifling importance." But they emphatically rejected the idea promoted by White, that upper-class Englishmen are arbiters of the language. "To declare a single standard of speech is impossible," Matthews asserted. Given the spread of English to all parts of the world, "the only possible standard for English speech," Lodge declared, is the usage of the best writers and the best-educated speakers "without regard to where they may have been born or to where they live." He objected to the term "the Queen's English" because the majority of English-speakers were not subjects of England's queen. But he rejected the term not to separate American English from British English but to affirm the unity of the language of all English speaking peoples.[17]

In an undated entry in his "Savings Bank" notebook, Howells defined Americans as a "new people without a new language."[18] He did not advocate the establishing of a separate language; he referred to "American English" or "continental English," not to "American" or "the language of the United States." But he is distinguished from Matthews, Lodge, Lounsbury, and Higginson by his stress upon the differences rather than the likenesses between American and British English. His cardinal principle, the opposite of White's, was that Americans should *not* look to England for their standard of good English. If Americans attempt to conform to British usage, Howells argued, "we shall be priggish and artificial." Instead, writers should strive to write "good American English—the only kind of English that Americans can be expected to write 'like natives.'"[19] In *A Fearful Responsibility*, when the American girl, Lily Mayhew, visits the Elmores, an American family in Venice, Howells notes: "Now it was not only English they spoke, but that American variety of the language of which I hope we shall grow less and less ashamed" (p. 23).

Howells devoted several essays in *Harper's Weekly* to mild ridicule of Americans who would abandon "their national speech" in favor of "a certain prevalent dialect of the English language" spoken by the British upper class. He joined Matthews and Lounsbury in regretting the replacement of *sick* by *ill*, observing that the Americans outdid the British by converting *ill* into the modifier of a noun (the ill man). He was willing to accept the British spelling of words like *honour* and *traveller*, but only because neither American nor English spelling was logical, and the English "are too wrong-headed to conform to ours." When *honor* appeared without the *u* in a British publication, Howells humorously despaired of our ever "keeping up with the English in the last refinements of Form."[20]

Howells also stressed the differences between American and British English by noting the failure of British writers to represent American speech accurately. He wondered at the talk of the American colonel in Bulwer's *The Parisians*, "so preciously unlike the sort of American talk which it is supposed to represent." He noted that E.F. Benson, who surpassed Reade, Trollope, and Dickens in portraying Americans, let one of his educated Americans say, "I want to know." He criticized Grant Allen for making his upstate New York characters in *Babylon* speak a mixture of Pike and blue grass dialects. "His people are Americans of the sort that the accurate English eye has seen and the delicate English hand has drawn ever since we were first portrayed in *Martin Chuzzlewit*." In a letter to E.C. Stedman, Howells described an English doctor who "tells me he will 'pull round.' Of course he means 'through,' but you can't expect an Englishman to speak our language correctly."[21]

The least objectionable English characters in Howells's fiction are those like Lord Rainford in *A Woman's Reason* and Lydia's uncle in *The Lady of the Aroostook* who try to speak to Americans in their own language but often encounter "unresponsive blankness" (p. 242) when they talk of "keeping the ball rolling" or being "up a stump" (p. 249). Lydia's English uncle, who keeps a notebook of Americanisms, and her aunt, an American, who instructs Lydia that she must say *ill* because "sick is an Americanism" (p. 276), are both comic figures. The uncle is a genial harmless soul, however, who in his enthusiasm for America does not repudiate his own country, as does his foolish wife, who tells Lydia, "You've no idea how droll our customs seem here; and I much prefer the English" (p. 246).

Similarly, Marian Ray, in *A Woman's Reason*, adopts English habits of speech after a few months abroad, returning to America "quite English in her intonation," in enjoyment of "the difficulty, which sometimes besets American sojourners in England, of distinguishing herself from the aristocracy, or at least the landed gentry" (pp. 63, 380). In his one-act comedy "A Letter of Introduction," Howells satirizes both Americans who substitute English words for American (e.g., *boxes* for *trunks*), and the priggish English visitor who earnestly inquires the meaning of American slang (*paint the town red, bark up the wrong tree, take the cake*), perceives the drollery of expressions some moments after he hears them, and asks his American hosts: "Is that peculiar dialect used by your California writers spoken in the cities?"[22]

Repeatedly, Howells insisted that American life was essentially different from English life and that no foreigner could fully comprehend or recreate American civilization "necessarily springing from our own peculiar conditions and impossible from any others." He also reminded Americans that English larks and nightingales and cowslips did not belong in pictures of their native land.[23] In *Years of My Youth*, he recalled that when he sought to render in poetry the beauty of the Ohio fields and woods, his father "guarded me against translating it in the terms of my English poets....He contended that our own birds and flowers were quite as good, besides being genuine." (pp. 82-88).

Because he believed the language of Americans to be the ever-changing product of conditions unique to them, he believed inevitable the divergence of American and British English and welcomed it. He rejoiced to see "our inherited English ...constantly freshened and revived from the native sources" and declared that if American English becomes as different from the "English of the scholasticists as the rehabilitated Norse is from the Danish, we do not think that will be cause for grief, but the contrary." More emphatically, but with the characteristic touch of humor, he affirmed: "The American who chooses to enjoy his birthright to the full, lives in a world wholly different from the Englishman's and speaks (too often through his nose) another language." Unlike Lowell, who rests his defense of dialect in *The Biglow Papers* on the claim that "the Yankee often has antiquity and very respectable literary authority on his side," Howells not only felt no need to establish a British pedigree for native words and idioms; he identified American English with the primacy of the continental as opposed to the insular: "Our continental English will differ more and more from the insular English, and we believe that this is not deplorable, but desirable. Our tongue will always be intelligible enough to our cousins across the sea."[24]

Brander Matthews identified literature as the most powerful of the forces uniting the speakers of one language: "Until it has a literature...a language is not conscious of itself...and it is by its literature chiefly that a language forever binds together the peoples who speak it." If the Americans and the English speak essentially the same language, as he affirmed, it followed that the literature of America and England was one literature—English literature. "Although it has ceased absolutely to be British, the chief literature of North America is still English, and must remain so, just as the chief literature of South America is still Spanish." As the English language has rooted itself in many parts of the world, so English literature, "still alive and sturdy after a thousand years," survived transplantation to flourish in the United States. The same view was expressed by Henry S. Pancoast, who, in *An Introduction to American Literature* (1898), defined his subject as "simply the American branch of English literature set by colonization in fresh earth...the continuation of English literature within the limits of what has become the United States."[25]

The potency of the view these men represented is evident today in the universities and colleges in which American literature is still taught in departments of English literature. In the 1890s a number of universities were just beginning to offer an elective course or two in American literature.[26] The Modern Language Association, founded in 1883, published 286 articles in the first twenty volumes of its journal (1885-1905), three of which were devoted to American literature.[27] Another article, "Language in a New Country," reduced American English to the status of a "colonial language" in a state of "arrested development" because it showed features of English dialects of earlier centuries.[28] The view that American literature was but a branch of English literature (and therefore subordinate to and dependent upon the parent stem) prevailed in the literary magazines. White insisted that Americans were merely "transplanted Europeans" and dismissed as "factitious" the separate identity of American literature. "English literature is the literature of all English-speaking peoples."[29] In one "Editor's Study" in *Harper's*, Charles Dudley Warner declared that literature by Americans about American life "is coming to have a stamp of its own that is unlike any other national stamp." But in a later "Study," although he acknowledged the existence of a "literature that is distinctively American," he insisted that "in the largest perspective there can be but one literature of the English-speaking race, with no separate limbo to be styled American."[30]

Underlying the definition of American literature as a branch of English literature were two premises: that language is an expression or function of race, and that the United States is essentially an Anglo-Saxon country, its defining element being the Americans of British stock, united to the British by Anglo-Saxon institutions, political and cultural traditions, and ideals. As German scholars and philosophers, such as Fichte, Friedrich von Schlegel, A. Kuhn, and Jakob Grimm, exalted the German language as the bond uniting all Germans in a race superior to others, so Americans, if somewhat less ardently, affirmed the identity of language and race. In White's words, "language belongs to race, not to place." Brander Matthews insisted that "language cannot but be a most important witness when we wish to inquire into the special peculiarities of a race." In the vigor of the English language he saw reflected the hardiness and independent spirit of the Anglo-Saxon race. William Dwight Whitney, Professor of Sanskrit and Comparative Philology at Yale, found in the study of language proof of the existence of "favored races." To trace "the history of language" is to "see how its growth has gone hand in hand with the cultural development of the race."[31]

Those who embraced the trinity of language, literature, and race also urged the primacy of racial ties binding America and England. Higginson anticipated the prevailing sentiment at the turn of the century when he celebrated both the independent vitality of American culture and "this broad Anglo-Saxon manhood which is the basis of our national life." Scholars and editors of the national magazines and newspapers as well as political and military figures such as Lodge, John Hay, and Alfred Thayer Mahan, celebrated the bonds of language and race joining the United States and England in an Anglo-Saxon partnership. "The literary history of America," Barrett Wendell concluded in his book of that title (1900), "is the story, under new conditions, of those ideals which a common language has compelled America, almost unawares, to share with England."[32]

George William Curtis, during his thirty years' tenure in the Editor's Easy Chair of *Harper's*, insisted upon the necessity of friendship with the English, "a people of our own race and tradition"; he accused England of playing the part of a "political Tartuffe" during the Civil War, but declared that conflict between the United States and England would also be civil war. "We are mainly sprung from the Anglo-Saxon stock. Our language, our history, our political, social, and moral traditions are all derived from that civilization." Brander Matthews, a prominent spokesman for the Teutonic origins theory, which held English, Americans, and Germans to be descendants of the Anglo-Saxon "race" described by Tacitus, identified the United States as "one of the wide series of Anglo-Saxon states which now encircles the globe."[33]

Among the many proponents of some form of Anglo-American union was Howells's long-time friend John Hay, who, during his tenure as ambassador to Great Britain (1897-98), declared his mission "to do what I can to draw closer the bonds that bind together the two Anglo-Saxon peoples" and affirmed "a sanction like that of religion which binds us to a sort of

partnership in the beneficent work of the world." The pro-
motors of an Anglo-Saxon union included not only the imperi-
alists such as Carnegie, Sumner, and Hay, but the one-time
celebrators of the American spirit such as Higginson, who in
1906 favored a "wide and comprehensive tie which shall bring
the whole English speaking world under some general name,
yet leave the various parts to entire individuality."[34]

Pro-British sentiment in America was fostered at the turn of
the century by gratitude for the friendly actions of Britain
during the Spanish-American War, by the desire of Americans
to gain power in world politics through military alliance, and
by Americans' fear of the growing numbers of non Anglo-
Saxon peoples in the United States, which impelled Americans
of English stock and their supporters to try to reinforce their
position by strengthening their ties with England. In promoting Anglo-Saxon unity, writers also celebrated the powers of
the "Anglo-Saxon mind" and the "Anglo-Saxon character,"
claiming that Anglo-Saxons surpassed all other races in virtue,
intelligence, and political genius. British and American advocates of imperialist expansion and conquest justified their
aims on the grounds that the welfare of all peoples rested upon
the dominance of the Anglo-Saxon nations. In the words of the
New York lawyer John R. Dos Passos, "the unification of the
English-speaking peoples means the elevation and enlight-
ment of mankind, the mitigation of suffering, and the opening
of new roads to human happiness."[35]

Exponents of Anglo-Saxon power and superiority naturally
asserted the primacy of the English language in glorifying
Anglo-Saxon conquest and colonization. Fitzedward Hall predicted that if any language ever became universal it would be
English. Lodge, a leading advocate of annexation of the Philippines, exulted that "English is the language of a conquering,
colonizing race," as did Brander Matthews, who noted approvingly that Anglo-Saxons showed "no slackening of their
determination to reach out and to possess themselves of more
and more territory." Matthews prophesied that by the year
2000 English would claim more speakers than any other language except the Russian, which he dismissed as representing

"another civilization in a more or less remote part of the globe." Likewise, John Fiske predicted that by the end of the twentieth century English would be the language of "every part of the earth's surface not already covered by a well-established civilization." Lafcadio Hearn believed that Fiske's prediction would be realized if the influence and wealth of England did not decline.[36]

Glorification of English, the "conquering language," was accompanied by celebration of Anglo-Saxon words, judged superior in strength and "manly vigor" to words of Greek or Latin or French origin. The Saxonist revival in England led by William Barnes, the Dorset poet and philologist, had supporters in America. The Shakespeare scholar Horace Howard Furness, in a letter to the president of the Board of Education of Philadelphia, applauded the "great and healthy and growing interest in the early structure and history of our own language." In studying it, he asked, "are we not acquiring at the same time a knowledge of the bone and sinew of our own strong, sturdy English? a knowledge that will help us throughout life to express our thoughts in honest, homespun, vigorous phrases?" Like Barnes, the American linguist Elias Molee argued that a Saxon vocabulary was more democratic than Latinate English because better understood by the common people.[37]

The study of Anglo-Saxon words became the province not of ordinary readers, however, but of specialists in universities, where by the 1890s Old English literature and language dominated the curriculum of many English departments. The University of Chicago, for instance, in 1897 offered two courses in American literature and six in Old English. Professor James M. Garnett of the University of Virginia recommended that a course in Anglo-Saxon be required for both the bachelor's and master's degrees, because in the language one touches "the qualities of the Anglo-Saxon mind, the plain, straightforward common-sense, the earnest vigor, the patient endurance characteristic of the people." During the twenty years (1885-1905) that *PMLA* published its three articles on American literature, it published twenty-four articles on Old English literature.[38]

The popular magazines enthusiastically supported the Anglo-Saxonists. A writer in *Godey's Lady's Book* approvingly quoted the dictum of T.L.K. Oliphant, who, in *Sources of Standard English*, likened Early Middle English to a "fine stone building" weakened when "bricks from France replaced part of 'the good old masonry.' " According to Charles Dudley Warner of *Harper's*, "the shorter the words, the more of Anglo-Saxon vigor." Other writers in *Harper's* extolled the "true vocabulary" of a "real speaker," i.e., "the language of the dogmatic will, the resolute purpose, the imperial soul—the noble, glorious, old Anglo-Saxon." They urged ministers to speak in "the simple, vigorous Saxon of the Bible and the heart," declared it "a general rule, that the best English is that in which Saxon-derived words are used the most freely," and urged the study of Anglo-Saxon in colleges and universities on the grounds that "the terse forms of the Anglo-Saxon element afford the most potent words and phrases for popular address" and are "the most important element in our native tongue." *Saxon* was modified by such adjectives as *pure, good, clean-cut, noble, honest, courageous, steady, vigorous, manly,* and *glorious. Saxon* connoted northern forests, rugged strength, simplicity, staunch and sturdy men "with granite and iron in them."[39] A few writers reminded readers that polysyllabic Latinate words were as essential to the English language as Anglo-Saxon monosyllables, and that words derived from the Anglo-Saxon were not innately superior to words from the Latin.[40] But defenders of the virtue of the Latin were outvoiced if not outnumbered by the champions of Anglo-Saxon strength.

Although Howells went further than Matthews, Lowell, and Higginson in stressing the differences between American and British English, until the turn of the century his view of the cultural and racial ties between the two nations was not markedly different from theirs. It is true that his anger, roused by British sympathy with the Confederacy, endured for years after the Civil War. In *A Fearful Responsibility* (1881) he portrayed the English painter Rose-Black as an offensive boor who provoked him to observe sarcastically "how forbearing and generous and amiable Englishmen are" (p.100). In the same year he exclaimed in a letter to Higginson: "*What* a great thing it is not to be an Englishman! It's a sort of point of nobility." Savage attacks upon Howells appeared in the British quarterlies after publication in the *Century* (Nov. 1882) of his essay pronouncing the art of Henry James superior to that of Dickens and Thackeray, and exacerbated feelings of hostility on both sides. In his "Editor's Study" Howells denounced British literary criticism as arrogant, provincial, and egotistical, related American literature to the traditions of Continental, not English, literature, and applauded Mark Twain's attack on the British monarchy and aristocracy in *A Connecticut Yankee*.[41]

During the 1880s and 1890s, when his criticisms of the English were sharpest, however, Howells was also asserting the unity of the Anglo-Saxon peoples in references to "our race," "we Anglo-Saxons, both British and American," "our Anglo-Saxon civilization," "the two branches of the Anglo-Saxon race." He designated London and Boston as "the aesthetic capitals of our race," described American writers from Franklin to Emerson and Lowell as "Englishmen rooted in another soil and blossomed in another air," and argued that American literature was not an outgrowth of the folklore of the Red Indians, but was "a condition of English literature."[42]

His "Editor's Study" of May 1886 praised Froude's *Oceania* for showing "the real solidarity of the Anglo-Saxon civilization, and the simultaneity of its characteristics." In another "Study" (Nov. 1891), he denied that Americans had either a language or a literature "wholly their own" and insisted that "for all aesthetic purposes the American people are not a nation, but a condition. They are the old, well-known Anglo-Saxon race, affected and modified by the infusion of other strains, but not essentially changed by these." Although his designation of England as "insular" and the United States as "continental" expresses his sense of the primacy of America, as late as 1898 he was referring to "our branch of English fiction" and to the "parent stock."[43] In *Miss Bellard's Inspiration* (1905), when the American girl Lillias proposes to break with her estimable English suitor, Edmund Craybourne, telling him,

"We are not only of different natures, but different races," Howells presents the response of the Englishman as the more sensible": "I had always supposed the Americans and English were of the same race—the Anglo-Saxon race. Or if you won't allow that, we're certainly of the same human race" (p. 183). The resolution of their differences in a renewal of their engagement and the promise of a happy marriage seems to confirm the rightness of his view.

The contradictions in Howells's attitudes are not to be reconciled. But there was no inconsistency in his attitude toward the ideas of Anglo-Saxon dominance and the supremacy of English as the conquering language. He emphatically, without qualification, rejected these imperialist ideas. He utterly repudiated Lord Rosebery's vision of a political union of America and England, declaring that it was worth the price of a war for independence to be rid of the British aristocracy, the state church, and the "grotesque idolatry of sovereign worship." He was a vice-president of the New York Anti-Imperialist League; in letters and essays he denounced American annexation of the Philippines; he referred sardonically to the "*rapprochement* of the two great Anglo-Saxon nations for the exploitation of weaker peoples," and condemned Cecil Rhodes's dream of a "universal Anglo-Saxon empire" as a "cheap and vulgar hallucination." Far from asserting the superiority of Anglo-Saxons to all other peoples, Howells asked why the Anglo-Saxons, known to the world as the exponents of money and force, "should stand at the head of human affairs." The vision of English as the universal language left him cold. "We...do not share the wish of these that English should prevail to the exclusion of other tongues. English has its virtues, but it is well known that it is not so clear as French, so mystical as German, so musical as Italian, so dignified as Spanish. We should be extremely sorry if these languages should finally fall mute.... Rather than this should happen we would be willing that the orthography which prevents the universalization of English should continue a stumbling-block forever."[44]

During his years at the *Atlantic* (1866-81), when his ties to Boston and Cambridge were strongest, Howells saw America as an Anglo-Saxon stronghold menaced by invading immigrants, particularly the "Celtic army" and its "besieging shanties" (*Suburban Sketches*, p. 71). In later years, he modified his view, seeing not a conflict in which one force threatens the other, but a process of "successive assimilations" as one race follows another. In 1909, in an address to the New York Society for Italian Immigrants, he identified Italians as the most recent actors in the process, which began in New York with the Dutch, who were assimilated by the English, who in turn received the Irish, who were followed by the Germans, Slavs, and Italians.[45] Rather than America's roots in England, Howells, in his later years, stressed "our multiplicity of origin" and the identity of America as "a mixture of the plebian ingredients of the whole world." Although in one "Editor's Study" he declared that immigration had not changed the fundamentally Anglo-Saxon character of the American people (Nov. 1891), in another "Study" he declared that "the ideal America, which is the only real America, is not in the keeping of any one race; her destinies are too large for that custody; the English race is only one of many races with which her future rests" (March 1889).[46]

Howells had cordial relations with a number of English writers, including Edmund Gosse, William Archer, and Thomas Hardy. But his position in the 1870s as defender of Anglo-Saxon power in America reflects his ties to his New England friends such as Lowell and Norton more than it reflects any sense of a bond with the English. He acknowledged that the American of English extraction might on his arrival in England feel his English and his American forebears "join forces in creating an English consciousness in him," but after several months in England in 1904 Howells felt the sense of difference deepened by what bound the two nations: "I rather think my race and language alienated me the more from our parent English." He later praised Hardy for not writing about Americans, who although of the "same speech, race, and religion" as the English are too different from the "ancestral stock" to be other than foreign to the English.[47]

Howells desired the friendship of England and America

which would preserve the integrity of the United States and "replace the old grudge with memories of good done together for the whole race." But more than the partnership of two countries he sought amity among all nations. Rather than the bonds uniting Americans and English he fostered the bonds uniting all peoples. He judged patriotic literature "distinctly inferior" to that which appeals to us "not as Americans, or Englishmen, or Frenchmen, or Russians, or Spaniards but as civilized men." Although he believed in inherited racial traits, he disliked the way nations claimed for themselves virtues "which belong rather sparingly to the whole of humanity; they speak of English fairness, and German honesty, and American independence, and they really make themselves believe that other people are destitute of the qualities which they severally arrogate to themselves."[48]

Howells objected to Taine's method of literary analysis, believing that his famous theory of race, milieu, and moment failed to account sufficiently for the artist's individuality. "Rigorously applied, [Taine's theory] would make us expect to find all the artists of a given people at a given time cast in one mould." Howells might also have objected to Taine's theory on the ground that it failed to account for the many resemblances Howells noted between peoples of different races, times, and places. Seeing in Central Park the Egyptian obelisk given by the Chedive, Howells reflected on the "essential unity of the civilization beside the Nile and beside the Hudson." In a review of Domingo Sarmiento's autobiography, he stressed the resemblances between the early careers of Abraham Lincoln and the Argentine leader, while acknowledging the "ineffaceable differences between the two men of race, religion, and traditions." Howells documented the universality of human nature in two articles on humor, in which he developed the thesis that "humor is human and not national," that to speak of French or Spanish or German humor is misleading for "essentially they are all alike." What most interested him in Switzerland was that a foreign country could be "so kindred in ideas and principles to ours."[49]

The masterpieces of realism produced in the nineteenth

century by Europeans and Americans proved that artistic ideals were not confined by national boundaries. In his "Editor's Study," Howells repeatedly celebrated the "universal impulse" realized in the works of Zola, Turgenev, Tolstoy, James, Hardy, Ibsen, Bjornson, Valdés, and Galdós. He praised T.S. Perry for his "sense of simultaneity of the great literary movements or aspects." He noted in Balzac's *César Birotteau* and Gogol's *Dead Souls* likenesses that illustrated "the simultaneity of the literary movement in men of such widely separated civilizations and conditions."[50]

In a devastating review of Wendell's *A Literary History of America*, Howells charged its author with "mistak[ing] the nature of our literature" and insisted that American literature, as "the daughter or the granddaughter" of English literature was interesting only in its "inequality or unlikeness" to its parent. This view seems in conflict with his belief that the literary critic should emphasize what unites, not what divides, mankind, that he should demonstrate the "final unity of human nature, in which all the strangest and remotest things are akin."[51] But American literature was a special case. To demonstrate its universality, Howells believed, the critic had first to affirm its identity as the product of unique conditions. Only then could the critic secure for American literature its place of equality with all other literatures, including that of England.

The statements of Howells's contemporaries, such as Lodge, Hay, Matthews, Wendell, and Pancoast, illustrate the observation of Howard Mumford Jones that after the Civil War the prevailing view of American literature changed radically.[52] Instead of urging American writers to assert their independence of British models, instead of calling for a national literature expressive of the American spirit, as Emerson, Bryant, and Channing had done, most men of letters, inside the universities and out, treated American literature as an inferior branch of English literature, deserving at most of one or two elementary courses in a college curriculum. In their literary histories they made English literature the standard by which they judged American literature, and they emphasized the literature of New England, which seemed to them most like English literature.

At times Howells appears to have shared their point of view, but taking the whole body of his writing, his references to America's literary dependence on Britain are far outweighed by his defense of the integrity of American English and American traditions. He did not venerate the British Empire; he did not believe that "our true place in literary history is as one of the literatures of this greater England."[53] He did not deny the national spirit; he worked, instead, to preserve and fortify it.

Chapter Four

Realism and Dialect

Fifty years after Emerson in 1837 delivered his oration "The American Scholar" to the Phi Beta Kappa Society of Harvard, Howells in his "Editor's Study" of October 1887 quoted the famous declaration: "I ask not for the great, the remote, the romantic;...I embrace the common; I sit at the feet of the familiar and the low." Like Emerson half a century earlier, Howells in his letters, fiction, and criticism exhorted American writers to turn their backs on the past, to cast away foreign models, to seek to capture the essence of the commonplace, and to create their own tradition in the representation of American life. As late as 1888, he complained that Americans were still "literary colonists," dominated by the English point of view, bound to "something worse than a literary past; we have a second-hand literary past, the literary past of a rich relation." Repeatedly he insisted that only from American life, from "wilding native growths," could a national literature come. He valued the "frank and self-reliant spirit" of western writers, the first, he believed, to escape the "colonial tone of deprecation, of apology" in treating American subjects.[1]

In urging American writers to make their own tradition, Howells was not only writing his declaration of American literary independence; he was affirming a literary philosophy in which political and artistic ideals were inseparable. When he asserted that "literature must be native to the soil...essentially of the people, of the land and time in which it is produced," he was upholding principles of truth and equality fundamental in his concept of realism. The ruling idea of his criticism is that fiction is justified by its realism, its truth to actual life, that the illusion of reality depends upon "the faithful, almost photographic delineation of actual life." Realism, which is "nothing more or less than the truthful treatment of material," is achieved not by the writer who looks to literature for reflections of life, but by the writer who goes directly to the life he knows, "who attempts to report the phrase and carriage of every-day life, who tries to tell just how he has heard men talk and seen them look."[2]

As this statement shows, language—"how men talk"—is of primary importance to the realist. If fiction is justified by its truth to the reality of everyday life, by "the respect for probability, the fidelity to conditions, human and social," then language that reflects those conditions must be rendered with fidelity. Often Howells defined realism in terms of language. The signs of "absolute and unswerving realism" are characters who speak "out the heart of human passion in the language of life." Howells praised the Norwegian exemplars of realism such as Ibsen, Bjornson, and Boyesen, who in creating character returned to the people "to study their language at its source on their lips." He urged American writers of fiction and drama to let their characters "speak the dialect, the language, that most Americans know—the language of unaffected people everywhere." Characters could be fully realized, he believed, only if they were rooted in their surroundings and shown to be the outgrowth of the conditions that have created the culture of a particular society or region. "The prime condition of their being themselves is that they shall be of their circumstance."[3] If language is created by and is expressive of the environment that shapes the characters, then the representation of their language becomes important in establishing the connection between characters and their circumstances.

The importance of language is further enhanced by Howells's conception of realism as an objective, dramatic rendering of characters which sustains the illusion of their independent existence. The realist "detaches, or seems to detach himself completely from his work, and to let it stand and go its way alone." In contrast to romanticism, which Howells equates with the undramatic and the subjective, realism achieves "that apparent self-being which is the perfect artistic illusion or the effect we call reality." He often compared the novelist to the dramatist or the actor whose "office is to make his audience feel the character and understand it," not by addressing the audience but by realizing the identity of the character.[4] By what they say, characters in fiction as well as drama reveal not only their motives, personality, range of interests, and habits of thought, but also their origins, social class, and degree of refinement. Diction, grammar, and syntax become an index to the attributes of a character and his society.

The principles of realism that Howells espoused governed his position on what proved, toward the end of the nineteenth century, to be a controversial topic—the use of dialect in literature. Howells defended dialect, believing that it creates a sense of reality, defines characters and their culture, and revitalizes our "inherited English" by the infusion of new words. He believed dialect to be an essential resource particularly for American writers, whose country, with its "vast spaces" and regional differences, forbade the creation of the "great American novel" and fostered instead an "intense localism" in its literature. "We are an intensely decentralized people in our letters as well as in our politics, and the justification of dialect is to be found not in this quarter or that, but everywhere that our authors have honestly studied the local life."[5]

As assistant editor and later editor of the *Atlantic Monthly,* Howells was always hospitable to works in dialect. In early reviews, he praised in Henry Ward Beecher's *Norwood* "certain felicity" in the use of Yankee dialect to express "the flavor and color of New England life"; he commended F.H. Underwood's *Lord of Himself* for its artistic portrayal of poor whites in Kentucky, whose "dialect is faithfully caught"; he extolled Lowell's mastery of dialect in *The Biglow Papers* and recommended his introduction to the second series as giving "more portable, trustworthy knowledge of Americanisms than is elsewhere to be found."[6] In 1872, Howells wrote a favorable review of Edward Eggleston's *The Hoosier Schoolmaster*, quoting a passage of Flat Creek idiom to illustrate a power to suggest through dialect the society of the Indiana frontier. According to Kenneth Lynn, Howells's decision to review *The Hoosier Schoolmaster*, "the most far-out work of fiction ever considered for mention in the *Atlantic* up to that time," marked the direction of Howells's editorial policy.[7] Among the works of fiction that Howells accepted for the *Atlantic* during his decade as editor were more than fifty stories and sketches containing dialect by Mark Twain, Bret Harte, Sarah Orne Jewett, Charles Egbert Craddock, Constance Fenimore Woolson, John De-Forest, Harriet Beecher Stowe, and Rose Terry Cooke.

Several years later, in his first "Editor's Study" (Jan. 1886), Howells affirmed the convictions that had guided his editorial policy: "Without asking that our novelists of the widely scattered centres shall each seek to write in his local dialect, we are glad...of every tint any of them gets from the parlance he hears....when their characters speak, we should like to hear them speak true American, with all the varying Tennessean, Philadelphian, Bostonian, and New York accents." He cared enough for fidelity to the "local dialect" to identify errors in the fiction he admired and praised in reviews: he questioned the use of *thar* and *whar* on the "New England tongues" of Mary E. Wilkins's characters; he identified as a "false note" Edith Wyatt's substitution of the Dundreary *w* for the *r* in her rendering of the Boston accent; and he wondered whether the contractions in the dialect Crane used in *The Red Badge of Courage* were to be heard in people's speech.[8]

Shortly before Howells became editor of the *Atlantic*, his fellow writer John Hay urged him to write a novel of western life, citing the "ravenous market" for works in dialect. In *Roadside Meetings*, Howells's friend and protégé Hamlin Garland recalled the public demand for "local-color recitals"—stories and songs in dialect—which turned lecture platforms, theaters, and magazines into "exponents of local-color art" and by the 1880s created a "cult of the vernacular," of which Richard Watson Gilder, editor of the *Century*, was "high priest." According to Charles Dudley Warner, Howells's successor in the

"Editor's Study," the writer in 1892 could produce "more mar-
ketable local color in a dialect than in any other things that can
be acquired."[9]

By the early 1890s, however, a reaction against dialect had
set in. Reviewers and essayists in the popular magazines complained that writers had overused dialect, that they relied on it
as a substitute for imaginative power in "working up" a lo-
cality. Warner, for instance, objected to the use of dialect as a
commodity by those who thought they might "somehow dye
the language and make it more expressive to the reading eye."
According to the popular novelist John Kendrick Bangs, "the
best books have had no dialect in them, and many of our worst
books have it in plenty." Frederic Bird, in *Lippincott's*, advised
writers: "Avoid dialect; as a main reliance, its day is done." The
subject provoked surprisingly vehement outbursts. T.C. De-
Leon in *Lippincott's* condemned dialect writers as "a curse to
the rising generation" and dialect fiction as an "epidemic," the
result of the "malarial influence of imitation," requiring "the
application of many a fierce blister of criticism." Even James
Whitcomb Riley, who affirmed the power of dialect to convey
"a positive force of soul, truth, dignity, beauty, grace, purity,
and sweetness," deplored the number of writers who, lacking
knowledge of the "inner character" of those they portrayed,
produced "rank abomination[s]" that "insulted, vilified, and
degraded" dialect and its speakers. The most distinguished
critic of dialect fiction, Henry James, protested against the
"complete debasement" of colloquial speech by such writers as
Charles Egbert Craddock and Sarah Elliott, whose works, to
James, were "suggestive of how little the cultivation of the
truth of vulgar linguistics is a guarantee of the cultivation of
any other truth."[10]

Always an advocate of the vernacular, Howells continued to
champion George Washington Cable, Craddock, Madison
Cawein, Thomas Nelson Page, James Whitcomb Riley, and
other writers of dialect. In June 1895, he devoted three articles
in *Harper's Weekly* to the merits of dialect, which he defended
as "part of the world-wide movement in fiction towards
greater naturalness and lifelikeness." He invoked the greatest

writers of dialect—Shakespeare, Dickens, Hardy, Ibsen, Goldoni, George Eliot—then conceded that, given the public's hostility to dialect, the writer might be well advised to use it sparingly, but insisted "when it comes to sacrificing a precious artistic effect...dialect must be used and used unsparingly." Here as elsewhere he took his characteristic position as mediator between opposing traditions: he celebrated both the masterpieces of European realism and American works in the vernacular that set themselves in opposition to European civilization.

Although Howells vigorously supported writers of dialect, in defending their art he made qualifications. He distinguished between the dialect of a character like Hosea Biglow and the "grotesque spelling" of such humorists as Artemus Ward, Petroleum V. Nasby, and Josh Billings, whose techniques he dismissed as "clownish tricks" and "orthographic buffoonery." (Howells later relented toward the humorists: "They were of the genuine American strain, and while they overworked their bad spelling in the genial cause, their will was always good.") He further distinguished dialect from vulgarisms and the cant peculiar to thieves and gypsies. True dialect was "descriptive of generic facts and ideas" and thus to be distinguished from the broken English of partly Americanized immigrants. Howells never argued that dialect automatically produced verisimilitude or the reality of a character. Believing that dialect should suggest the "personal rather than the provincial character of the speaker," he objected to Eggleston's apologizing for the oddity or rudeness of his characters' speech. Howells's ideal was Lowell's Hosea Biglow, whose speech was not rude or uncouth but "natural, pure, solemn, and strong," and who expressed the wit, humor, and sentiment of a whole civilization.[11]

If dialect reveals the distinctive features of a particular society or culture, dialect is also, in Howells's view, a means of uniting people of different cultures. His idea of realism rests on the conviction that people are bound to each other by their humanity, that in the speech and manners of a particular class or group are revealed universals of human nature. "What is true to humanity anywhere is true everywhere." To be true to one region is to be true to "human experience everywhere." He observed that Ibsen's plays, notable for their fidelity to actual speech, represent through their truth to the provincial scene "conditions universally human and not Norwegian merely." He argued that the so-called narrowness of American writers such as Sarah Orne Jewett, Edward Eggleston, and Charles Egbert Craddock was a virtue, not a defect, that a work depicting a New England village, a farm in the Indiana back country, or a settlement in the Tennessee mountains might be as broad as life, for "each man is a microcosm."[12]

Howells defined the realist as one who "feels in every nerve the equality of things and the unity of men." The duty of the realist is to "widen the bounds of sympathy" by revealing the conditions of a particular society so that readers, perceiving the likeness to themselves in others seemingly alien to them, may be "humbled and strengthened with a sense of their fraternity." Repeatedly Howells asserted as the primary function of literature this power to reveal to people their common humanity and urged writers to portray "those finer and higher aspects which unite rather than sever humanity." He celebrated the democratic impulse as opposed to the aristocratic spirit encased in pride of caste and taste. He venerated Ibsen, Tolstoy, Turgenev, and Goldoni because they achieved the "highest effect" of art—"to make one live in others" by creating in characters of societies perhaps remote from the reader's experience "eternal human types whose origin and potentialities everyone may find in his own heart." He envisioned American writers as a great partnership together "striving to make each part of the country and each phase of our civilization known to all the other parts."[13]

The ground of Howells's belief that fiction is the greatest of the arts, realism its highest expression, is given in his definitive statement of the writer's office:

Human nature is the same in all environments, and the chief delight that an author can give the reader is the delight of discovering it the same under all the masks and disguises that novel conditions have put upon it; of finding himself, his motives, principles, passions reflected in people of a wholly different tradition and physiognomy. This perpetually fascinates and perpetually satisfies; this forms the solidarity of all the arts, and the universality of fiction, which is the highest of the arts.

It is one of the most edifying facts in the prevalence of realism, which is the supreme phase of the highest art, that it has in a manner brought all the world together through just this loyalty to environment.[14]

Howells's faith in the power of realism to promote brotherhood seems based on an unswerving allegiance to principles of unity and equality which he championed throughout his life. Yet his theory of realism, when put into practice, reveals an inherent conflict. For Howells, "loyalty to environment," which fosters unity and a sense of kinship, required that the language of characters faithfully reflect their conditions, social and geographical. But as his own fiction shows, nothing more immediately establishes differences among characters than different habits of speech. Unless all the characters speak in the same way, dialect at once divides the speakers of the standard language from the nonstandard speakers. Howells himself in his essays on language distinguished different groups—the semi-cultured, the pseudo-cultured, the half-bred, the well-bred—by their speech. When he portrayed himself as "the elderly essayist" who had "judged the moral and social status of people by their saying 'different than' " and viewed with disbelief the spread to the "elect" of this "monstrous perversion" he was humorously exaggerating discriminations and distinctions he made in all seriousness.[15]

The collision of contradictory ideals is evident in *Harper's Magazine*, with which Howells was so long associated. On the one hand, the editors of *Harper's* championed national unity, insisted that no section could isolate itself from the whole, and repeatedly affirmed that the purpose of the magazine was to unite Americans, dissolve sectional antagonisms, bring all parts "ever nearer the main currents of our national unity, and "become a bond of sympathy and union among men of various climes and pursuits."[16] Yet for seventy years the "Editor's Drawer" printed innumerable anecdotes and verses in dialect in which certain groups, especially Negroes, Hard-Shell Baptists, rural Yankees, and the Irish, are made comic by their speech.

The force of the stigma attached to nonstandard English has already been seen in the scores of articles appearing in *Harper's* and elsewhere instructing readers in the "educated" pronunciation of words and warning them against the errors of the unlettered, the rustic, and the vulgar. Occasionally someone pointed out that an ungrammatical speaker was not necessarily a fool, that "crudity of diction is not always indicative of crudity of thought." In one "Editor's Study," Charles Dudley Warner obsrved that dialect may be the "chief badge" of a people's identity expressive of their nonconformity to the ways of the outside world. But Warner expressed the prevailing sentiment when in another "Study" he referred to speech as the means by which people try to efface a "vulgar beginning" and by which their humble origin may be betrayed despite "the most careful circumspection and training."[17]

For more than a hundred years, Americans had upheld the ideal of uniform pronunciation. In 1783, Noah Webster, in a letter to the New York Legislature, defined the aim of his new *American Spelling Book and Grammar*: "to render the pronunciation of [the language] accurate and uniform by demolishing those odious distinctions of provincial dialects which are the subject of reciprocal ridicule in different states." In *Notions of the Americans* (1828), James Fenimore Cooper warned against regional variation, which might produce "a dialect distinct from that of the mother country," and observed with satisfaction that "the distinctions in speech between New-England and New York, or Pennsylvania, or any other State, were far greater twenty years ago than they are now. Jacob A. Cummings emphasized in his *Pronouncing Spelling Book*, "the great importance of preserving uniformity in our country, and of avoiding what already begins to be called northern and southern pronunciation." For professors of rhetoric and writers on etiquette alike, the ideal was the speaker whose pronunciation did not reveal his origins because he had removed from his speech "all geographical sign-boards labelling a man's provinciality." According to A.S. Hill, the best speech is that which is "most free from local or professional peculiarities, and conforms most closely to the language as used by men and women of culture." Mrs. Burton Kingsland advised readers of *Correct Social Usage* to "avoid the pecularities that mark you as from any special district."[18]

In diverging from these views Howells upheld the principle of unity in diversity. He could affirm this principle without inconsistency when he portrayed regional differences in the speech of educated Anglo-Saxon Americans of the same social class. But in his portrayal of speakers of nonstandard English, the contradictions implicit in his definitions of realism become apparent.

Chapter Five

The Problem of "Negro Dialect" in Literature

Nowhere was the unifying force of language more vigorously asserted by Howells's contemporaries than in their definitions of race. According to Brander Matthews, a "community of language" was more potent than any other community in creating "the unrelaxing bonds that hold a race firmly together." But to define language as the "uniting bond between men" was also to acknowledge its power to divide people of different tongues. In the words of Charles Dudley Warner, precisely because language is "the final expression of national life and of thought," language is "a veil between the races, never quite thin enough, with the utmost familiarity, to be transparent."[1]

Warner is referring here to languages of different nations, which he declares can never be translated. But American writers reinforced barriers between speakers of English by creating dialects for certain groups within the United States. Many nationalities, such as the Irish, Germans, Italians, French, and Chinese, were identified in stories and poems by the words they mutilated and the syntax they skewed. Even more familiar to readers was the dialect fashioned for uneducated blacks, who far outnumbered characters of any other non-Anglo-Saxon group in American literature. Howells's belief in the power of dialect to unite readers in the recognition of their common humanity thus receives its severest test in the writing, including his own, which purports to render the speech of blacks.

During the twenty-five years before Howells wrote his first criticism of a black writer, a review of Paul Laurence Dunbar's poetry (1896), the popular literary magazines published hundreds of stories, anecdotes, sketches, poems, and installments of novels portraying black characters speaking in dialect. The writers of prose fiction, notably Mark Twain, George Washington Cable, and Joel Chandler Harris, created the most memorable black characters—Jim in *Huckleberry Finn*, Bras-Coupé in *The Grandissimes*, and Uncle Remus—but the writers of dialect verse established the literary conventions governing the portrayal of black characters and their speech. Between 1875 and 1880, *Scribner's Monthly* published more than a dozen poems in Negro dialect by Irwin Russell, who in such verses as "Uncle Cap Interviewed," "Novern People," and "Mahsr John" set the pattern followed by Thomas Nelson Page, A.C. Gordon, and others. The dialect speaker in their poems—more often than not an aged black man called Uncle, occasionally a preacher, sometimes blind, usually born in slavery—recalls the happiness of life before the war with his "marster and mistis," extols their virtues, and laments his freedom. He praises his old master as greater than "Washintum an' Franklum' an' sech genuses as dose" ("Mahsr John"), explains why life is so much better for Negroes in the "Souf" than in the "Norf" ("Novern People"), tells his children to "be 'spectful to all de white people you see" (Russell, "Precepts at Parting"), says of himself "Dis hyar nigger am quality" because his owners "wuz ob high degree" (Page, "Uncle Gabe's White Folks"), and mourns a son who died saving the white master's son, who in turn died of grief in losing his black friend (A.C. Gordon, "Kree").[2]

Although Russell, Page, Gordon, and their school celebrated the absolute devotion to each other of black servants and white masters, the poets also assumed an unbridgeable gulf between blacks and whites. Russell marvels at the difference between his Negro characters and his white readers, in his longest, most idyllic picture of plantation life, "Christmas Night in the Quarters" (1878). Scenes rendered in thick dialect depicting plantation Negroes dancing, singing, fiddling, and telling tales of ghosts and conjurors alternate with stanzas in the standard English of a white observer who invites the reader to "Observe them at their Christmas Party. / How unrestrained their mirth—how hearty: / How many things they say and do, / That never would occur to you."[3]

In his introduction to *Poems by Irwin Russell*, Joel Chandler Harris declared Russell a pioneer in realizing "the literary possibilities of the negro character" and praised as "the most wonderful thing about the dialect poetry" its "accurate conception of negro character." Harris's most famous character, Uncle Remus, teller of the folktales in dialect published in *Harper's* and the *Century* in the 1880s and later collected in three volumes, seems cast in the mould of Russell's aged black speakers devoted to their white benefactors and yearning for the past. Although, as Louis Rubin observes, he is the champion of the weak and vulnerable when he recounts the triumphs of Brer Rabbit over his aggressive adversaries, he is described by Harris as "kindly and venerable," "the type" of his race, who had no desire to be free, has "nothing but pleasant memories of the discipline of slavery," and shares with his mistress, Miss Sally, "all the prejudices of caste and pride of family that were the natural results of the system."[4]

This statement perfectly describes the black speakers in Page's *In Ole Virginia* (1887), generally considered to be his best work. The narrators of "Marse Chan," "Unc' Edinburg's Drowndin'," and "Meh Lady," former slaves who loved their white masters, completely embody the values Russell and Harris had identified with the Negro dialect speaker: undying fidelity to the master and all his family, everlasting gratitude for their never-failing kindness and affection, pride in their own servile status because they served "de quality," and conviction that the Negroes were happiest in slavery.

Also flattering and reassuring to white readers was the

reverse of the picture—the caricature of the Negro as a comic rather than pathetic figure, the credulous buffoon dressed in gaudy colors, ignorant, superstitious, prone to lying, chicken-stealing, and misuse of big words—the stock figure familiar to audiences of the minstrel show. The popular literary magazines in Howells's era perpetuated the stigma of dialect in its crudest form in the publication of jokes and cartoons in which Negroes exhibit ignorance, greed, stupidity, and servility in grossly fractured English. Month after month, the "Editor's Drawer" of *Harper's* and the "Bric-a-Brac" department of *Scribner's* printed poems and anecdotes about black preachers, waiters, and servants who are made ridiculous by their malapropisms and mispronunciations and failure to understand requests in the simplest English. One of Russell's blacks talks in court of the "Deestric Turner"; a black gardener in a cartoon tells white visitors that the architecture of a building is "ob de Modren French Rem'niscences"; a black waiter in a hotel apologizes for his delay in serving long-term guests: "I had to wait on de *transoms* first." As late as 1920, *Harper's* offered readers of "The Editor's Drawer" examples of "the magniloquent language in which our 'colored brethren' are so apt to indulge"—language supposedly comic in itself.[5]

The magazines perpetuated other stereotypes in dialect verses and jokes about tight-fisted Scots, rapacious Jews, cloddish Germans, and thick-headed Irishmen, but the Negro was more often caricatured than the white European. A favorite form of anecdote was the dialogue between a black servant and a white employer, who is shown to be wiser than the black. For instance, a black freedwoman admits that she was fooled into a bad marriage because her husband was "edicated" and "come co'tin' of me" with words "out do *jogafy* and *some* out de *dicshunary.*" Here and elsewhere, the prevalence of "eye dialect"—the rendering of a word phonetically which, like *dicshunary*, may represent what most people, educated or not, would say—heightens the effect of illiteracy. Preceding this anecdote from the "Editor's Drawer" of *Harper's*, August 1888, is a little essay on "naturalization" which asks whether one may give up "the instinctive tendencies of one race and take up those of another" and concludes: "One is likely to remain in the inmost recesses of his heart an alien."[6]

In the dialects of black figures ridiculed or sentimentalized in the magazines, twentieth-century readers have found elements more malignant than the crudities of other dialects. The deviations from standard English not only mark black figures as inferiors and aliens, as the lingos of the comic Germans and Irishmen establish their inferior status; according to recent scholars, both black and white, the Negro dialect fashioned by post–Civil War writers is itself a symbol of servitude, reflective of the white's desire, conscious or not, to enslave the Negro through language which at best connotes the simplicity of the faithful slave, at worst the primitive lusts of the criminal. Jean Wagner, for instance, maintains that Negro dialect—"an instrument of oppression when handled by white writers"— perpetuates myths about the Negro and is itself a myth fostered "to ensure that the mark of oppression should attach to him indelibly." Acknowledging that Uncle Remus is "finely conceived," Sterling Brown nonetheless criticizes Harris for using his dialect narrator as "the mouthpiece for defending orthodox Southern attitudes." Brown, Benjamin Brawley, and others stress the power of dialect to deprive the Negro of his humanity by perpetuating the familiar stereotypes: the Contented Slave, the Wretched Freedman, the Tragic Mulatto, the Comic Negro, the Exotic Primitive, the Brute Negro. Louis Rubin, in demonstrating the power of southern white writers to transcend the racial stereotypes in such works as *Huckleberry Finn* and *The Grandissimes,* acknowledges that even Mark Twain and Cable were confined by circumstances and literary convention while the black figures constructed by Page and his school "exist entirely as extensions of the white man's identity and requirements."[7]

Harris and Page and their followers naturally did not see their use of dialect as an act of oppression and self-justification. They identified themselves with the local color writers of other regions and defended their dialect as essential to a realistic picture of the Negro's life and character. Page insisted that his Negro dialect accurately reflected the "Negro's habits of thought...which I have endeavored to reproduce." In a letter to E.L. Burlingame (November 14, 1888), Harris wrote in reference to the language of the Aunt Minervy Ann stories: "I am very fond of writing this dialect. It has a fluency all its own; it gives a new coloring to statement, and allows of a swift shading in narrative that can be reached in literary English only in the most painful and roundabout way." He defended dialect in general as "the natural vehicle" of the most popular forms of American humor; he defended the Negro dialect in the Uncle Remus tales as necessary to his purpose of giving the "genuine flavor" of plantation life and preserving the old folktales in the language in which "they have become a part of the domestic history of every Southern family." He insisted on the difference between the dialect of Uncle Remus and that of "the Hon. Pompey Smash" and "the intolerable misrepresentations of the minstrel stage." He accounted his dialect a failure if it did not represent the Negro's "quaint and homely humor" or convey "a certain picturesque sensitiveness—a curious exaltation of mind and temperament not to be defined by words." Anticipating Howells's defense of regionalism and dialect in the "Editor's Study," Harris also affirmed that through "localism," reflecting the "tone and color" of the particular region, the writer of dialect helps to unite Americans by making the people of different parts of the country known to each other.[8]

The enthusiastic reviews of the fiction of Page and Harris, the publication of three volumes of Uncle Remus tales, the number of dialect stories and poems in the magazines indicate that many readers liked their contemporaries' depiction of the plantation Negro and saw nothing pernicious in his dialect. In an article in the *Southern Bivouac*, Charles Foster Smith stressed the contribution of dialect to the "wonderful advance" made by Harris and Cable over earlier southern writers. Charles Coleman, writing on southern literature in *Harper's*, May 1887, asserted the value of dialect in revealing the people of different regions to each other and declared Page's "Marse Chan" to be "the most exquisite story of the war that has yet appeared."[9] (This issue also included, in its "Editor's Drawer," an anecdote about a "Nigger with a Card," another in which a white child asks her mother if God, who made all people, thought Negroes were *pretty*, and a third in which an old black cook, against her mistress's advice, leaves to marry "Uncle Peter" and discovers him to be exactly what her mistress had said, "a stingy old miser," who hires her out to do laundry.) Readers who wanted to believe that southern whites treated Negroes well, or who believed that Negroes were a biologically inferior race, happiest in slavery and forever doomed by congenital deficiencies to inferior status, would not object to pictures of Negroes living in happy dependency upon benevolent masters.

Not all nineteenth-century readers shared Page's and Harris's ideas about Negro dialect. In praising *Uncle Remus: His Songs and Sayings* as a humorous but serious work, a reviewer in the *New York Evening Post* (Dec. 6, 1880) objected to "the comic aspect necessarily given to the book by its illustrations and by the look of dialect in print."[10] Annie Steger Winston, in an article on "The Democracy of Fiction" in *Lippincott's Magazine*, observed that many Negroes speak "passably good English," argued that dialect often reflects class spirit rather than concern for realism, but thought it unlikely that "any truly Southern writer" would discard "the badge of inferiority to be found in dialect" and admit the Negro to "the equality of good English."

Years before George Philip Krapp and Sumner Ives observed that the speech of uneducated Negroes and rustic whites is very similar, contemporaries of Harris and Page called attention to the similarity, noted that writers seldom represented the provincialities of upper-class white southern speech, and protested that in misspelling words like *was* and *enough*, which blacks and whites pronounce in the same way, writers made the speech of blacks seem more illiterate than it was. Writing in *Lippincott's*, William Cecil Elam maintained that dialect assumed to be peculiar to the Negro was in fact "equally the lingo of the wholly uneducated and socially degraded white," observed that the Negro talks "more or less" like the whites he hears most often, and condemned the practice of writers who upgraded the speech of whites as they debased the speech of blacks. "The treatment accorded the two races in this murdering of the language is analogous to that dispensed to murderers under our old colonial laws, which allowed benefit of clergy to whites and denied it to negroes."[11]

The widely used term "Negro dialect" was condemned by the novelist Charles Chesnutt, who declared that the term denoted not a dialect at all but simply English rendered "as an ignorant old Southern Negro would be supposed to speak it."[12] Page himself, in defending his use of dialect against the charge of inconsistency, acknowledged that the Negro "gets his language from his associates," that his dialect "is in a constant state of mutation," and that, therefore, "there is no fixed dialect, and certainly no negro language." Page's defense of his dialect was followed a month later in the *Critic* by "A Protest against Dialect," in which a correspondent from Richmond asked why dialect writers "spell phonetically words which a Negro pronounces exactly the same as a white man does....A white man reporting a Negro's *speech* has no business to write as the Negro would *write*." He advised that dialect be dropped and declared that he lost half the pleasure in Page's "Marse Chan" "through the outlandish lingo put into old Sam's mouth." Page could hardly have improved upon the response to the Richmond critic, signed by a "Southern Matron" of Hampden-Sydney College: "The 'dialect tale' *cannot* be told in 'simple English, pure and undefiled,' as far as negro dialect is concerned. It is almost a language in itself; and the old negroes pronounce very few of our common words as the white man does." After praising the "genuine negro dialect, coming from the faithful negro's loving heart" in "Marse Chan," she declared this dialect to be "one of the glories of our Past."[13]

Readers may judge the power of dialect in creating an impression of character by considering Mark Twain's portrayal of the slave Roxana in *Pudd'nhead Wilson*. Roxana, who is only one-sixteenth black, looks, in Twain's words, "as white as anybody," but she speaks the "basest dialect of the negro quarter."

If readers imagine Roxana as black, not white, they acknowledge that it is her speech, not the description of her appearance, that defines her.

In his defense of literary dialects, Howells made no distinctions between the southern writers and those of New England
and the West. Apparently he saw nothing more invidious in the
speech of the plantation Negroes of Page and Harris than in the
Pike County dialect of Bret Harte's ballads or the Hoosier
speech of Eggleston's Back Creek characters. Although he repudiated the position of white supremacists like Page, who
insisted upon the Negro's "incapacity to rise" and upon "the
absolute and unchangeable superiority of the white race,"
Howells responded to the dialect fiction of the southern writers as they wished readers to respond. He judged Page's best
stories to be those in dialect because "his art in these is freest
and finest....I cannot think of another writer who has so deli-
cately and yet so honestly employed the Negro parlance for the
expression of the finer and nobler intentions." For Howells, the
dialect that separates the former slave from his master in
James Lane Allen's "Two Gentlemen of Kentucky" did not
prevent the author from showing that "at heart they are broth-
ers and equals."[14]

Howells most fully defined the grounds of his defense of
dialect in his review of Paul Laurence Dunbar's second volume
of poems, *Majors and Minors*, printed in Dayton in 1896. Such
was the power of Howells's critical influence that his full-page
review of the poems, published in *Harper's Weekly*, June 27,
1896, transformed the obscure twenty-three-year-old operator
of an elevator in an office building in Dayton into a nationally
known figure and established the point of reference for later
critics.

As Dunbar's title indicates, his poems are of two kinds: the
"Majors" in standard literary English and the "Minors" in
dialect. Howells's preference for the dialect poems as superior
in interest and literary merit to the others is the central critical
judgment of the review. He believed that Dunbar was like
Robert Burns in that each was least himself when he wrote

poetry in standard literary English. Although he recognized in Dunbar's "Majors" evidence of "honest thinking and true feeling," he found little to distinguish them from the verses most young poets write. In Dunbar's dialect poems, however, Howells felt the force of "a direct and a fresh authority" which revealed as never before the essence of the black character, "the heart of primitive human nature in [the poet's] race." He distinguished the sentiment of Dunbar's poems from the "too easy pathos of the pseudo-negro poetry of the minstrel shows," declared Dunbar the first Negro "to study his race objectively," but also claimed for him the same virtues of humor, sympathy, and tenderness he found in the white southern writers, and concluded that Dunbar "makes a stronger claim for the negro than the negro yet has done."[15]

This review, parts of which appeared in Howells's introduction to Dunbar's *Lyrics of Lowly Life*, shows as clearly as anything Howells wrote how he tried to reconcile the seemingly contradictory principles of unity and diversity. He valued Dunbar's dialect poetry as "expressions of a race-life from within the race"; he attributed Dunbar's rhythm and lyrical sense to his racial heritage. But he also affirmed the greater importance in Dunbar's poetry of the conscious art through which universal truth is expressed. For him, Dunbar's poetry revealed not only "the simple, sensuous, joyous nature of his race" but, to his surprise, a common ground of feeling between black and white. "I have sometimes fancied that perhaps the negroes *thought* black, and *felt* black; that they were racially so utterly alien and distinct from ourselves that there never could be common intellectual and emotional ground between us....But this little book has given me pause in my speculation. Here, in the artistic effect at least, is white thinking and white feeling in a black man, and perhaps the human unity, and not the race unity, is the precious thing, the divine thing, after all."[16]

Here Howells sets "white feeling" as the standard by which "human unity" is defined. In his introduction to *Lyrics of Lowly Life*, Howells placed black and white on the same plane: the poems are "an evidence of the essential unity of the human race, which does not think or feel black in one and white in another, but humanly in all." But, in Howells's view, "essential unity" comprehends distinctive racial qualities which should be preserved: "There is a precious difference of temperament between the races which it would be a great pity ever to lose."[17] Better than the poems in literary English, Howells believed, Dunbar's dialect poetry expressed the writer's individuality, embodied the essential qualities of his race, and revealed the spiritual unity of mankind.

Dunbar's response to Howells's recognition is a good example of the debt of gratitude that becomes the burden of a grievance. Dunbar credited Howells's review in *Harper's Weekly*, which brought him two hundred letters of congratulation, with establishing his literary reputation. Several days after the review appeared, he wrote to Howells, "Now from the very depths of my heart I want to thank you. I feel much as a poor, insignificant, helpless boy would feel to suddenly find himself knighted." Howells entertained Dunbar at his house on Long Island that summer, recommended him to Mark Twain's lecture agent, Major James Pond, and wrote to Ripley Hitchcock at Appleton's: "I believe a book of entirely *black* verse from him would succeed." When Dunbar went abroad, Howells gave him letters of introduction to British publishers.[18]

In thanking Howells for writing the introduction to *Lyrics of Lowly Life*, Dunbar wrote: "My affairs have very materially changed for the better, and entirely through your agency." But soon, while writing respectful, guarded letters to Howells from England, he was complaining to friends that because of Howells's review, editors refused to print anything but his dialect verse. To one correspondent he accused Howells of "[doing] me irrevocable harm in the dictum he laid down regarding my dialect verse." In his poem "The Poet," he lamented that the world "turned to praise / A jingle in a broken tongue." Another poem in literary English, which begins "We wear the mask," expresses Dunbar's view of the race's "joyousness" that Howells found in the dialect poems.[19]

Did Howells do Dunbar "irrevocable harm" by praising his poetry in dialect? Howells alone was not responsible for editors' requests for dialect. Three years before Howells reviewed *Major and Minors*, Dunbar complained to his friend, the Ohio poet James Newton Matthews, that editors "won't take anything but dialect so I have no market for anything else." Nor did Dunbar consistently repudiate his dialect poetry or place a low value on it. Although one interviewer quoted him as saying "I am tired, so tired of dialect," he is reported to have told others that "It took me some time to realize that my natural speech is dialect" and that "my fondest love is for the Negro pieces....These little songs I sing because I must. They have grown instinctively in me." As Dunbar's biographers, Benjamin Brawley and Virginia Cunningham, have noted, Dunbar was fascinated by dialects and liked to try to identify people by their speech. Dunbar acknowledged James Whitcomb Riley as one of his masters and wrote poems suggestive of Riley, such as his tribute "James Whitcomb Riley," in the dialect of rural whites, as well as imitations of German, Scottish, and Irish dialects. What Dunbar apparently resented and lamented was the failure, as he saw it, of editors to recognize his gifts as a poet in literary English, and for this failure he blamed the most influential of his critics.[20]

Dunbar's readers do not deny the importance of Howells's review but they differ in assessing the validity of Howells's judgments and the merits of Dunbar's poetry in dialect. James Weldon Johnson, a friend and champion of Dunbar, took issue with Howells in his preface to *The Book of American Negro Poetry* (1931), where he maintained that the Negro dialect in the poems Howells praised fosters the stereotype of the Negro as a comic or a pathetic figure, restricts the poet to conventional scenes of plantation life, and subjects him to the limitations of "an instrument with but two full stops, humor and pathos." Johnson objected to Howells's comparison of Dunbar and Burns, arguing that, unlike Burns, Dunbar wrote in a dialect not developed by his own race but imposed from without, the literary convention of an alien culture. J. Saunders Redding, in *To Make a Poet Black,* attacked Howells's comparison on the same grounds: that Burns's dialect was the standard of a whole people, whereas Dunbar's was "not native" but "synthetic," a "bastard medium" contrived for "Northern whites to whom dialect meant only an amusing burlesque of Yankee English."[21]

Others, too, have argued that Howells, in claiming that Dunbar's dialect poetry revealed the heart of his people, praised Dunbar for what he failed to achieve, that Dunbar's dialect was not authentic speech at all but "a phony Negro dialect," a fabrication expected by white readers and interpreted by them as Dunbar's acknowledgement of his inferiority and his acceptance of the stereotypes. In Wagner's words, the dialect Howells praised was "at best a secondhand instrument irredeemably blemished by the degrading themes imposed upon it by the enemies of the black people." Howells's critics argue that his recognition of Dunbar injured the poet by making a specious dialect the measure of his worth.[22]

Dunbar's dialect poetry has had many defenders who also endorse Howells's judgment that Dunbar made his distinctive contribution to American literature in his Negro dialect poetry. Dickson Bruce, Jr., quotes a number of black writers, the poet's contemporaries, who praised Dunbar's dialect poetry as an accurate representation of antebellum plantation life and preferred it to the poetry in literary English. Chidi Ikonné has declared that Howells justly praised Dunbar for striving in his dialect poems to view his race objectively. According to Darwin Turner, Howells "evaluated Dunbar's talents perceptively" when he judged the dialect poems superior to those in standard English. Benjamin Brawley has commended "the excellent spirit" in which Howells wrote of black-white relations, has endorsed his comparison of Burns and Dunbar, and has praised the poems in Negro dialect for their "delicate and sympathetic irony"—a quality often noted in Howells's work. In the opinion of James Stronks, Howells's review was "a priceless boost to Dunbar's career" and "possibly the greatest single event in American Negro literature to this day."[23]

Both the critics and the defenders of Howells can find support for their views in his writings on Dunbar. In referring to Negroes as "those people," Howells revealed his sense of distance from them; in attributing to the poet's race "a simple, sensuous, joyous nature" in which "the range between appetite and emotion is not great," he projected the familiar image of the unreflective primitive Negro. But Howells also declared Dunbar to possess powers of feeling and imagination that mark the great artist in any language. He judged Dunbar not only as a black poet—as "the first negro who has been able to deal objectively with negroism"—but as an "absolute poet" whose "excellences are positive and not comparative."[24]

Howells's reference to "white feeling" in Dunbar's dialect poems suggests that it was the poet's generally acknowledged affinities with white dialect poets, especially Riley, that paradoxically allowed Howells to feel himself drawn to the heart of what was to him an alien race. But Howells never urged black writers to model themselves upon whites. In fact, he anticipates the writers of the Harlem Renaissance in conceiving the ultimate achievement of blacks to be the creating of an original art, to be judged and valued, like any expression of an independent, native culture, for itself and not dependent on any other. In his praise of the stories of Charles Chesnutt, which he judged "remarkable...above most short stories by people entirely white," he declared that blacks "may create a civilization of their own, which need not lack the highest quality." This statement, immediately preceded by Howells's reference to "that sad solidarity" from which blacks have "no hope of entrance into polite white society," may seem to offer only a substitute for the social equality Howells does not foresee or advocate—analogous to the "separate but equal" doctrine. But in his literary criticism, Howells stressed the equality, not the separateness, of the races. Writers like Dunbar and Chesnutt showed capacity equal to that of whites to rise to the top in "that republic of letters where all men are free and equal." Although Howells believed that Chesnutt's novel *The Marrow of Tradition* was flawed by its "awful bitterness," he saw in its power the promise of work "that will scarcely be equalled in our fiction" and a "portent of the sort of negro equality against which no series of hangings and burnings will finally avail."[25]

In praising the work of black writers, Howells exposed himself to the charge that he did not understand the problems they faced in the post–Civil War era. Chesnutt, who like Dunbar won his first success in the portrayal of dialect speakers but chafed at the limits imposed by dialect, expressed gratitude for Howells's praise of his work but rejected Howells's belief that no "color line" in literature impedes the black writer. "I am pretty fairly convinced that the color line runs everywhere so far as the United States is concerned." Later writers, such as Houston Baker, Bert Bender, and Addison Gayle, have accused Howells of failing to perceive the plight of the black writers who to gain a hearing were forced to use a dialect that debased the people of their race.[26] Nothing in his reviews of Dunbar and Chesnutt, it is true, suggests that Howells was aware of their feelings about dialect or saw it as anything but an essential element in their art. But he was not blind to the position of the black writers in America. In *Their Silver Wedding Journey* (2:401), his spokesman, Basil March, reflects on Germany's neglect of Heine, who perhaps had not even a "step-fatherland" in the country he mocked as well as loved. March then admits to himself that "if he were a negro poet he would not feel bound to measure terms in speaking of America, and he would not feel that his fame was in her keeping."

Chapter Six

Language, Race, and Nationality in Howells's Fiction

The equality of races Howells believed to prevail in "the republic of letters" is absent in the society he portrayed in his fiction and essays. Unnamed blacks—usually waiters, janitors, or servants—appear briefly in several of Howells's novels (e.g., *Their Wedding Journey, A Hazard of New Fortunes, An Open-Eyed Conspiracy*), but blacks are prominent figures in only one work of fiction, *An Imperative Duty,* and in two essays: the first of the *Suburban Sketches,* which portrays the black cook, Mrs. Johnson, and "Police Report" (1882), which records the testimony of four black litigants in a Boston court. Of all the black figures, only a lawyer in "Police Report" speaks the English of educated whites or appears as their equal in intelligence or social rank.

Howells's portrayal of blacks documents actual conditions and also reflects attitudes and assumptions he shared with his contemporaries. Although he affirmed the unity of mankind, he accepted the widely held belief that race determines temperament and that national or ethnic groups are differentiated by inherited racial traits. Accepting the premises of racial determinism, he accepted the common racial stereotypes such as those by which white writers distanced themselves from the black characters they created. In his portrait of Mrs. Johnson in *Suburban Sketches,* for instance, Howells wed dialect to the type of the black primitive who has inherited "the Ethiop's supple cunning and abundant amiability" (p. 28), who exhibits a "ragged gayety, which comes of summer in the blood" (p. 20), and who reveals to the head of the white household she serves "how slightly her New England birth and breeding covered her ancestral traits, and bridged the gulf of a thousand years of civilization that lay between her race and ours" (p. 21).

To Howells as the observer of the court trials in "Police Report," the grammatical lapses of the black witnesses as well as their color make comic the "little drama" of domestic strife to which actors of "another complexion" might have given the intensity of tragedy. "I suppose it will be long before these poor creatures will cease to seem as if they were playing at our social conditions, or the prejudices and passions when painted black will seem otherwise than funny.[1] Basil March, in *An Open-Eyed Conspiracy*, registers a similar impression when at a hotel in Saratoga he sees a cast of black performers in "East Lynne," feels the artificiality in their attempts to assume "white" character and imitate "our convention," and concludes that the "African race" lacks "histrionic talent" (pp. 104-05). Rather like Howells in his preference for Dunbar's dialect poetry, March prefers "the most amiable of the human race" (p. 107) in what he considers "their own kindly character," as singers of spirituals and performers in walk-rounds (p. 104).

Howells most fully represents black characters in his short novel *An Imperative Duty*, set in Boston, in which a beautiful young girl, Rhoda Aldgate, brought up to believe that she is white, learns that she is the daughter of an octoroon, vows melodramatically in the shock of discovery to go South to serve "her people," but is persuaded by a young white doctor, who loves her despite her "taint," to marry him instead. Although the full force of white prejudice vents itself in Dr. Olney's initial revulsion when he learns the truth and in Rhoda's horror and loathing of her new-found race, grotesque and hideous in her eyes, the blacks are given a dignity lacking in the figures in the police court. The blacks in *An Imperative Duty* gain by the presence of the Irish—lower on the scale of intelligence and decorum, as represented by a thick-headed hotel servant baffled by the doctor's request to fill a prescription and by working girls, "thin and crooked," who embrace their "fellows" in public and babble in voices "at once coarse and weak" (pp. 4, 7). In contrast, black girls Olney observes dress stylishly, act decorously, and speak in "very thin, high piping voices that had an effect both of gentleness and gentility" (p. 8).

When Rhoda, after learning the truth, wanders in shock and despair into the black district, she encounters no lustful stereotypes but a contrasting type, an aged mulatto woman "from Voginny" who in a voice of "motherly kindness" tells Rhoda that the people she sees in the street are going to "a kyind of an evenin' meetin' at ouah choach to-night" (p. 61). The submissiveness with which she quotes scripture, tells Rhoda, "Them's the words, lady; the Lawd's own words," and meekly sighs, "Somebody's got to be black, and it might as well be me" (p. 62), is as typical as "the mild, sad face we often see in mulattoes of that type" (pp. 60-61).

The black student from a southern college who preaches in the church to which the old woman takes Rhoda is likewise a type but not a caricature. What is most interesting about him is the theme of his sermon. Four years before Booker T. Washington, in his famous Atlanta address, advocated reconciliation of the races through white assistance to blacks and black submission to the realities of white dominance—a policy Howells emphatically endorsed[2]—Howells portrayed a divinity student who likewise preaches reconciliation but without the eloquence of a great orator. Although Rhoda hears in his voice plaintive caressing notes like "some rich, melancholy bell," "the peculiar gift of his race" (p. 64), he reveals a common order of mind as he preaches benevolence in English neither flawless nor illiterate: " 'you got to commence doing a person good if you expect to love them as Jesus loved us when he died for us. And oh, if our white brethren could only understand— and they're gettin' to understand it—that if they would help us a little more, they needn't hate us so much, what a great thing,' the lecturer lamely concluded—'what a great thing it would be all round!" (p. 65).

Howells's black speaker is neither the comic grotesque whose "colored eloquence" amused magazine readers, nor the inspired evangel like Dunbar's minister in "The Miracle at Mount Hope," who "forgot his carefully turned sentences" and transported his congregation with words "like winged fire."[3] Howells's divinity student is not satirized but he is not individualized either. Significantly, in Rhoda's eyes, "he had no discernible features"; his profile is but a "wavering blur against the wall" (p. 63).

An Imperative Duty breaks with convention in its portrayal of the love of a white man for a woman of mixed blood. The assurance of their happy marriage sets Howells's treatment of miscegenation apart from earlier depictions, from the most celebrated, in *Uncle Tom's Cabin* and *The Grandissimes*, to the now-forgotten, in such novels as *The Chamber over the Gate* and *Towards the Gulf*, both of which Howells reviewed in the "Editor's Study" in 1887, three years before he wrote *An Imperative Duty*. Through the character of Dr. Olney, Howells deflates the melodramatic view of the "tragic mulatto" which Rhoda tries to take. Olney also rejects the popular notion of atavism that grips Rhoda's aunt in the fear that savage traits of Rhoda's ancestors will reappear in her or her children. But the doctor, who rejects the probability of "reversion," also refers repeatedly to the black as the "inferior race type." Although Howells does not caricature his black figures he creates no fully realized black characters to replace the types.

Most of the other non-Anglo-Saxon figures in Howells's fiction and essays, like the black figures, occupy a place low on the social scale and speak a nonstandard English that not only signals their inferior social status but in itself calls to mind the familiar stereotypes of racial jokes and cartoons. The thick-headed Irishmen in "Police Report"—a witness whose dullness obliges the magistrate to put a simple question to him seven times, and a vagrant who blankly replies "sor?" when asked if "habitually intoxicated" (p. 5)—are the prototypes of Irish characters in the novels and plays: the hotel servant in *An Imperative Duty*, tipsy bellicose travellers in "The Albany Depot," the thieving tramps in *Out of the Question*, a woman arrested for drunkenness in *The Minister's Charge* who wails over her three helpless "childer" and begs "your hanor" to "make it aisy" (p. 60).

The primitive nature of the "little Canuck," Jombateeste, in *The Landlord at Lion's Head* expresses itself in his fragments of broken English. In a conversation about the afterlife he offers his opinion of the Egyptians: "They know—they feel it in their bone—what goin' to 'happen—when you dead....Got it from the "Ebrew. Feel it in 'is bone" (pp. 191, 192). The more highly developed nature of the French Canadian tavern keeper Bird in *The Quality of Mercy*, depicted as talkative, hospitable, and honest, is reflected in his speech, which departs from standard English mainly in the matter of the *h*; he talks of "more gold in the 'ills" and admits, "I am too hold" (p. 189). Higher on the social scale in the same novel, the Quebec-born priest Father Etienne, who ministers to the defalcator Northwick, is represented as speaking an English without any regional peculiarities, as undefiled as his "pure and unworldly heart" (p. 204).

Likewise, Howells renders the speech of upper-class Englishmen—even the most detestable, such as Rose-Black in *A Fearful Responsibility*, without phonetic rendering of vowels or substitution of *w*'s for *r*'s. He is faithful, however, to the linguistic habits of the Cockneys in *Their Wedding Journey* and the young man in *The World of Chance* "whose Cockney origin betrayed itself in an occasional vowel and aspirate (p. 120). Cockney dialect serves a dramatic purpose in *The Rise of Silas Lapham*, when the fraudulent character of the purportedly English agents is revealed to the reader, if not to Silas, by the speaker who momentarily forgets to drop his *h*'s and then corrects himself.

Howells rarely represents the phonetic deviations of the English spoken by Italians, such as those who "practice the language" at the Venetian palace of Lydia's aunt in *The Lady of the Aroostook*. That they are not native English speakers is apparent when they say on meeting Lydia, "very please, very honored, much," and on bidding her goodbye, "I shall come a great deal to see you" (pp. 267, 264). But the Italians are not stigmatized by the solecisms and the eye dialect that disfigure the speech of Irish and black figures.

Of all the non Anglo-Saxon figures in Howells's fiction, only two have roles of central importance: the Italian priest Don Ippolito in *A Foregone Conclusion* and the German socialist and scholar Lindau in *A Hazard of New Fortunes*. In these two novels we may compare the effects produced by the foreign speaker whose words in English as well as in his native tongue are represented by standard English and the speaker whose foreign accent is reproduced in a word-for-word phonetic transcription of his speech.

Throughout *A Foregone Conclusion*, the protagonist Don Ippolito is said to speak in Italian and in English to the other main characters: the American girl Florida Vervain, to whom he gives Italian lessons and whom at the climax of the novel he astounds and horrifies by his declaration of love; her mother, a foolish, kind-hearted woman whose near-sighted vision corresponds to her failure to see the priest's futile passion for her daughter; and the American consul Ferris, who introduces the priest to the Vervains, likewise falls in love with Florida, and marries her several years after Don Ippolito's death. In the opening scene, in which the priest seeks the consul's aid, Ferris, upon hearing that Don Ippolito learned English from an Irish priest, is able to identify "a fine brogue superimposed upon his Italian accent" (p. 13). But Howells does not represent either the brogue or the Italian accent when Don Ippolito speaks in "his patient, conscientious English" (p. 78); he merely acknowledges "certain blunders which it would be tedious to reproduce" (p. 78). Nor does Howells indulge in the irritating practice of inserting foreign words and phrases (with a translation) into English speech to suggest foreignness. The "mixed language" the characters speak at the Vervains' is represented only by Don Ippolito's forms of address: *Madama* and *Madamigella*, by which, as Howells noted in his journal, the priest "compromises between the conventional English and Italian address."[4] Howells's use of standard English throughout the novel is in keeping with Ferris's insistence that the portrait of an Italian priest, such as he is painting of Don Ippolito, "doesn't need any tawdry accessories" (p. 74). In any case, Howells's use of standard English to render Don Ippolito's speech in both English and Italian did not prevent Henry James from feeling in the priest "not only a very vivid human being, but a distinct Italian, with his subtle race-qualities artfully interwoven with his personal ones."[5]

Standard English in *A Foregone Conclusion* is a flexible medium which through rhythm, diction, and syntax conveys the breathless emphases of Mrs. Vervain, the abrupt directness of Florida, and the colloquial ease of Ferris, who tells Don Ippolito that "In America…they don't care a fig for passports" (p. 6), confesses that the priest "stuck in my thought" (p. 56), tells Mrs. Vervain, "You've done it!" (p. 57), and wonders what Don Ippolito meant "by pumping him in that way" (p. 87). The ceremonious speech of the Italian servants, whose habitual use of ceremonial forms Howells noted in *Venetian Life*,[6] is represented in their requests to Ferris to "Favor me above," and to visit Don Ippolito "if such a thing were possible in the goodness of your excellency" (p. 232). Don Ippolito's speeches in both English and Italian unroll in fluent sequences of adjectives, parallel clauses and rhetorical questions, suggestive of both the rhythms of the priest's Italian and the carefully worded constructions of English spoken by a foreigner moved to theatrical pose in times of strong feeling. The most famous character in *The Merchant of Venice*, the play to which Ferris once refers, comes to mind when Don Ippolito passionately asks of the consul whether a priest "has…not blood and nerves like you? Has he not eyes to see what is fair, and ears to hear what is sweet?" (pp. 190-91). Although, like Shylock, Don Ippolito is given English words to plead his kinship with his listener, he no less than Shylock is isolated from the other characters, who feel him always as alien to themselves.

Howells's contrasting method of representing the English of a European speaker is best seen in *A Hazard of New Fortunes*, published in 1890, when the popular and critical protest against dialect was reaching its height. As if to assert the value of dialect in the face of objection, Howells in this novel bestows distinctive habits of speech on more central characters than ever before. The cast includes, in addition to the ebullient and slangy Fulkerson, a Paris-trained artist from upstate New York, who speaks English "with quick, staccato impulses, so as to give it the effect of epigrammatic and sententious French" (p. 105); a southern colonel and his daughter from "Charlottes-boag" in whose "broad-vowelled, rather formal speech" one hears "odd valuations of some of the auxiliary verbs, and...total elision of the canine letter" (p. 113); a new-rich family of Pennsylvania Dutch and German extraction whose two uncultivated daughters provide numerous examples of General Low Colloquial; and Lindau, the German scholar and political agitator, who is represented as speaking English with such a thick accent that the reader almost has to translate his words.

Of all the characters, Lindau is the most seriously compromised by his speech in that in its effect it jars the most with the sentiments and ideals it conveys. A socialist who fought with the revolutionists in Berlin in 1848, emigrated to the United States, and joined the Union army in the Civil War, when he lost an arm, Lindau in the novel attacks the evils of the capitalist system, cries out against the oppression of the poor, and affirms the ideals of justice and brotherhood in mutilated English in which every metamorphosed vowel and consonant is rendered. When March asks him why he lives in poverty and squalor on Mott Street, he replies: "I tidn't gome here begause I was too boor to life anywhere else...I foundt I was begoming a lidtle too moch of an aristograt. I hadt a room oap in Creen-vidge Willage, among dose pig pugs over on the West Side, and I foundt...that I was beginning to forget the boor!" (pp. 189-90). Only once in the novel, when Lindau speaks in German, is he allowed the dignity of standard English by which his speech in his native language is rendered.

Howells's phonetic rendering of Lindau's English can be defended on several grounds: unlike Don Ippolito, a native of the city in which his story is set, Lindau in New York is a foreigner whose alien speech seems the correlative of his own sense of alienation from American society. Lindau's linguistic peculiarities along with those of other characters also contribute to the impression of the "vast hive of populations" (p. 182) that make New York a "cosmopolitan Babel."[7] Finally, dialect prevents Lindau, who voices many of Howells's convictions but sanctions violence that Howells condemned, from appearing to be Howells's spokesman. Lindau seems to be drawn from several Germans Howells knew in his youth: a bookbinder with whom he read German literature (as March in his youth read Heine with Lindau), an editor in Columbus, who like Lindau "stood behind the barricades in Berlin," and a jeweler and watchmaker, also a political refugee after 1848, who died in the Civil War and whose ghost, according to Howells, became "a loved and honored character in *A Hazard of New Fortunes*."[8] Lindau has "the noble, partriarchally bearded head" of the watchmaker, but the artist who hires him as a model is representing it as the head of Judas, and Lindau's incitement of striking motormen leads directly to the death of the other idealist, Conrad Dryfoos, whose ineffectual fanaticism makes his relation to Christ as ambiguous as Lindau's relation to Judas.

Lindau is a tragic, not a comic, figure of finer intelligence and moral sense than a political fanatic like Ansel Denton in *The World of Chance*, who does not bear the stigma of dialect. But Lindau's speech, which Fulkerson amuses himself by imitating, is comic in its effect, more fitting for a type like Trina's German father in *McTeague* than the "sensitive and cultivated man" that March identifies in Lindau. For the creation of characters whom the reader will remember for their thoughts and feelings rather than their oddities of speech, Howells's method in *A Foregone Conclusion* is to be preferred.

Whenever dialect in Howells's fiction reinforces a racial stereotype, it violates two of his principles of realism: that human nature is essentially the same in all times and places and that human character is not fixed but variable: "now noble, now ignoble; now grand, now little; complex, full of vicissitude."[9] The divergence between the principles of unity and equality Howells affirmed in his criticism and his portrayal of non-Anglo-Saxons is especially marked in his treatment of Jews and their culture.

On the rare occasions when Jewish figures appear in his fiction, they conform to the stereotype of the vulgar mercenary shopkeeper who sacrifices principle for profit. In *Their Wedding Journey*, the Marches hear "two Hebrews" talking of the "glothing business," the elder explaining to the younger in language designed to appear as unattractive as the sentiment, that manipulating customers is the key to success: "Id's easy enough to make a man puy the goat you want him to, if he wands a goat, but the thing is to *make him puy the goat that you wand to zell when he don't wand no goat at all*" (pp. 42-43). Should the reader be in doubt, the narrator explains that "he seemed to be speaking of a garment and not a domestic animal" (p. 42). Later, a "shrill-voiced, highly dressed, much-bedizened Jewess" is pictured in rowdy quarrel (p. 71). In casual remarks, Howells's characters reinforce the stereotypes identified with the dialect in *Their Wedding Journey*. In *A Foregone Conclusion*. Ferris observes of a Venetian landlord: "The man's a perfect Jew—or a perfect Christian, one ought to say in Venice; we true believers do gouge so much more infamously here" (pp. 56-57). Another American consul, in Vienna, refers to the Viennese shopkeepers as "the most notorious Jews in Europe."[10] Mrs. Bolton, the farmer's wife in *Annie Kilburn*, when asked where to buy children's clothes, responds, "There's a Jew place. They say he cheats" (p. 234).[11] Basil March, on shipboard in *Their Silver Wedding Journey*, converses with a Jewish passenger who, although agreeable, talks only of business and leads March to "[philosophize] the race as so tiresome often because it seemed so often without philosophy" (2:454).

In Jewish writers, however, Howells discovered qualities of feeling and imagination denied by the stereotypes. He found in Heine, "a poet of alien race and language and religion...a greater sympathy than I have experienced with any other. Perhaps the Jews are still the chosen people, but now they bear the message of humanity, while once they bore the messages of divinity." He valued Fanny Hurst, Israel Zangwill, Morris Rosenfeld, and Abraham Cahan for their depiction of Jewish life expressive not only of "racial traits" but of the universal qualities of humor, tenderness, and pathos. For Howells the critic, the Yiddish of Morris Rosenfeld's "Songs from the Ghetto" was not the dialect of comic stereotypes but "the speech of an oppressed people," possessed of the beauty and pathos of a language "probably reaching its supreme effect in the moment before it is lost in the world of American English about it."[12]

Howells's receptiveness to dialect in Jewish literature is most fully demonstrated in his criticism of the fiction of Abraham Cahan, the Jewish writer whose career owed most to Howells's recognition. A year before Howells launched Dunbar's career with his review in *Harper's Weekly*, Howells read Cahan's first published English story, "A Providential Match" in *Short Stories* (February 1895), was so impressed by it that he sought out the thirty-five year old Russian immigrant writer, urged him to write a novel of ghetto life, read and discussed the completed manuscript with Cahan, suggested the title, *Yekl: A Tale of the New York Ghetto*, and after recommending the manuscript to several New York publishers, finally placed it with Appleton's, who published it in 1896. Howells then published in the *New York World* (July 26, 1896) a long review, "New York Low Life in Fiction," of unqualified praise of *Yekl* and Stephen Crane's *Maggie*, brought out by Appleton's the same year. Like Dunbar, whose *Majors and Minors* Howells had reviewed the month before, Cahan credited Howells with making him known to the American public. In his autobiography, he referred to Howells's article as a "sensation" which resulted in interviews with reporters and the syndicating of an illustrated feature story about him in Sunday papers all over the country.[13]

In his review, Howells applauded both Cahan and Crane for achieving in their pictures of poverty and squalor the kind of artistic beauty expressed through the writers' truth to human characters and their conditions. He connected the two works in observing that in both the representation of the corrupted English of the streets moved one to ask (as Henry James was later to ask in *The American Scene*): "What will be the final language spoken by the New Yorker? We shall always write and print a sort of literary English, I suppose, but with the mixture of races the spoken tongue may be a thing composite and strange beyond our present knowledge."[14]

Howells found *Yekl* "full of indirect suggestions on this point." In fact, in this novel, which portrays the Americanization of a young Russian Jewish immigrant in New York who in the process is confirmed in his native vulgarity and self-ishness, language is as important to the characters as in any work of fiction Howells reviewed. Yekl and his friends struggle to learn English at an academy where the language "was broken and mispronounced in as many different ways as there were Yiddish dialects represented in that institution."[15] Although, as Cahan observes, dwellers in the Jewish quarter of New York—"a vast and complex city within a city"—are isolated from the "English-speaking portion of the population" (p. 51), Yekl, who wants before everything to be an American, is quick to add American slang ("greenhornsh," "monkey beeshnesh," "by gum," "Betch you' bootsh") to his stock of "mutilated English" (p. 3). When his wife, who speaks no English, comes from Russia to join him three years later, he rails at her slowness in learning the words he tries to teach her and signals his wish to detach himself from her by speaking English in her presence to the woman he has taken up with in New York.

While some reviewers, like Howells, regarded the Yiddish dialect as valuable in creating the impression of actual life, others objected to its ugliness and to the tediousness of its constant use. Cahan himself called it "gibberish"; in response to the criticism he dismissed the dialect as "no more than a cheap bit of comedy" and vowed to "avoid such 'dialect' in my subsequent English stories."[16] Cahan's next book, *The Imported Bridegroom and Other Stories of the New York Ghetto*, published in 1898, contains five stories, in which immigrant Yiddish characters of the East Side, including a tailor in a sweat shop, a peddler, a marriage broker, and factory workers, speak a quaintly formal literary English, far removed from the mutilated English of *Yekl*. Howells praised these stories as warmly as he had praised *Yekl:* "No American fiction of the year merits recognition more than this Russian's stories of

Yiddish life, which are so entirely of our time and place, and so foreign to our race and civilization."[17] The statement expresses Howells's sense of distance from a culture he felt alien to his own; it also shows that for Howells a writer's power to evoke the distinctive qualities of a people's life did not depend on dialect.

The fiction of Cahan illustrates the primacy of language in the lives of the foreign-born seeking to become Americans. For a character like Yekl, who declares, "Once I live in America...I want to know that I live in America" (p. 9), knowledge of English is the essential condition of transforming himself from an alien to an American. Howells makes the same point in *Their Silver Wedding Journey*, in his portrayal of the German businessman Stoller, the son of German immigrants, who in his childhood in Indiana suffered so keenly from the boys' mockery of his speech that he repudiated the German language: "He hated his native speech so much that he cried when he was forced to use it with his father and mother at home; he furiously denied it with the boys who proposed to parley with him in it on such terms as 'Nix come arouce in de Dytchman's house' " (1:262). One price of his "dear-bought Americanism" (2:265) is that when he places his daughters in German schools he cannot speak the language he now considers is desirable, because fashionable, for them to learn.

Whether the ability to speak English, however imperfectly, is enough to make the child of immigrants an American is a debatable point in *Their Silver Wedding Journey*. When Mrs. March asks if Stoller is an American, Burnamy, the young man in his employ, answers "with an uneasy laugh: 'Why I suppose so....His people were German emigrants who settled in southern Indiana. That makes him as much American as any of us, doesn't it?' " To this, Mrs. March "answered with her eight generations of New England ancestry, 'Oh, for the West, yes, perhaps' " (1:251-52).

In this exchange, Howells represents the conflicting points of view to which he gave allegiance in his fiction and criticism. He repeatedly affirmed his belief in the unity of the American people, bound in one nation by common traditions and ideals. Although America was decentralized, comprising many regions, each with its own distinctive features, there existed, Howells believed, a national spirit and character distinguishing Americans from other nationalities. In attacking the idea of a political union of America and England, Howells asserted the integrity of the American nation against forces destructive of its identity. "Whatever tends to distinguish Americans from one another, and separate them into classes, threatens the perpetuity of the commonwealth by making its citizens unknown to one another. Its safety is mainly in that unity of tradition which as yet is of such integrity with us that no word of national import needs translation, in all the length and breadth of the Union, from the original accent in which it was uttered."[18]

Many of Howells's statements, however, belie his idea of America as a united people. In an essay in which he compares Americans to "the children of one family," he distinguishes between "natives" who being free to choose their vocations are "masters of circumstance" and the "various sorts of aliens" who do menial work in America and remain "slaves of conditions." He applied the term "American" selectively, as in his account of people at Rockaway Beach which distinguishes Americans from Germans, Irish, and Jews.[19] In *Their Silver Wedding Journey*, the alien presence is symbolized for Basil March in Carlsbad by a "tablet dedicating the American Park…which is signed by six Jews and one Irishman" and by a band playing a potpourri of American songs, only one of which, "Dixie," March regards as "the least characteristic or original." When Mrs. March asks him if the "Washington Post" is not American, March replies, "Yes, if Sousa is an American name; I should have thought it was Portuguese" (2:7).

The Marches and almost all of Howells's central characters are of English stock, descended from several generations of native-born Americans. Many of his characters live in New England towns which they see transformed after the Civil War by the influx of Irish, French Canadians, and Italians. In *Indian Summer*, the minister, Mr. Waters, sojourning in Florence, declares that he will never return to his native New England: "Half the farms in Haddam are in the hands of our Irish friends, and the labor on the rest is half done by French Canadians" (p. 125). The lawyer, Ralph Putney, tells his friend Annie Kilburn, newly arrived from Rome, that the old New England village of her birth no longer exists. "There *is* no old Hatboro' any more....we live now in a sprawling American town; and by American of course I mean a town where at least one-third of the people are raw foreigners or newly extracted natives" (p. 117).

In American cities, the number of foreigners was larger, the heterogeneity greater. What most impresses the Marches when they arrive in New York in *A Hazard of New Fortunes* is the "quality of foreignness" in the city; in the streets they see "Italian faces, French faces, Spanish faces" (p. 55). The frequenters of Maroni's restaurant, a meeting place for the characters, are "of all nationalities and religions" (p. 82). For the Marches, the word "American" defines not the whole but only a part, to which the other parts are foreign. In Greenwich Village, they enjoy a "lingering quality of pure Americanism," preserved by the neat brick houses and the sound of church bells, but the tenements and new apartment buildings "implied a life as alien to the American manner as anything in continental Europe" (pp. 298-99). Riding in an elevated car filled with Neapolitan construction workers, March listens to "the jargon of their unintelligible dialect" and with irony that cuts two ways wonders "what notions these poor animals formed of a free republic from their experience of life under its conditions" (p. 182).

Howells's letters, essays, and fiction reveal that he shared with his New England friends such as Lowell, Aldrich, and Norton the fear that immigrants would supplant the old stock and undermine American life. In "A Pedestrian Tour" (1869), Howells pictures decaying houses in Cambridge, once carefully maintained by native New Englanders, now fallen to the "Celtic army," which has wrought a change for the worse in the population, lent itself to political corruption, supported "tottering priestcraft," and threatened the end "of us poor Yankees as a dominant plurality" (*Suburban Sketches*, pp. 70,

68). A few months before he published the sketch, he wrote to his father that he planned to sell his house on Sacramento Street to escape the Irish, whose presence, he believed, would lower the value of all property in the neighborhood.[20]

In important respects, however, Howells's position differed from that of his New England contemporaries. Although he was sympathetic to some of the views of nativists like John Fiske, N.S. Shaler, and Henry Cabot Lodge, unlike them Howells did not participate in the Immigration Restriction League; in his writing he did not support efforts to impose quotas or otherwise restrict immigration. He did not assert that the Germanic peoples were more desirable immigrants than the Slavs and Italians or more readily to be assimilated in American society. Observing "the mixture of races and tongues" in the New England manufacturing towns, he placed on an equal plane all the newcomers: "Greeks and Assyrians, and Arabs, and Poles and Irish and Germans, all dwelling there in a common beginning of American citizenship, each no less and no more at home in the alien conditions than another."[21] In *A Traveller from Altruria*, he created an ideal realm where no immigrants threaten the "Utopian dream of brotherly equality" (p. 165); but seven years later, in the introduction to *Through the Eye of the Needle*, he criticized not conditions in America but the anomalies of Altruria, the ideal, where people "are forced to discourage foreign emigration, against their rule of universal hospitality" (p. 273).[22] Rather than blaming strikes and riots on foreign workers and their leaders, Howells attacked the root of the evil in the whole competitive system, in which foreigners and natives alike were exploited. In *A Hazard of New Fortunes*, it is the rapacious speculator, Dryfoos, not Howells's spokesman, Basil March, who fulminates against labor unions and accuses foreigners of fomenting strikes.

Howells had his preferences among national groups. His letters, fiction, and travel essays show a greater liking and admiration for the French, Italians, and Russians than for the Germans, Irish, and Japanese.[23] As a writer, however, he desired not to suppress any racial group but to promote in all dwellers in America a spirit of unity fostered by common ideals and traditions. In his relations with foreign-born writers in America he encouraged accommodation to American life. He urged his friend and protégé, the Norwegian novelist Hjalmar Boyesen, to perfect his English, encouraged him to write a novel "such as only a man of two hemispheres like yourself can write", and warned against too long an absence from America, for "you fairly belong to us now" and can be assured of success "if you live—and live in America." In his review of *Yekl*, Howells praised Cahan for being "thoroughly naturalized to our point of view; he sees things with American eyes, and he brings in aid of his vision the far and rich perceptions of his Hebrew race, while he is strictly of the great and true Russian principle in literary art."[24]

Like Howells's introduction to Dunbar's poems, this statement attests to Howells's belief that literature can promote national unity and also preserve racial character. He argued that given the social and political decentralization of America no one writer could comprehend the whole, that in the truthful depiction of the different regions and ethnic groups lay "the highest promise of a national literature." Cahan, Dunbar, Boyesen, and Cable, in representing the distinctive culture of Jews, blacks, Scandinavians, and Creoles in America, revealed to their readers the universal in the alien and so fostered a spirit of unity. Howells championed political and economic equality for all "adoptive Americans" but he believed equality compatible with the expression in literature of the writer's racial heritage: "If we come to look at a man in his relation to aesthetics, we perceive a certain inalienable propriety in his being of this origin rather than that."[25]

Howells often noted the absence in America of a class structure like that of England, which in English fiction shaped character, determined ideals and ambitions, and distinguished members of society from one another. One could argue that in its racial diversity America offered to the writer a picture of comparable variety and density, in which characters may assimilate new ideals and change their conditions in a way not possible to those in the class system of a hereditary monarchy.

Much in Howells's writing suggests an unresolved conflict between racial attitudes and democratic ideals. In his fiction, he emphasized the barriers between races, the differences in temperament and conditions that separate one people from another. His only two foreign characters of central importance, the Italian priest, Don Ippolito, and the German socialist, Lindau, both die in the knowledge that they cannot realize their ideals and aspirations in America. In his literary criticism, however, Howells insisted that unity and diversity could coexist, that literature revealed the power of individual genius, preserved the distinctive character of the different races, promoted a spirit of national unity, and bound all people by showing them that under the differences of temperament and conditions "human nature is everywhere eternally the same."[26]

Chapter Seven

Language and Class
in the Early Novels

When Howells in his essays and reviews defended the use of dialect in fiction, he was usually referring to speech that identifies people with a particular race or region. But his own fiction illustrates the observation of George Philip Krapp that the most pervasive form of nonstandard speech is "class dialect which distinguishes between popular and cultivated or standard speech."[1] Many of Howells's characters speak nonstandard English that has no racial or geographical significance. Almost always, however, provincialisms and solecisms, whatever the race or place of the speaker, signal a social position inferior to that of the standard speakers.

Although Howells did not use dialect extensively until *The Minister's Charge*, his twelfth novel, he was from the beginning a careful recorder of the locutions and accents of different social classes. His first long narrative, *Their Wedding Journey*, which he described to his father as "a new species of fiction," dependent not on plot but on "the interest of character seen and described," renders the speech of a variety of people seen and heard by Basil and Isabel March on their trip to Niagara Falls and Canada. The narrative, intended to be "a faithful study of our American life,"[2] thus offers a good test of Howells's premises: that a truthful representation of the ordinary and everyday reveals the universality of human nature and thus unites people of different cultures in the recognition of their kinship; that the novelist can therefore affirm the ideals of unity and equality and also represent the traits, including habits of speech, that distinguish people from each other.

The first paragraph of *Their Wedding Journey* introduces the Marches in their role as representative Americans, as they are about to embark on the kind of journey thousands before them have made, the wedding trip to Niagara Falls. Not only do the Marches typify American localities, she from Boston, he an adoptive Bostonian from the west; they are universalized when they fondly imagine themselves as Adam and Eve possessing their world in the newness of their love. A journey such as the Marches undertake was Howells's favorite device for bringing all kinds of people together, in trains, boats, and hotels, where they are subject to the same delays and dangers and reveal themselves by the way they act and speak.

In introducing the Marches, Howells also introduces the potential source of conflict in his philosophy of realism when he states his purpose: "to talk of some ordinary traits of American life *as these appeared to them* (p. 3, emphasis added). The Marches do not regard themselves as ordinary, and nothing so convinces them of their distinction as the sight of "ordinary traits." At the start of their journey, Isabel tells her husband: "We shall go just like anybody else—with a difference" (p. 3), and they cultivate their sense of difference throughout the journey. With Basil, Isabel repeatedly forbids herself displays of affection in public for fear of appearing "bridal," like other newlyweds. She and Basil gratify their sense of superiority by comparing what they see to scenes in Europe, presumably unknown to less sophisticated travelers. They are slumming when they take the daycoach rather than the parlor car, not to save money but to capture "the spirit of ordinary American travel" (pp. 52-53). They view passengers on the boats and trains with amusement or disgust or pity, but rarely with any sense of fellow-feeling, of being "humbled and strengthened with a sense of their fraternity." They detach themselves from others either by romanticizing them, as they fabricate a tragic history for a shabbily dressed young man with a sensitive face (p. 44), or by belittling them, as they perceive a couple of newlyweds, "two hopelessly pretty brides, with parasols and impertinent little boots" (p. 77). Displaying the "patronizing spirit of travellers in a foreign country," they take a "keen interest" (p. 9) in everyone they see, but remain "mere observers of their kind, more or less critical in temper" (p. 11). Less complacent than his wife, who is self-conscious but rarely self-critical, Basil March can at least feel his failure to enter in spirit into others' lives. In passages Howells deleted from the manuscript Basil reflects upon the lack of sympathy between classes and the difficulty of understanding people of other (i.e., lower) classes;[3] he is aware that he and Isabel "come to Niagara in the patronizing spirit in which we approach everything nowadays" (pp. 103-04); he struggles to comprehend the suffering of the man in a steamboat collision on the river, but acknowledges that "the poor wretch seemed of another order of beings" (p. 50).[4]

As narrator, Howells is aware that the Marches' sense of superiority often produces effects of smugness or triviality that make them, no less than the people they scorn, fit subjects for a satirist. But when he juxtaposes the Marches' standard American English with the debased speech they hear on the trains and boats he justifies their claim to superior culture. In most of the fragments of talk, which one reviewer considered "the life of the work,"[5] the nonstandard speakers betray not only social inferiority but moral unworthiness, revealing themselves as callous or silly or boisterous or otherwise unfit for polite society represented by the Marches. An insolent hotel clerk ignores a guest to say to a friend, "Well, she's a mighty pooty gul, any way, Chawley!" (p. 62). (One may wonder what lies behind the "any way.") Sharing the deck with the "two Hebrews" talking of the "glothing business" are a flirtatious girl and a salesman of the "second or third quality" (p. 41), who exchange tasteless banalities while fancying themselves engaged in clever repartee. At Quebec, the carefree talk of a Cockney theatrical troupe, which "babbled on over dislocated aspirates," has "the romantic freedom of violated convention" (p. 152). The women, dressed like actresses playing society women on the stage, talk of what they will give "at Montre-

hal"—appropriately a play about transformation, "Pygmalion" (probably W.S. Gilbert's *Pygmalion and Galetea*, first per-
formed in 1871). But "oo's to do Wenus?" asks one when told
that "Hagnes" has gone to New York. "Bella's to do Wenus,"
says another, to cries of protest: "W'at a guy she'll look!
...Bella's too 'eavy for Wenus!" (p. 153).

Speech betrays the true station of a tall, distinguished-
looking man on the boat to Quebec, whom Mrs. March takes to
be a foreign nobleman of "high birth and long descent" (p. 117).
Like the man in Coleridge's anecdote who at a dinner party
preserved his air of distinction until he praised the apple
dumplings ("Them's the jockeys for me"[6]), the man on the river
boat sustains illusion until he says, "in the best New York State
accent", "Pretty tejious waitin', ain't it?" (p. 118). After this, the
Marches never give him another thought.

Howells also identifies the social grade of travelers by noting certain of the words they use. The Marches are clearly
superior to three passengers observed in the Albany station:
"that kind of young man who is called by the females of his
class a fellow, and two young women of that kind known to him
as girls" (pp. 7-8). The ensuing scene foreshadows Howells's
mature technique of presenting parallel actions as parodies of
each other. The young man's "robust flirtation" (p. 8) with one
girl burlesques the happiness of another young couple, who
earlier had been seen as a "travesty" of the first wedding
couple, the Marches. "Our temporary state...is often mirrored
in all that come near us" (p. 7), the narrator observes, a truth
that is illustrated by the talk on the Hudson River boat where
"each group had its travesty in some other; the talk of one
seemed the rude burlesque, the bitter satire of the next" (p. 44).

Such words as *travesty, burlesque,* and *satire* suggest the
satirist's categories, as do *vulgar, grade, class, station,* and *quality,* which indicate Howells's awareness of social differences.
Howells proposed to celebrate "the poetry of the commonplace," but the recurring words *common* and *commonplace*
usually denote something cheap, vulgar, or banal, lacking in
distinction, inferior to its opposite. The French Canadians at
Quebec "are nearly always of a peasant-like commonness, or

where they *rise above* this, have a bourgeois commonness of face and manner" (p. 124, emphasis added). Howells refers sarcastically to the "common admiration" (p. 48) with which all the passengers except Basil March listen to the self-important man pontificating on the steamboat collision. At Niagara, the "sacred grove beside the fall was profaned by some very common presences indeed" (pp. 76-77). The conditions uniting people are usually distressing, like the dirt and heat of the day car which reduce the passengers to "common bodily wretchedness" (p. 70).

Of course, class differences were part of the American scene and so must be noted in "the faithful study of American life" that Howells wished to write. But he held himself aloof from uncouth Americans like the salesman and his unrefined companions, although, as T.S. Perry noted, Howells shows no ill-nature in his portrayal of them. He viewed his subjects with the detachment of a genial satirist who did not "have the improvement of my nation greatly at heart," as he admitted in a letter to Bayard Taylor. "I'm afraid that I'm always more amused than shocked by outrageous things such as American travel abounds in."[7] After recording the witless badinage of the salesman and the girl in *Their Wedding Journey*, detached amusement moves Howells to exclaim: "Ah! poor Real Life, which I love, can I make others share the delight I find in thy foolish and insipid face?" (p. 42). Howells seems never more superior to ordinary people than when he asserts their literary value and affirms his bond with them:

As in literature the true artist will shun the use even of real events if they are of an improbable character, so the sincere observer of man will not desire to look upon his heroic or occasional phases, but will seek him in his habitual moods of vacancy and tiresomeness....I never perceive him to be so much a man and a brother as when I feel the pressure of his vast, natural, unaffected dullness. Then I am able to enter confidently into his life and inhabit there, to think his shallow and feeble thoughts, to be moved by his dumb, stupid desires, to be dimly illumined by his stinted inspirations, to share his foolish prejudices, to practise his obtuse selfishness. Yes, it is a very amusing world, if you do not refuse to be amused. [p. 55]

Even if Howells is mocking himself for the confidence with which he presumes to enter another's life, his power to satirize himself is but another evidence of superiority.[8]

Surprisingly, one of the admirers of the book was Theodore Dreiser, who read some of Howells's novels in the 1890s and in a letter to a *Kansas City Post* reporter (Oct. 15, 1914), included *Their Wedding Journey* in a list of some dozen novels that constituted "quite the sum of my American literary admirations." In *Forgotten Frontiers* (1932), Dorothy Dudley reported that although "today" Dreiser expressed contempt for Howells's novels he acknowledged that Howells "did one fine piece of work, *Their Wedding Journey*, not a sentimental passage in it, quarrels from beginning to end, just the way it would be …really beautiful and true." Fryckstedt believes that Dreiser actually had in mind *A Modern Instance*, which more nearly corresponds to Dreiser's description. But in a letter to George Ade (1942), Dreiser again singled out *Their Wedding Journey* as one of the books that "were the beginning of my private library of American Realism."[9]

The importance Dreiser attached to *Their Wedding Journey* reminds us that Howells, as he said, was creating a new kind of narrative, that simply in portraying (in whatever spirit) "an ordinary carful of human beings" (p. 55) he was asserting their worth as literary subjects. When he apostrophized "poor Real Life" he not only expressed his sense of superiority to the underbred but emphasized his daring in presuming to make literature of Real Life's "foolish and insipid face." But one has only to compare Howells's chapter "A Day's Railroading" with Dreiser's most famous scenes of train journeys in *Sister Carrie* to realize how different are the impulses that drew the writers to the ordinary and the commonplace. Both see the value of their subjects as social history; both have the historian's care for accuracy and fullness of documentation. Dreiser sees vulgarity and mental weakness as clearly as Howells does, but he enters into the lives of the kind of people that the Marches and the narrator of *Their Wedding Journey* only view with amusement from the outside; Dreiser's sense of identification with his main characters forbids his being merely amused by them or designating them as "poor Carrie" and "poor Hurstwood."

In defending the commonplace as worthy of the "true artist's" study, Howells has invited comparison with Walt Whitman, whose fifth edition of *Leaves of Grass* appeared in 1871, the year *Their Wedding Journey* was serialized in the *Atlantic*. In his pioneering study of Howells's early work, Fryckstedt maintains that *Their Wedding Journey* had "deep roots in the soil of democratic and equalitarian idealism that inspired many of the poems in *Leaves of Grass*."[10] But plants rooted in the same soil may be quite different. Instead of scenes like those in "Song of Myself" in which the poet unites himself to the laborer, the hunted slave, the maimed fireman, and the wounded soldier; instead of the long catalogues by which Whitman created all Americans equal, drawn inward to himself as he "tend[ed] outward to them," Howells in *Their Wedding Journey* depicts a variety of people identified as socially or morally inferior to more sophisticated and enlightened observers, including the narrator, who invites the reader to view with amused detachment, as if watching a stage performance, the vagaries and crudities of the lesser actors. In *Their Wedding Journey* Howells comes closest to the spirit of *Leaves of Grass* when Basil March counters Isabel's objection to the name "Sam Patch" in a poem by insisting upon the poetic value of common names and facts: "We shall never have a poetry of our own till we get over this absurd reluctance from facts, till we make the ideal embrace and include the real, till we consent to face the music in our simple common names, and put Smith into a lyric and Jones into a tragedy" (pp. 68-69). But "face the music" also means to confront the worst; the "facts and dreams" Basil longs to see "continually blended and confronted" (p. 69) he is unable to fuse except in sentimental fancies that separate him from others; and what he hears on the night boat is not America singing but "the voice of the common imbecility and incoherence" (p. 47).

The voice of judgment in *Their Wedding Journey*, however, does not proceed from mere snobbish pleasure in the consciousness of superiority. In fact, Basil seeks refuge in irony when he feels powerless to assert himself in the presence of ill-mannered people like the hotel clerk. Consciousness of one's superior place in the social order is self-sustaining in a wider context defined in recent criticism. As several scholars have shown, the book is not a lighthearted picture of the notorious "smiling aspects" of American life.[11] Rather, the narrative evokes the nightmare world of suffocating heat, poverty, and death in the modern city and confronts travelers with the perilous in the natural world, where people are scalded to death in steamboat wrecks and are dwarfed by the colossal falls where thousands have perished. To sensitive, impressionable observers, like the Marches and Howells himself, a social order with its hierarchy, its codes and conventions is a defense against the terrors of existence, a means of controlling the irrational within human nature, of asserting the power of human reason in the face of natural forces indifferent to humankind, like the thundering falls of Niagara, where Basil with self-protective irony reflects upon "some potent influence undermining our self-satisfaction; we begin to conjecture that the great cataract does not exist by virtue of our approval" (p. 104). The power of the social order is dramatized in the tensest scene in the book, when Isabel collapses in uncontrollable panic on Goat's Island and Basil, helpless to aid her, knows his own moment of real terror. Only the chance arrival on the island of another tourist, Fanny Ellison, proves "sovereign" against her fear. The presence of the woman, who Isabel says "is so much like *me*," restores her to her habitual regard for convention and enables her to "[dash] her veil over her face" and cross the bridge to the shore (p. 93).

Analysts of *Their Wedding Journey* have noted the pull of conflicting feelings and attitudes within the narrator: his long-

ing for the picturesque diversity of European culture, coun-
tered by his faith in the greater promise of American civilization; his responsiveness to the sentimental and idealistic,
which his intellect condemns as false to life, resulting in a
"continuing struggle between his head and his heart." A review
of *Their Wedding Journey* in the *North American Review* by the
editor, Henry Adams, suggests another kind of conflict. To
Adams, Howells's book was unrivaled in its "extreme and almost photographic truth to nature" and in its "idealization of
the commonplace."[12] But "commonplace" speakers could not
be idealized when "truth to nature" demanded the rendering of
nonstandard speech.

In *A Chance Acquaintance*, his next long narrative, published serially in the *Atlantic*, January through June 1873,
Howells once again had to choose between verisimilitude and
an idealized treatment of his subject. This time, however, he
sacrificed strict realism to his primary purpose: to embody in
his heroine, Kitty Ellison, in their purest form the democratic
ideals he identified with the American West. Appearing briefly
in *Their Wedding Journey*, Kitty confounds Isabel March by her
intelligence, refinement, and "charm of manner," remarkable
in a provincial girl from Eriecreek, New York (p. 109). Likewise, the aristocratic Bostonian, Miles Arbuton, who, in *A
Chance Acquaintance*, meets Kitty on the boat to Quebec and
falls in love with her almost against his will, "wondered at the
culture she had somewhere, somehow got" (p. 93). Howells not
only made Kitty his most attractive champion of the democratic ideal but gave her antecedents, tastes, and opinions like
his own. Growing up in frontier towns where she received little
schooling, like Howells she has educated herself by wide reading. After her father, a country editor like Howells's father, dies
in Kansas, a martyr to the antislavery cause, she is welcomed
into the family of her uncle, a doctor, whose house in Eriecreek
has been a station on the Underground Railroad. In Eriecreek,
"socially as well as politically...almost a perfect democracy"
(p. 37), Kitty has imbibed her uncle's "fierce democracy" and

"extreme theories of equality," including the conviction that "a belief in any save intellectual and moral distinctions was a mean and cruel superstition" (p. 37).

Howells placed her in an even more favorable light by making complete the contrast between her and her suitor. Representing the most class-conscious element of Boston society, Arbuton is an "exclusive by training and by instinct" (p. 40). Kitty is open, warm, responsive; Arbuton is cold, supercilious, aloof. When he lapses from his habitual reserve, he tries to "congeal again" (p. 20). When he fails of perfect politeness, he suffers not from the pain inflicted upon others but from the wound to his own self-esteem. Kitty begins her journey with "the unsnubbed fearlessness of a heart which did not suspect a sense of social difference in others, or imagine itself misprized for anything but a fault" (p. 37). Arbuton begins his journey with "a conscience against encouraging people whom he might have to drop for reasons of society" (p. 11). Kitty's drollery, expressive of her enjoyment of the incongruous and the eccentric, displeases Arbuton, to whom "humor always seemed...something not perfectly well bred" (p. 47).

Henry James, who read *A Chance Acquaintance* in the *Atlantic*, applauded the portrayal of Kitty but thought Arbuton "decidedly a shade too scurvy," and wished that Kitty, not Aron, had precipitated the break by an affront to him. Howells's drama, James assumed, "was the irreconcilability of the two results of such opposed antecedents and not a verdict on one or the other."[13] But Howells did intend a verdict upon both characters and meant Kitty to be superior to her patronizing suitor. The narrator's comments, Kitty's observations, and Arbuton's own words and acts all reveal a man of undeveloped heart and little imagination, eager to scorn those lacking "the proper associations and traditions" (p. 16), superior only by his own snobbish standard to Kitty, whose imagination, kindled by everything she sees, creates a bond of sympathy with others. Even Arbuton, in his moment of greatest insight, acknowledges her superiority when, after ignoring Kitty in the presence of fashionable friends, he "perceived that throughout that ignoble scene she had been the gentle person and he the vulgar one" (p. 160). Unlike those male characters, such as Basil March, Colville (*Indian Summer*), and Percy Ray (*The World of Chance*), to whom Howells also gives his own antecedents, tastes, and ambitions, Kitty Ellison is presented without irony, wholly admirable in her loyalty to her principles and in her courage to act upon her just perceptions of Arbuton's character and her own.

Further proof of Howells's wish to favor his heroine is his gift to her of flawless English. She has grown up with her Eriecreek cousins, who say "I reckon," and with them she has "rattled on in a free, wild, racy talk" (p. 39), but in the novel she says nothing wild or racy, and her speech is marked by none of the rusticisms and grammatical lapses to be expected in a country-bred girl. She never says, "I want to know" or "don't know as"—locutions by which Howells's provincial characters most often betray themselves. Nor does Kitty express herself in girlish clichés like the character she foreshadows in her innocent self-reliance, James's Daisy Miller, who finds Europe "perfectly entrancing" and tells her patrician suitor, Winterbourne, that he was "awfully mean up at Vevey....You wouldn't do most anything."[14] As James Tuttleton has observed, Howells settled for a "limited realism" in rendering Kitty's speech, "willing to surrender verisimilitude to his larger purpose—to demonstrate the superiority of simple American manners over the veneer of conventionality that conceals the moral corruption of European society."[15]

Because Howells wished to show Kitty the equal of Arbuton in refinement and gentility, he not only spared her the dialect speaker's "badge of inferiority," but made her speech as polished as his. Ardent reading of books in her uncle's library has helped to give her "a great liveliness of mind" (p. 39) which reveals itself in wit beyond Arbuton's gift. She knows eighteenth-century poetry well enough to quote a passage from Pope's "Essay on Man" to cap one of Arbuton's remarks. She can return answers to him with the same neatness of expression, in phrases that balance his. When he says to her: "I am very sorry...to have been the means of a mistake to you to-day," she responds: "And I was dreadfully ashamed to make you the victim of my blunder" (p. 20). As she can perceive the droll in painful situations, so she can play on words in highly charged moments. When Arbuton tells her that he failed to write *Miss* before her name on the wall of the chateau they visit, she replies, "I dare say it won't be missed!" (p. 139).

Halfway through the novel, Kitty writes a long letter to her cousins in a style more reminiscent of William Dean Howells than of a young girl like Howells's sister Annie, who also wrote of a journey to Quebec and of whom Howells admitted there were "some faint outlines" in Kitty.[16] The vocabulary of Kitty's letter is simple, but witty turns of phrase display a sophisticated use of rhetorical devices and a control of tone that mark the practiced stylist. Kitty describes soldiers in the barracks when they are "off dignity as well as off duty" (p. 75), a nun who looks "as comfortable and commonplace as life-after-dinner" (p. 76), and Kitty's cousin with a sprained ankle, who has passed beyond "the first enthusiasm of her affliction" (p. 73). Durham Terrace in Quebec is "a formal parade in the evening"; in the morning, "the resort of careless ease" (pp. 74-75). She adds *disagreeabilities* (p. 81) to Howells's store of coinages, and like Howells she is attentive to the speech of others, quoting one of the priests who "all speak English, with some funny little defect" (p. 78). Howells wrote to James that in Arbuton and Kitty he had "confront[ed] two extreme American types: the conventional and the unconventional."[17] Kitty's speech and writing are unconventional only in the sharpness of insight and originality of expression which Arbuton could not match if he would.

Both Elinor Howells and James thought Kitty too pert in her conversation with Arbuton. As ready to acknowledge the merits of another's criticism as James was to defend the merits of his own view, Howells wrote to James that Elinor "agrees with you about Kitty's pertness" and explained: "I meant her to be everything that was lovely, and went on protesting that she was so, but she preferred being saucy to the young man, especially in that second number....She cannot very well help 'sassing' him, though she feels that this puts her at a disadvantage, and makes her seem the aggressor."[18] In the last installment of the serial (June 1873), Kitty apologizes to Arbuton: "I think I was very pert with you all day,—and I don't think I'm pert naturally,—taking you up about the landscape, and twitting you about the Saguenay scenery and legends, you know" (p. 152).

In revising the text of the serial, Howells was, as he told James, "able to check the young person a little before handing her down to the latest posterity in book form."[19] The changes, however, are fairly minor. In the serial Kitty says to Arbuton: "I suppose we ought to congratulate the first American landscape that's ever reminded you of anything" (*Atlantic* 31:183). In the book, her words are less personal: "Then you've really found something in an American landscape. I suppose we ought to congratulate it" (p. 29). Her challenge to Arbuton in the serial, "I suppose you've no fault to find with the Rhine scenery. That has tradition enough, hasn't it?" (31:192), becomes simply, "I suppose...the Rhine has traditions enough, hasn't it?" (p. 43). Interestingly, pertness or *sauce* was the one blemish Howells found in the wit of Jane Austen's Elizabeth Bennett, the character most likely to have been a model for Kitty, whose relations with Arbuton suggest those of Elizabeth and Darcy.[20]

Several of Howells's contemporaries, like James, objected to the portrayal of Arbuton. The reviewer in *Harper's* found him a "sorry representative of a Boston aristocrat." (47:461). Oliver Wendell Holmes would accept Arbuton only as "*a* Bostonian, not *the* Bostonian." None of these readers, however, objected to the portrayal of Kitty as unrealistic. James, who objected to Arbuton's "peculiar shabbiness," found Kitty "singularly palpable and rounded," and envied Howells "the delight of feeling her grow so real and complete, so true and charming." In his essay on Howells in the *Century*, T.S. Perry equated realism with the democratic spirit which reveals "the emptiness of convention and the dignity of native worth" and maintained that in *A Chance Acquaintance* "Mr. Howells's realism is untiring" (23:684).[21]

That readers did not question Kitty's perfect diction is not surprising, for Howells was observing a well-established con-

vention, which allowed to lowborn characters of superior virtue the grace of flawless speech. Dickens, for instance, let the
sometime inhabitants of London's underworld, such as the
foundling Oliver Twist and Lizzie Hexam, the daughter of a
Thames riverman (*Our Mutual Friend*), speak perfect English
as the mark of their gentility. Closer to home, Edward Eggleston, in *The Hoosier Schoolmaster*, which Howells reviewed in
1872, portrayed a bond servant, Hannah, who not only speaks
perfect English in a household where everyone else speaks the
base dialect of Back Creek, but defeats everyone, including the
schoolmaster, in the annual spelling match.

Howells granted the habit of correct speech to the western
hero as well as heroine. In his first three-act play, *Out of the
Question* (1877), the westerner Stephen Blake, one-time steamboat mechanic and inventor of an "improved locomotive driv-
ing wheel,"[22] who eventually wins the hand of Leslie Bellingham, daughter of a patrician Boston family, is at first rejected by her mother and aunt as "out of the question," but
proves himself worthy in deed and character by passing every
test of a gentleman including the "test of talk." He not only
gives up his room at the crowded summer hotel to Leslie's
mother and aunt, rescues Leslie from tramps, and is discovered to have saved the life of Leslie's brother Charles during
the Civil War; his speech is unfailingly dignified, courteous,
resolute, and grammatical without a trace of the slang spoken
by westerners like Fulkerson and Willis Campbell in Howells's
later works. To Mrs. Bellingham, who at first declares that
marriage to a man without family or social position is "simply
impossible," Leslie protests: "He used words more refined and
considerate than any I ever dreamt of....he talked splen-
didly....If you could only hear him talk as I do" (p. 54). Leslie's
aunt, unbending, like Arbuton, in her class prejudice, insists
that Blake is not a gentleman, but Charles Bellingham (who
appears in *The Rise of Silas Lapham* as the kindliest member of
the Coreys' circle) defends Leslie's choice in words that suggest
James's "nature's nobleman," Christopher Newman: Blake
"was from first to last one of those natural gentlemen that
upset all your preconceived notions of those things....I never

saw a trait in him or heard a word from him that wasn't refined" (p. 61). His voice, Bellingham concludes, is "the most sympathetic voice in the world" (p. 62).

Cast from the mould of perfection, Blake is even more completely idealized than Kitty. But in creating such figures Howells not only asserted the democratic ideal of equality which he and Perry identified with realism; he promoted the ideal by exposing the forces in American society that denied the ideal. To Abraham Cahan, *A Chance Acquaintance* was "preeminent" among Howells's works in exemplifying his "realistic instinct" becaue it exposed the reality which "lays bare the fictiousness of American equality."[23] The ideal qualities of Blake and Kitty make those who see them as social inferiors seem all the more benighted. Idealism, not strict realism, thus enabled Howells in *A Chance Acquaintance* to write the book which, he believed, "sets me forever outside the rank of mere *culturists,* followers of an elegant literature, and proves that I have sympathy with the true spirit of Democracy."[24]

In "Private Theatricals," serialized in the *Atlantic* in 1875-76 and published as *Mrs. Farrell* in 1921, Howells for the first time portrays characters of rural New England, among whom he would make his finest distinctions in rendering degrees of culture through dialect. "Private Theatricals" is a psychological study of thwarted passion, not a novel of manners in which action turns on class differences, but the New England farmhouse filled with summer boarders where the drama unfolds brings together different social types more sharply contrasted than those in *A Chance Acquaintance.* The summer visitors, including the main characters—the young widow, Mrs. Farrell, and her two tormented lovers, Easton and Gilbert, whose friendship she half willfully destroys—are city-bred members of genteel society, fluent even in the throes of passion, grammatically secure whatever moral weaknesses their words betray. One's sense of their fevered passions is heightened by the presence of the family serving them, the Woodwards, born of old Yankee farming stock described by the narrator as "a signally silent race" (p. 3) who seem "weatherbeaten in mind as in face" (p. 4) and who from their summer boarders "learn no greater glibness of tongue, or liveliness of mind, or grace of manner" (p. 4). Nehemiah Woodward, once a country preacher whose sermons, "of lead," were "too dull even for the inarticulate suffering of country congregations" (pp. 5-6), silently works the family farm in West Pekin, a decaying village of empty houses, exhausted orchards and crumbling stone walls. Only the influx of summer boarders breaks "the dreary solitude of the country life" (p. 3).

The narrator observes that the village women are more intelligent and quick-witted than the men (p. 4), but Mrs. Woodward and her daughter Rachel are alike taciturn, exhibiting that reticence inseparable from what Mildred Howells in her introduction to the novel called "their stern uprightness and self-restraint" (viii). The "angularity of rectitude" which Gilbert marvels at in Rachel best reveals itself to him in her speech. He tells his aunt: "You can see before she speaks how she is considering her phrase, and choosing just the words that shall give her mind with scriptural scruple against superfluity" (p. 185). A talented artist who wants to draw animals but not people, Rachel seldom expresses her feelings in words, hides her love for Mrs. Farrell's suitor, Easton, and only once gives voice to a "torrent of feeling from a source habitually locked under an icy discipline" (p. 147).

Because neither Rachel nor her mother harbors social ambitions or seeks equality with the people they serve (Mrs. Woodward keeps her family rigidly separated from them), the provincialisms of their speech do not stigmatize them; indeed, their dialect reinforces the effect of their stern morality and self-respect by enforcing the contrast between their granite-like restraint and the lovers' shifting passions of jealousy, longing, and despair. That Mrs. Woodward in one speech says "you was," "you'd ought to be very certain," "she wanted I should let her," and "I don't know as" (pp. 255-56) does not undermine her moral authority. Rachel, who teaches the village school in the winter and approaches nearer standard English in her speech, is not diminished by her rusticisms: "we did think some of sending it there" (p. 107); "She's not so well as common" (p. 113), "I don't know as they could rightly be called lessons" (p. 110); "I don't want you should speak to me about it again" (p. 256). Such locutions would brand the speaker an outsider in Arbuton's world, but do not render her unfit to speak for Howells in her own world. As Mrs. Farrell, although morally devious, is the first of his characters to enunciate his principle of complicity—"Nothing that's wrong can be one's own affair, I suppose; it belongs to the whole world" (p. 228)—, so Rachel, though she says *as* instead of *that*, is the first to voice his principle of moral responsibility, when she says of Mrs. Farrell: "She did more than she meant, and I don't know as we ought to be made to answer for more harm than we mean" (p. 253).

During the 1870s, when Howells was writing "Private Theatricals," he was also publishing sketches and stories by Sarah Orne Jewett, who likewise recorded the dialect of rural New Englanders portrayed from the point of view of the summer visitor to their towns and villages. The difference between the two writers is instructive. Repeatedly, Jewett expressed her abiding affection and respect for the country people, affirming her mission to "teach the world" of "their grand, simple lives." The standard English of the narrator in *The Country of the Pointed Firs* inevitably separates her from the people of Dunnet Landing, but she longs to enter into their lives, and she feels the pain of exclusion rather than the pride of her superior culture when she perceives herself an outsider. Howells does not mock the provincial characters in "Private Theatricals" or deny them virtue and wisdom. But neither he nor the summer guests of the Woodwards seek to remove the gulf that separates them from the provincial speakers. No genteel character in "Private Theatricals," or in any other novel by Howells, ever feels in the presence of country people as the narrator of *The Country of the Pointed Firs* feels with Mrs. Blackett of Green Island, that "[her] world and mine were one from the moment we met."[25]

Lydia Blood, the protagonist of Howells's next novel, *The Lady of the Aroostook* (1879), is his most attractive heroine of marked provincial New England traits. Like Rachel Woodward, Lydia has grown up in a rural community, one as desolate and forsaken as West Pekin, has taught the village school, and has exhibited a notable artistic gift, although her rich contralto voice with its "quality of latent passion" (p. 120) suggests a power to excite desire in others that Rachel lacks. Like Rachel, Lydia is distinguished by proud reserve and unbending moral rectitude. Like Kitty Ellison, she wins the love of an upper-class Bostonian whom she meets on a journey. In her story, however, Howells for the first time used dialect to characterize his protagonist and underscore social differences among the central characters.

Unlike Kitty Ellison, Lydia is first portrayed in her provincial setting, before she embarks on her journey and meets her aristocratic suitor. The isolated world of South Bradfield, Massachusetts, which has shaped her speech, is evoked in the first scene in the voices "arid, nasal, and high" (p. 6) of Lydia's aunt and grandfather as they bid her goodbye on the afternoon of her departure for Europe. The Yankee dialect, praised by John Hay as "better than I have ever seen in print before,"[26] renders the homely aphorisms of Lydia's aunt ("I ain't one to think that eatin' up everything on your plate keeps it from wastin' "), the grandfather's complaints of "be'n so put about," and their wish that Lydia's ship were going "straight to Venus" instead of "Try-East" (pp. 2, 24, 2).

The dialect, by which Howells claimed only to catch "the conscientiously-cunningly-reluctant, arbitrarily emphatic Yankee *manner*,"[27] acquires charm in the expressions of hearty good will uttered by the benevolent Captain Jenness of the *Aroostook*. Provincial and upper-class speech are first contrasted when Dunham, one of Lydia's fellow passengers, addresses her grandfather in "the firm, neat tone which she had heard summer boarders from Boston use" (p. 13).

Lydia's speech, which never lapses into the ungrammatical, more nearly resembles the correct English of her Boston suitor and fellow passenger, James Staniford, than it resembles the dialect of South Bradfield. But Lydia occasionally betrays herself by a rusticism, which Staniford notices. When during their first meal on the *Aroostook* Lydia cries "I want to know" (p. 55) in answer to Staniford's observation about the weather, he at once puts her beyond the pale, observing to his friend Dunham, "We cultivated Yankees and the raw material seem hardly of the same race" (p. 59). With Dunham he harps mercilessly on her "wanting to know"; in disdainful phrases he casts the rural suitors that he imagines Lydia has repulsed— "fellows, as they call themselves, like girls that have what they call go" (p. 84). He mockingly calls her Lurella, telling Dunham, "You have no idea of the grotesqueness of these people's minds" (p. 59). Likewise, Howells as narrator adopts Staniford's viewpoint, if not his tone, in relegating her to a class from which he too distances himself: "It is the habit of people bred like her to remain silent for want of some sort of formulated comment upon remarks to which they assent" (p. 106).

As Staniford persists in dwelling on "Lurella's" social deficiencies, the reader perceives that he indulges in his contemptuous analysis to conceal from himself and his friend his growing attraction to her. His desire for her is quickened when she sings. Her voice, symbolizing the union of seductive physical beauty and moral innocence, "rang far off like a mermaid's singing, on high like an angel's" (p. 113). Passion overcomes prejudice and his contempt disappears. When Lydia says "how" instead of "what," he "did not recoil at the rusticity" (p. 159). Later, when Lydia describes a woman as "very fine-appearing," he observes that she uses countrified phrases only when she represses her true feelings. "When she spoke her mind she used an instinctive good language" (p. 215).

It is part of Lydia's innocence that she perceives no social difference between herself and Staniford, that she asks her worldly aunt in Venice if he is "suitable," his family "nice," and does not understand what prompts the answer: "He's only *too* suitable...at home he wouldn't have looked at a girl like you" (p. 287). But eventually Staniford himself seems to lose all awareness of any social difference between them, and when Lydia enters Venetian society, her unbending reserve, which might be taken for rustic awkwardness, is admired as self-possession by her socially conscious aunt, who confirms the truth spoken by Lydia's aunt in South Bradfield: "She's a born lady, if ever there was one" (p. 46).

In his portrayal of Lydia, Howells balanced the demands of realism and democratic idealism, remaining faithful to the provinciality of his heroine yet investing her with a kind of dignity which makes those who hold themselves her social superiors seem unworthy. Lydia never exhibits the ready wit of Kitty Ellison or the conversational ease of Mrs. Farrell. She never acquires the polite formulas by which feelings are masked or simulated, and Dunham's observation to Staniford that Lydia lacks the "responsive quickness" of the "women we know" (p. 92) remains true to the end. But because Lydia has the refinement of the "born lady" and does not even conceive of social ambition, the provincialisms of her speech do not disfigure her. According to one reviewer, who found Lydia "rare and charming," "distinctly and honestly countrified without a tinge of vulgarity," her provincialisms give her "an individuality and a quaint half-awkward grace such as some English novelists have drawn from a use of the Scotch dialect or of a foreign accent."[28]

Howells ends the novel with Lydia and Staniford married and bound for California. They go west not because Lydia is unfit for Boston society—even at his most critical, Staniford recognizes that Lydia has "the genius of good society" and tells Dunham, "Give that girl a winter among nice people in Boston, and you would never know that she was not born on Beacon Hill" (p. 72). As John Crowley shows, all the places portrayed in the novel—South Bradfield, Boston, and Venice—are merely "half-way stations," insufficient as homes of the "ideal couple," whose marriage transforms Staniford from a supercilious idler to a purposeful man.[29] Only in the west can Lydia and Staniford escape the corruptions of European society, the barren isolation of rural New England, and the stultifying conventions of Proper Boston, identified at the end with the invalidism of Dunham's sickly wife.

Edwin Cady has noted an important fact about the first phase of Howells's career, which culminated in the publication of *The Lady of the Aroostook*. During the 1870s, the years of his editorship of the *Atlantic*, when his ties to Boston were strongest (and his mistrust of aliens most evident), he portrayed those characters—Kitty Ellison, Stephen Blake, and Lydia Blood—who most fully prove the superiority of the westerner to the Bostonian in true virtue and courtesy.[30]

Interestingly, the idealization of western protagonists and their speech occurs in the works depicting courtship, not married life. As Richard Bridgman has shown, Howells in *Their Wedding Journey* creates a realistic picture of husband and wife by capturing in their conversations the qualities of middle-class American speech. By creating dialogue in which speakers emphasize key words, repeat certain sounds and words, use coordinate rather than subordinate conjuctions, and avoid "set speeches," Howells, along with Henry James and Mark Twain, pioneered in the development of a colloquial style, evolved from "a nation's common fund of language," expressive of "the mass norm."[31] But neither the idealization of speech nor the creation of a colloquial style hides the gulf between the social classes in Howells's fiction. The conversation of the Marches, grammatically correct, however sentimental or smug its tone, always keeps its distance from the mutilated speech of the uncouth. The very fact that Howells insisted on the linguistic propriety of Kitty, Blake, and Lydia, that he kept provincialisms to a minimum or excluded them altogether from their conversation, attests to the importance he placed upon their success in passing "the test of talk."

Chapter Eight

Language and Class
in Novels of Country and City

When Henry James praised Howells's early novels, he often expressed his faith in his friend's power to go farther, to convert into literature more of the American experience. He pronounced *The Lady of the Aroostook* "the most brilliant thing you have done," then urged Howells to "attack the great field of American life on as many sides as you can. Plunge into it, don't be afraid, and you will do even better things than this." Several months later, in a letter dated July 22, 1879, when he had learned of the subject of Howells's next novel, *The Undiscovered Country*, centering on the relationships of a spiritualist, his daughter, and her lover, he commended the donnée as "very promising," although he confessed "an intense aversion to spiritualistic material which has always seemed to me terribly sordid and dreary." (Several years later he would convert such material into the brilliant satire of *The Bostonians*.) "But your subject has the merit of being real, actual and American, and this is a great quality," he concluded. "Continue to Americanize and to *realize*: that is your mission;—and if you stick to it you will become the Zola of the U.S.A.—which I consider a great function." After reading the first installment of *The Undiscovered Country* in the *Atlantic*, January 1880, he wrote enthusiastically to Howells: "You have something really new and unworked." He thought the conception of Egeria, the spiritualist's daughter, "a most interesting invention—a real *trouvaille*."[1]

Egeria, whose mesmeric trances symbolize her surrender to

her father's will, derives from Priscilla in *The Blithedale Romance*, Howells's favorite of Hawthorne's works. Dr. Boynton, blinded by his obsession until near death, when he condemns himself a vampire for his coercion of his daughter, has attributes of Priscilla's masters, Westervelt and Hollingsworth, as well as Hawthorne's Faustian scientists, such as Aylmer and Rappaccini, whose victims are beautiful young women.[2] Boynton's antagonist, the journalist Ford, who eventually marries Egeria, somewhat resembles Holgrave in *The House of the Seven Gables*, as Egeria, in her association with light, brightness, and the healing influences of nature, resembles Phoebe Pyncheon. Possible antecedents of Dr. Boynton, Egeria, and Ford also include the scientist Gifford, his daughter, and the mesmerist-medium in James's story "Professor Fargo." Egeria shares with Kitty Ellison and Lydia Blood physical beauty, moral purity, normal emotions, and the power to reclaim young men, at least temporarily, from the barrenness of snobbery or cynicism.

What are "new and unworked" in *The Undiscovered Country* are not the roles of the three central characters but their relationship to realistically conceived settings—Boston, the New England countryside, and the Shaker village, where the characters of romance origins encounter a greater variety of social types than Howells had yet portrayed. For the first time, he set main portions of a novel in a city, making Mrs. LeRoy's seedy boarding house, where a dozen people gather in the first scene for a séance, a microcosm of Boston's class structure. The lapses in the taste and grammar of Mrs. LeRoy's clients do not appear to affect their destinies, nor does the one representative of fashionable Boston, Ford's friend Phillips, exhibit Staniford's interest in class differences revealed in speech. But the boarding house, located on a "shabbily adventurous street" (p. 45) abounding in "material tokens of a social decay" (p. 2) and notable for the number of doorplates with *Madam* attached to English surnames, owes much of its sleazy, vaguely disreputable character to the solecisms, vulgarity, and bombast uttered in its parlor. The tone is set by the quack medium, Mrs. LeRoy, a blunt-spoken woman from the West, unabashed when called

a charlatan, who later offers to give Ford a "see-aunts," exclaims "Laws no!" and tells him that the Boyntons "ain't coming back" (p. 107). Among the guests at the séance are a
pompous self-appointed authority on spirits who offers a
"lavish display" (p. 17) of false teeth as he uncoils a succession
of inflated phrases until forced to stop and grope for a word.
His jocular and irreverent opposite, Mr. Hatch, foreshadowing
Fulkerson, calls departed spirits "those scamps" (p. 19); says
"I'm there, doctor, every time," when told to take his place
between two of the ladies; admits that "I can't help running
over a little" (p. 20); and invites the company, "Ladies, join me
in loud cries for Jim" (p. 26).

When the Boyntons leave Boston and, having taken the
wrong train, wander helplessly through the Massachusetts
countryside in a snowstorm, they encounter villagers whose
debased expressions of suspicion and hostility prove that the
country offers no idyllic retreat from the corruptions of the
city. At a country store, the Boyntons are told that "them
Shakers at Vardley keeps a house a puppose for lodgin'
tramps" (p. 131); a farm woman demands of Egeria, "You
hain't any of them that's escaped from the reform school?" (p.
133); the harsh-faced keeper of a disreputable tavern tells
Boynton, "I hain't got any hoss in now" (p. 150), and insists,
"There hain't been no murder—not in *my* time" (p. 157).

But Howells does not make dialect an invariable sign of evil
nature. The benevolent Shakers, who come to the rescue of the
Boyntons, nurse Egeria through a long illness, and keep her
and her father in their community through the spring and
summer, also speak the vernacular of the countrybred and the
unlettered. In his essay "A Shaker Village" (1876), based on his
family's summer visit in 1875 near the Shakers of Shirley,
Massachusetts, Howells noted that except for their use of *yea*
(pronounced *yee*) and *nay*, the Shakers' speech "does not...vary
from the surrounding Yankee."[3] In the novel, the isolated community of celibates and communitarians is attached to the
world they have renounced by the speech of the Shakers, who
say "you hain't," "without you feel," and "I don't know as you'd
ought"; observe that Boynton isn't "over and above strong" (p.

209); and remark that the community "hain't had a good fit of sickness on hand for quite a spell" (p. 169). One of the sisters tells Egeria that the man she once hoped to marry and his wife "live out in Illinoy"—a rare instance in Howells of eye dialect in which the accepted pronunciation of a word is rendered phonetically only in nonstandard speech. Brother Elihu, however, befitting his position of authority in the village, instructs the Shakers and defends their way of life to outsiders in English spoken with "neatness and point" (p. 177), as Howells's friend in the village at Shirley, Elder Fraser, in addressing the Sunday meeting, "enforced his faith in language which, while it was always simple, was seldom wanting in strength, clearness, and literary excellence."[4]

The three main characters, Dr. Boynton, Egeria, and Ford, are uprooted, without attachment to any social group, living in the marginal world of boarding houses, in Boston but not of it. Although of provincial origins, they speak without a trace of the vernacular by which they could be readily classed. Ford has broken his ties with his native village to become "an impassioned cockney," but his intelligence, his ironic wit, and his literary ambitions qualify him as a speaker of the standard of educated society. As a medical doctor, Boynton can be assumed to have the education and culture that separate him from Mrs. LeRoy and the village illiterates. But like "the windy verbiage" of James's Professor Fargo, who "caressed his rounded periods,"[5] Dr. Boynton's discourse is inflated by "rotund phraseology" (p. 232) which strikes even the unsophisticated Shakers as "pretty glib" (p. 169). Only with his recognition of his moral offense against Egeria does he understand the self-delusive power of his "rhetorical ecstasies" (p. 72). He cries to Ford, "Oh words, words! Phrases, phrases,—this glibness tires me to death! I can't get any foot-hold on it—I slip on it as if it were ice" (p. 366).

Henry James, who wrote less enthusiastically of *The Undiscovered Country* after he had finished it, praised the character of Boynton as "very finely conceived," but changed his initial opinion of Egeria, finding her six months later "the least individual and personal of your heroines."[6] But, as her name suggests, Howells intended to represent in Egeria not only a provincial New England girl who remembers her maternal grandfather's farm in Maine, but a symbolic figure of mythic dimension. Like the water nymph Egeria of Roman legend sought by King Numa for her powers of healing and prophecy, Howells's Egeria is consistently identified with natural beauty and fertility. In the wasteland of the city, in the winter, she falls ill; in the Shaker village she dies to her old life during her long fever, when she loses her telegenic powers. She recovers in the spring when orchards are in bloom, gardens are filled with canes of berries, meadows are green, and she herself seems "like some sylvan creature, a part of the young terrestrial life that shone and sang and bloomed around her" (p. 191). An artist or a poet might have figured her a youthful Ceres, Howells observes: "She looked so sweet and pure an essence of the harvest landscape, so earthly fair and good" (p. 213).

Were she conceived realistically at every point, Egeria, like Miss Thorn, the village school mistress who aids the Boyntons before they reach the Shakers, would reveal her provincial culture in her speech. But a heroine who partakes of the divine spirit of nature in a fable of death and rebirth inhabits a different realm from the country teacher, who says "I presume," "I don't know as," and "I want you should" (pp. 141-43). In other ways, however, Howells shows in Egeria the timidity, uncertainty, and social ignorance natural to a refined but unsophisticated country-bred girl. When she prepares to write a letter to Ford, she innocently buys paper of an "outlandish color and envelopes of a rhomboid shape" (p. 104); she omits the salutation, not knowing how to address him, and writes a hand "timid and feeble," lacking "the bold angularities of the fashionable female scrawl" (pp. 104-05). In conversations she speaks in short simple sentences, defers to her father and Ford and, with her lover especially, doubts her own powers of expression, saying of her attempts to describe her feelings, "I couldn't express it" (p. 303), "I know that I don't express it well" (p. 306), and "I don't know if I can tell" (p. 326). But in genteel nineteenth-century society, a young girl's unquestioning deference to the male was a sign of her good breeding, and, unlike

grammatical lapses, her ignorance of the proprieties of letter-
writing does not eternally brand her unfit for polite society.

A Modern Instance, which Howells began early in 1881,
shortly after the publication of *The Undiscovered Country*,
bears notable resemblances to that novel. Like Egeria and Dr.
Boynton, Marcia and her father, Squire Gaylord, a lawyer and
the leading citizen of his town, Equity, in Maine, are emo-
tionally bound in ties of mutual dependence, eventually
broken by the daughter's attachment to the man she marries.
In both novels the main characters leave their native New
England villages to live isolated lives in Boston rooming
houses. But *A Modern Instance* portrays the corruption, not the
salvation, of the main characters, the disintegration of a
doomed marriage made early in the novel, not a courtship cul-
minating in happy marriage at the end. The process of social
decay evident in *The Undiscovered Country* is more pervasive in
A Modern Instance, where in city and country alike commercial interests undermine religious belief, modern business cor-
rupts moral principle, marriages fail, and families break
apart. The degeneration of the protagonist, Bartley Hubbard,
reflects social malaise everywhere he appears—in Equity,
Maine, where he begins his career as editor of a village paper
and marries Marcia Gaylord; in Boston, where he sells his
services to a corrupt newspaper editor and, after a season of
ruinous prosperity, deserts his wife; in an Indiana divorce
court, where he attempts to convict Marcia of desertion; and in
Whited Sepulchre, Arizona, where he is shot to death by men
he has maligned in a newspaper.

According to William Lyon Phelps, Howells regarded *A
Modern Instance*, his darkest picture of American life, as
"undoubtedly my strongest work." H.H. Boyesen quoted
Howells as saying, when asked in an interview which novel he
regarded as his greatest, "I have always taken most satisfaction
in *A Modern Instance*. I have there come closest to American
life as I know it." John Hay, one of the first readers to recognize
its power, wrote to Howells on November 30, 1881, after the
first installment appeared in the *Century*: "The first part of the

'Modern Instance' seems to me to have a closer grip of realism than anything ever done in America."[7] Twentieth-century critics place *A Modern Instance* among Howells's most important works.

The "grip of realism" which Hay praised is revealed in ways not seen before in Howells's fiction. For the first time, he not only created in Bartley a leading male character who has neither the manners nor the nature of a gentleman; he presented a provincial heroine without idealizing her. Like Lydia Blood, Marcia Gaylord, who marries Bartley, has rustic manners and provincial habits of speech as well as beauty, but, far from being otherwise flawless, her possessiveness that flames into jealous rage when Bartley even converses with other women dooms their marriage from the start. In portraying the mundane life of a man and woman fortunate chiefly in their health and energy, Howells for the first time depicted the inwardness of a relationship over an extended period—the conversations at meals, the quarrels and reconciliations, all the day-to-day life of a couple known only to themselves.

Of all the elements of Howells's realism, speech is the most potent in placing characters on a social and moral scale. Reflective of social changes are the differences between the speech of parents and their children, in whom the provincial idioms of an older generation have diminished or disappeared altogether. Squire Gaylord and his wife say *ain't, hain't, don't know as, some those times, hadn't ought,* and *don't know but what,* except when the Squire pleads Marcia's case in the Indiana divorce court; then, miraculously, all traces of the vernacular disappear. Elsewhere, the Squire places himself by his ruminative nasal *m*'s prefixed to *yes* and *no,* a feature of backwoods speech noted by several British travellers in America.[8] Mrs. Gaylord's talk is enlivened by country expressions— "a master hand at tea," "make company," "'twas wearin' on her," "it worked me up considerable," "show out her feelings." Her daughter Marcia's talk is "thin and dry" (p. 176) with everyone but Bartley. Once, when excited, Marcia says "ain't," but otherwise her provinciality expresses itself in locutions like "I want you should" and "I presume," which never fall from the lips of Atherton, the Boston lawyer, and his class.

Olive Halleck and her brother Ben, Bartley's college friend whose guilt-ridden love of Marcia poisons his life, by choice remain apart from fashionable society, but they speak like its most cultivated members. Their parents, of country stock, long settled in Boston in unfashionable prosperity, have kept the idiom of their native village as well as the religious faith of their youth. In conversation with Bartley, Mr. Halleck exclaims, "You're right, I guess!" (p. 207) and refers to his wife as "Mother," of whom he says, "she keeps it about right" (p. 207).

Language also separates the Hallecks, parents and children, from the Hubbards' landlady, Mrs. Nash, another country-bred person and long-time resident in Boston. Conversing with Marcia and Bartley, who impress her as "a very pretty-appearing young couple" (p. 148), she speaks with "the lazily rhythmical drawl, in which most half-bred New Englanders speak" (p. 148). "I don't neve give board" (p. 150), she tells them; "I heard some my lodgers tellin' how they done" (p. 151); "I hain't never tried it myself" (p. 151). Later she exclaims to Marcia of Bartley, "Gaw, is he college-bred?...He ain't a bit offish. He seems *re'l* practical" (p. 154).

Of all the characters, Bartley Hubbard is the most difficult to place in the novel's class structure and his social position is the most anomalous. To the people of Equity he seems cosmopolitan and sophisticated with his city-tailored clothes and self-confident manner; at the Boston hotel, where he registers as "Bartley J. Hubbard and Wife" (p. 139), the clerk "knew him at once for a country person" (p. 139). As a newspaper reporter, he gains entrance into the homes, offices, and club rooms of the rich and socially prominent, but unlike Silas Lapham he makes no effort to become part of their world. Appropriately, his speech places him neither with the vernacular speakers nor with Ben Halleck and Atherton. He uses none of the provincial locutions (e.g., *don't know as, want you should*); he makes no blunders like Kinney, the loggers' cook, who says "you was," "I been," "some them little things," and "it would about broke my heart" (pp. 310-11). But Bartley's "free, joking way" (p. 20), admired by Mrs. Nash and the people of Equity, is alien to Ben Halleck and Atherton.

That Bartley belongs to no linguistic class is consistent with Howells's portrayal of him as a rootless figure, orphaned in childhood, growing to manhood without a sense of loyalty to any person or institution or tradition. Instead of beliefs and principles he has the chameleonlike power to play whatever part will win approval, to adopt whatever kind of language serves his purpose at the moment. It is one proof of the "smartness" so admired in Equity that as editor of their newspaper he can advertise the beauties of the town "with the zeal of a *condottiere*" (p. 29) in panegyrics verging on the burlesque. With equal ease, he adopts the language and the pose of a romantic hero in a sentimental novel when he intoxicates Marcia by telling her, in a "rich caressing voice" (p. 8), "You have always influenced me for good; your influence upon me has been ennobling and elevating" (p. 13).[9] With equal readiness he absorbs the language of Blackstone, which Squire Gaylord sets him to read: "The very language seemed to have been unbrokenly transferred to his mind, and he often gave the author's words as well as his ideas" (p. 21). In Boston for the first time, as a college student visiting the Hallecks, he had aped the manners of their fashionable visitors and "civilized himself as rapidly as his light permitted" (p. 26). When he returns to Boston after his marriage he sells slick newspaper features on various subjects filled with the "vivid and telling" sentences and "strokes of crude picturesqueness and humor" (p. 169) desired by editors and readers. Described by Ben Halleck, the character who has known him longest, as "a fellow that assimilated everything to a certain extent, and nothing thoroughly" (p. 213), Bartley not only regards language as something to be plundered, but appropriates the life story Kinney planned to write, sells it without a guilt pang for fifty dollars, then is mystified and exasperated when Marcia condemns the act as theft.

When Bartley speaks most naturally, without calculation, he expresses himself in colloquialisms and slang. He tells

Marcia, "I knew you were dead in love with me from the first moment" (p. 48); says of an Equity girl with whom he had flirted, "She flies at higher game than humble newspaper editors" (p. 69); and advises Kinney to "try some other tack" (p. 86). When Marcia says that she wants their daughter Flavia christened, he agrees: "Well, let's go the whole figure" (p. 255). After Halleck brings him home drunk, he says to him of Marcia, "I guess she must have smelt a rat" (p. 276).

In a passage in the serial which Howells removed from the book, he said of Bartley: "His college training had been purely intellectual; it left his manners and morals untouched, and it seemed not to have concerned itself with his diction or accent; so far as his thoughts took shape in words, he thought slangily."[10] In the novel, as in the serial, Bartley's thoughts at several points are phrased in language as little elevated as his sentiments. After declaring that Marcia's ennobling influence sustains his life as the oil in the lamp feeds the flickering flame, he goes to his hotel, consumes a hearty midnight snack of mince pie, toasted cheese, and milk, and reflects complacently that Marcia, "the prettiest girl in the place," had "fallen in love with him at sight" without "a word on his part that anyone could hold him to." "Bartley was still free as air; but if he could once make up his mind to settle down in a hole like Equity he could have her by turning his hand" (p. 19). Such thoughts, even more than his actions, expose his inherent cheapness and vulgarity, which justify the Squire's condemnation of Bartley to Marcia: "Don't you see that the trouble is in what the fellow *is*; and not in any particular thing he's done?" (p. 96).

With its many characters reflective of "a crude and partly brutal civilization," as Horace Scudder phrased it, *A Modern Instance* is a particularly good test of the degree to which Howells exhibits what he later called "a very essential matter" in the realism of the American novel: the "inherent, if not instinctive, perception of equality: equality running through motive, passion, principle, incident, character, and commanding with the same force his [the Realist's] interest in the meanest and the noblest, through the mere virtue of their humanity." The rest of the passage, which castigates those who long for the "ideal" in fiction, implies that equality is realized simply through a truthful representation of both high and low subjects. But Howells also attacks "the want of humanity" in English criticism "in sympathy only with class interests, growing out of class education, and admitting only class claims to the finer regard and respect of readers."[11] Here he includes in the idea of equality the writer's attitude by which the reader's response is shaped.

Does *A Modern Instance* betray the class consciousness Howells condemned? In representing Marcia's and Bartley's search for inexpensive rooms and meals in Boston, Howells draws close to his characters and enters into their concerns. He distances himself, however, when he observes that "three or four months after they came to Boston, they were still country people, with scarcely any knowledge of the distinctions and differences so important to the various worlds of any city" (p. 178). This may be accepted as a statement of fact, although it implies the superiority of the narrator who can make such an observation. The narrator assumes a tone of condescending irony when he notes that Bartley was "already beginning to get up a taste for art" (p. 178) and "boldly" praised the statue of Venus (fittingly) in the Public Garden (p. 204). He and Marcia, we are told, "thought it a divine treat" to let the organ in the Music Hall "bellow" over them at noon, and then, "upon the wave of aristocratic sensation from this experience" (p. 178), to go and dine at Parker's.

It is true that occasionally Howells allows his irony to reflect a satirical view of fashionable society as well. He refers to visitors of the Hallecks who were "infected with the prevailing culture of the city" (p. 26). He mildly ridicules the socialite Clara Kingsbury in her fear that her marriage to Atherton has weakened her "mental powers" because she has sacrificed to married happiness the purposes, "unquestionably large" if "somewhat vague," of her former life as well as such "great interests" as "the symphony concerts" and "Mr. Fiske's lectures on the cosmic philosophy" (p. 414). But, in recording the speech of the characters, he reserves for the vernacular speakers certain techniques that imply inferior status.

Usually Howells records his characters' colloquialisms without comment, but occasionally he inserts a parenthetical clause to disclaim responsibility for the idiom, as in a statement about Kinney: "Late in the fall, he went in, as it is called, with a camp of loggers" (p. 100). Several times he identifies a phrase as Bartley's: "He had had, as he would have said, a grand good time" (p. 16); "he loved to hear the Squire get going, as he said" (p. 33); "he dressed Flavia out to kill, as he said" (p. 289); "he meant to make a raise out of Ben Halleck, as he phrased it to himself" (p. 326). In Equity, he was popular because "he passed the time of day, and was give and take right along, as his admirers expressed it" (p. 20). Milder than James's "in the vulgar parlance," these tags separate the narrator from the characters, implying that he does not speak as they do.

In giving the speech of the "half-bred" Mrs. Nash, Howells not only records grammatical errors but revised passages in the serial to represent more fully the provincial features of her pronunciation as well. The way Atherton and Halleck and other upper-class Bostonians pronounce their *a*'s and *r*'s is not indicated, but in the novel Mrs. Nash is made to seem even more underbred when she is represented as saying *dollas*, *anotha*, and *yea* and emphasizing even more words than in the serial (*ruther, rule, thought*). Nor is the narrator's statement that Mrs. Nash "liked Bartley, as most people of her grade did, at once" (p. 148) calculated to elevate either character in the reader's eyes.

The most clearcut division of characters is made by the Boston lawyer Atherton, who insists to his wife that Halleck's love of Marcia while married to another man is an "indelible stain" (p. 453) and who argues that, because Halleck is known as a man of rectitude, a violation by him of principles which uphold the social order has far graver consequences than the transgressions of a man like Bartley Hubbard. "It doesn't matter much, socially, what undisciplined people like Bartley and Marcia Hubbard do," he instructs Clara, "but if a man like Ben Halleck goes astray, it's calamitous; it 'confounds the human conscience,' as Victor Hugo says" (p. 416).

Atherton's distinctions express a patrician view of society, most evident when he insists upon the difference between "natural goodness," comparable to "the amiability of a beast basking in the sun when his stomach is full," which he is willing to grant the Hubbards; and "implanted goodness," which saves Halleck from dishonor—"the seed of righteousness treasured from generation to generation, and carefully watched and tended by disciplined fathers and mothers in the hearts where they had dropped it" (p. 417). Implicit in Atherton's words, as Henry Nash Smith notes, is the existence of a moral hierarchy, its highest class, like a social aristocracy, inheriting its patrimony, "the seed of righteousness," which is then carefully nurtured to flower in the moral principles and self-restraint of its members.[12]

The author of *A Chance Acquaintance* and *The Lady of the Aroostook* did not regard "the seed of righteousness" as the exclusive property of the Boston Brahmins or of any class. But his treatment of the characters in *A Modern Instance* shows the strength of a tendency to make the most socially cultivated characters also the most morally enlightened. It is true that he undercuts Atherton's authority by letting Atherton enunciate his idea of "implanted goodness" while drinking tea with his wife in the "luxurious dining-room" of their house on the Back Bay (p. 413). But the action of the novel supports Atherton's distinctions. Although Ben Halleck is psychologically as well as physically crippled, enfeebled by his frustrated and guilt-ridden love, when "the enemy of souls put forth his power against this weak spirit" (p. 405), he triumphs. Bartley Hubbard, his opposite, hardly even conceives of a life in which opportunities to serve oneself are temptations to be resisted. When he appears in the divorce court, every vestige of good in him has disappeared; he is "the bulk," obscenely fat with "broad cheeks" and a triple chin (p. 438). Marcia has sufficient moral sense to condemn her husband's theft of Kinney's story, but she is twice compared to a savage in her ignorance of religion and literature (pp. 143, 254), and nothing she does disproves the description of her by friend, Olive Halleck after Bartley's desertion: a woman grown "commoner and narrower" in misfortune, "like a querulous, vulgar, middle-aged woman in her talk" (p. 401).

Although Howells allows even Clara Atherton to perceive the irony in the sight of Atherton pronouncing judgments on the impoverished Hubbards while supported in the utmost luxury by his wife's fortune, the narrator throughout presents Atherton in positive words not used of the Hubbards. His look is "at once kind and keen" (p. 184); in their concern for Marcia after Bartley deserts her, Atherton and the Hallecks are "good and faithful friends" (p. 393). The fact that Atherton is "playing with his spoon" when he instructs Clara in the idea of complicity—"We're all bound together. No one sins or suffers to himself in a civilized state" (p. 418)—does not lessen the importance of the idea in Howells's fiction. Since Bartley's monstrously fat body and beer-bloated face are meant to symbolize moral degradation, the contrasting image, Atherton's "slim, delicate hand" (p. 417), implies the moral opposite. In all these ways the novel supports Richard H. Brodhead's claim that Howells sought to invest in Atherton the authority of ethical and moral principles which, as the novel demonstrates, were losing force in modern society. "Atherton might be described as the means by which a lapsing social code rhetorically reconstitutes itself as a binding moral law, objectively sanctioned and universally enforceable."[13]

Significantly, the strongest resistance to Atherton in the novel comes not from an outsider but from one of his own class, Ben Halleck, who asserts that Atherton's arguments against divorce take no account of the reality of private experience, that the social order to which Atherton would sacrifice individual happiness is but a fabrication sustained by the hypocrisy of "sinners whose blameless life has placed them above suspicion" (p. 362). In other words, the conflict of views is contained within the society of the "genteel and grammatical"; the vernacular characters are excluded from the debate, and Ben Halleck, open in his denunciation of Bartley as he is secret in his love for Marcia, cannot unite his class with theirs. In Howells's next novel, *A Woman's Reason*, the contrast between classes is just as sharp, but his subject enabled him not to reconcile the ideal of equality with the principle of "implanted goodness" but to avoid the full exposure of the conflict.

A Woman's Reason (1883), coming between *A Modern Instance* and *The Rise of Silas Lapham*, two of Howells's most substantial works, has suffered by comparison. It has no memorable characters like Bartley Hubbard and Silas Lapham. It is weakened by the nearly eighty pages narrating the adventures of the hero shipwrecked for two years on an atoll in the Pacific, the most palpable example in Howells's work of the kind of contrivance he deplored in romantic novels. But the main subject of the novel is not trivial. In depicting the plight of a well-born young woman whose fashionable education in German and French, painting and music has failed to equip her to earn her living when the need arises, Howells made his most comprehensive study to date of the class distinctions and inequalities in American society. As the protagonist, Helen Harkness, left almost destitute by her father's bankruptcy and death, struggles in vain to support herself—by decorating pots, writing book notices, coloring photographs, and designing bonnets—she moves down in the social scale, from her father's house on Beacon Steps, filled with the spoils of his Far Eastern trade, to a boarding house, where a young art student and a journalist and his family also have rooms, and finally to the spare room in the cottage of her family's cook, from which the timely arrival of her fiancé, the shipwrecked hero whom she had believed dead, rescues her.

A Woman's Reason is notable also as the only novel of Howells in which the protagonist is a member of Boston upper-class society with the assumptions and prejudices of her class. (Grace Breen of *Dr. Breen's Practice*, the protagonist most similar to Helen in sensibility, comes from an "inland New England city" (p. 12) and is not concerned with questions of class in her dealings with the other characters.) For the first time, in *A Woman's Reason*, Howells presents a novel from the point of view of a character whose relations with those outside her circle are governed by a sense of status. The sense of superiority evident in the narrator's treatment of vernacular characters in the earlier novels thus becomes part of his main character's habitual way of dealing with others. After her father's death, Helen allows Margaret, their Irish cook, to pay the last round of the family bills because, as she explains to a family friend: "It isn't as if anybody else did it for me—any equal you know" (p. 96).[14] When the Misses Amy, decayed gentlewomen with whom she first seeks to board, patronize her by assuring her that, like them, "you won't keep *all* your acquaintance" (p. 153), she replies distantly, unwilling that they "should assume their equality in that fashion" (p. 153). When she meets the journalist Evans and his family, she keeps her distance, guided by her "strong impression that she was their social superior" (p. 167), showing "by a thousand little recoils and reserves, that her fellow-boarders and herself could never meet on a level" (p. 251). When Evans assumes equality by inviting her to share his amusement at their landlady's mispronunciation, Helen holds herself aloof, although out of politeness she laughs "for sympathy" at his mimicry: "Goes with the rooms on this floor; I always let 'em *on suit*; now, if you wanted anything *on suit*..." (p. 166).

She is as sensitive to distinctions made at the expense of her own class as she is ready to make them at the expense of others. When her English suitor, Lord Rainford, tells her that to him one trade is like another—"it appears all the same to-us"—, the "us" rankles. "When it came to herself, she had the national inability to accept classification" (p. 286). She is outraged when he refers to America as "a society where you are all commoners together" (p. 292); she perceives that "she had only been his equal as he ordained it" (p. 294). As she chafes at the sense of superiority he unconsciously reveals, so her fellow boarders at Mrs. Hewitt's resent her air of superiority. Miss Root, the country-bred art student, stiffens in offense when Helen, offering to help her fit a dress, says: "I used to help our cook with hers" (p. 321). Evans's ironical praise of Helen for receiving a check for book notices that he will have to rewrite gives him particular satisfaction, for he has felt her condescen-

sion and realized that, in their resentment of it, both he and
Miss Root have succumbed to "the self-flattery that comes
through the ability to patronize a social superior" (p. 326).

Instead of merely demonstrating the hollowness of convention and prejudice that would class Kitty Ellison below Arbuton, Blake below Leslie, Lydia below Staniford, Howells in
A Woman's Reason exposes the sense of status pervading all
classes of American society. What was implicit in *Their Wedding Journey*—that class consciousness and class distinction
belie Americans' professed belief in equality—is now made
explicit as characters call attention to the disparity between
practice and principle. When Lord Rainford says to Helen, "I
didn't find you such deeply-dyed democrats" (p. 276), she tells
him that Americans are democrats in their traditions but not
in their opinions and practice (p. 276). She discovers that her
generalization applies to all classes of American society, that
the working girls are "as full of prejudice and exclusiveness as
any one. I've never seen distinctions in society so awful as the
distinction between shop-girls and parlour-girls" (p. 389). She
betrays her own sense of status in feeling their social distinctions as "such a burlesque of ours" (p. 389).

By creating a protagonist with a keen sense of social superiority, Howells to some extent avoided conflict between his
democratic and his patrician impulses. He not only shifts to
Helen the burden of class consciousness but criticizes it
through his ironic treatment of her view of things. Like James
in his revelation of Isabel Archer in the early chapters of *The
Portrait of a Lady*, Howells lets his protagonist's thoughts betray her complacency, ignorance, and unquenchable sense of
her own superiority. At nineteen, after rejecting several pro-
posals, Helen "felt that she now knew the world thoroughly,
and while she was resolved to judge it kindly, she was not going
to be dazzled by it any longer" (p. 16). After humbling herself to
approach shop-people "on their own level" to offer her deco-
rated pots for sale, she wonders that "they should have shown
no sense of the sacrifice she had made, but should have tram-
pled upon her all the same" (p. 191). The narrator's mockery
lurks in his statement that Helen in meeting Mrs. Evans was

"painfully aware of not having heard of her" and that, when she learns that Evans is a newspaper editor, "she understood, of course, that they could never have been people that people knew" (p. 252). Helen can hardly be expected to feel otherwise, Howells observes: "It is impossible that one who has been bred to be of no use should not feel an advantage over all those who have been bred to be of some use" (p. 251).

In other passages the narrator's point of view is not so easy to determine. Does the account of Helen's effort to please the maids, second-girls, and cooks, for whom she makes bonnets after she has failed with her fashionable custom, reflect his view as well as hers: "Helen did her best to serve the simple, stupid things cheaply and well" (p. 373)? When the fashionable women who have known Helen are said to be glad "that the poor thing had found something at last that she *could* do" (p. 377), the phrasing is clearly theirs, not the narrator's, but the narrator's designation of one of Helen's customers as a "hapless creature," his use of quotation marks in referring to "salesladies," and his description of a "young coloured girl" sent forth from Helen's "resplendent in a white hat trimmed in orange and purple" (p. 374) indicate that the characterization of the girls as "simple, stupid things" is as much the narrator's as Helen's. These passages indicate that later, when Helen reflects that "for the last six months her relations had been with inferior people" (p. 380), the narrator again shares her view. It is Helen, not the narrator, who calls the social distinctions made by the working girls a "burlesque" of upper-class society, but her view duplicates Howells's view of Negroes engaged in what seems a burlesque of white society. He shares Helen's sense of distance from the provincial Miss Root, noting that Helen's appeal to the art student touched Miss Root, "or as she would have said, it made her feel for the girl" (p. 315). When Helen is unable to imagine herself working in a store, the narrator does not satirize her feeling that she can never be like those poor shop-girls "shrilly piping 'Ca-ish!' " while they "munched a surreptitious lunch of crackers and chocolate creams" (p. 317).

Helen's sense of status, which at times results in unconscious cruelty, does not survive in all its rigidity. Early in her social descent, when Lord Rainford describes a Customs officer named Kimball, who had told him that a deposit "wasn't necessary between *gentlemen*," Helen "laughed at the man's diverting assumption of a community of feeling with Lord Rainford" (p. 264). Months later, in the last chapter of the novel, when she meets Kimball, who has befriended her on several occasions and is now poverty-stricken himself, she no longer finds him laughable but is filled with sympathy, while her rich friend, Marian Butler Ray, on hearing of his words to Lord Rainford, exclaims "How amusing!" (p. 452). Of course, the fact that Kimball unquestioningly accepts his lowly place in the social scale and treats Helen with the deference due a lady from a one-time policeman and Customs officer, enhances for her his instinctive courtesy and good will.

In *The Rise of Silas Lapham*, his best known work, Howells again dramatizes the unbridgeable gulf between the social classes in Boston. But Silas Lapham is his only protagonist who actively strives to force his entrance into patrician society, here represented by the Coreys, whose son Tom eventually marries Silas Lapham's elder daughter Penelope. More than in any other work by Howells, manners determine the decisions and attitudes of the characters, as both the Laphams and the Coreys refer their actions to the code of behavior established by the upper class.

When Tom Corey proposes to enter Silas Lapham's mineral paint business, Tom's father, Bromfield Corey, stifles his misgivings and tells his son: "The suddenly rich are on a level with any of us nowadays. Money buys position at once" (p. 64). But the novel proves otherwise. Although Lapham believes that his fortune made in business will buy a place in the Coreys' world, after his humiliation at their dinner party he finally accepts what his wife Persis has argued from the beginning; that even after twelve years in Nankeen Square, the Laphams are still "country people" (p. 30), ignorant of the manners and traditions of the established families like the Coreys. Between them and the Laphams, Penelope tells her suitor, "there is too great a difference every way" (p. 356) for the families ever to understand each other.

The ineffaceable differences between outsiders and insiders, who can be allied only through the marriage of their children, are evident at many points—their houses, the schools their children attend, the places where the families spend the summer, the daughters' dresses, the way their mothers sign their letters. Most deeply ingrained are the habits of speech that separate the Laphams from the Coreys. The vernacular of Silas Lapham, essential to conveying his boastful pride, energy, and hearty good will, sets him forever outside the world of the Coreys, whose conversational ease, refined diction, and irreproachable grammar represent a barrier he can never pass.

As Janet McKay has noted, the solecisms and colloquialisms of Silas's dialect are most numerous in the first chapter, in which Bartley Hubbard interviews Silas for "The Solid Men of Boston" series as he had interviewed Ben Halleck's father in *A Modern Instance*.[15] Silas's first words in the novel, "Walk right in," convey his hospitable readiness to talk about himself, in colloquialism and slang as familiar as his story of his rise from poverty to wealth. He tells Bartley he "was bound to be an American of *some* sort, from the word Go" (p. 4); he went to the southwest when "Texas was all the cry" (p. 9), returned to New England to find more farms for sale "than you can shake a stick at" (p. 7), feared that the man who tested the paint from the newly discovered mine "was drawing a long bow" (p. 11), then had to "face the music" when the war "knocked my paint higher than a kite" (p. 15). Apparently unconscious that he deviates from any grammatical standard, he says "hain't," "I begun," "Don't know as," and "them houses," explains to Bartley how his father found paint "laying loose in the pit" (p. 7), and tells him "I aint a-going to brag up my paint" (p. 11). Surprisingly he consciously avoids anachronisms, saying of his father's determination to work the paint mine, "I guess, if they'd had the word in those days, they'd considered him pretty much of a crank about it" (p. 7).

Although, unlike Silas Lapham, his wife and two daughters are, as Bronfield Corey understands from Tom, "very passably grammatical" (p. 64), they would never be mistaken for members of the Coreys' circle. Like her husband, Persis Lapham says, "I ain't," "I don't know as," "I presume," and "I don't know but what." She affectionately mocks him in expressions like his, telling him, "I do believe you've got mineral paint on the brain" (p. 71), taunting him, "Do you suppose a fellow like young Corey...would touch mineral paint with a ten-foot pole" (p. 71), and threatening him, "if you try to get off any more of those things on me" (p. 85). Unlike Bartley Hubbard's slang, which usually proceeds from contempt and a cynical refusal to accept anything as sacred, the Laphams' colloquialisms, expressive of their vigor and forthrightness, do not debase them or their subjects of conversation.

Their grammar school education in Boston has brought the Lapham girls closer than their parents to the genteel standard. But Irene, whose beauty is her chief attribute until Tom Corey's choice of her sister calls forth her iron will, reveals her family's country origins when she says "I presume," "all about it is," "I want you should." She has few thoughts to express and few words to say what she does think, relying on "young lady" expressions in talking with Tom Corey. Her exclamations to Penelope, "Oh, you mean thing" and "You may try and you may try and you may try," later grace the conversations of the uncouth girls, Statira Dudley and 'Manda Grier, in *The Minister's Charge*. When Mrs. Lapham tells Irene in bald sentences that fall "like blows" that Tom Corey "don't care anything for you. He never did," Irene finds her only relief not in words but in physical activity, telling her parents, "I don't want any one should talk with me" (p. 245).

Penelope, who eventually marries Tom Corey, first charms him by her talk, which has something of her parents' colloquial ease and savor (she observes that her father is "on his high horse" and "don't pet worth a cent"). But she is betrayed by none of their rusticisms, which would disqualify her from marriage into the Corey family. Her speech bears out Oscar Firkins's observation about Penelope: "A consummate tact leaves the question of her refinement in lasting abeyance; she is never shown in circumstances where the author might have to choose between the sacrifice of her charm and the suspension of his realism."[16] Likewise, she is spared the curse of New England women—high-pitched nasal tones: "She had a slow, quaint way of talking, that seemed a pleasant personal modification of some ancestral Yankee drawl, and her voice was low and cozy, and so far from being nasal that it was a little hoarse" (p. 37). To Tom Corey, "that low, crooning note of hers was delicious" (p. 135). (*Delicious* is also the effect of Irene's beautiful coloring: "There is no word but delicious," p. 52.) As Tom, although not witty himself, can appreciate his father's witty irony, so he can delight in Penelope's gift, equally foreign to him, her droll mimicking, seemingly unstudied, unliterary, "hardly conscious" in its effect.

By endowing Penelope with the humorist's sense of the absurd and the actor's skill in representing it, Howells enabled her to win her place in Tom Corey's world by means other than perfect conformity to their way of speaking. In fact, her humorous drolling, which so charms Tom, reinforces his family's sense of her distance from them. Bromfield Corey, who, after Tom, best appreciates Penelope, "made a sympathetic feint of liking Penelope's 'way of talking' " (p. 359). Mrs. Corey, least responsive, finds her "pert," and Penelope, in explaining why his family would not want her as Tom's wife, tells him, "they don't understand my way of talking" (p. 358). (Habegger notes that *Pert* is also the nickname Silas affectionately gives his wife, and when applied to a woman's speech, implies a spunky, self-assertive assumption of equality.)[17]

In other ways, language reveals differences between the social classes. As Janet McKay shows, the Laphams, characterized by Howells as "blunt, outspoken people," converse in short simple sentences, often say "I guess," speak their minds directly, without reflection, and engage in no conscious ambiguity or play on words. In contrast, the Coreys, in their conversations, often circle around the subject, imply rather than state their meaning, and probe the meaning of each other's words.[18] Bromfield Corey refers to "my wife"; Silas refers to his wife as "Mrs. Lapham." In addressing his father as "sir," Tom Corey speaks "in an old-fashioned way that was rather charming" (p. 62). Silas Lapham's frequent iteration of *Sir*, directed to whatever man he happens to be addressing (yes sir, no sir, well sir), is a habit foreign to "really refined society," according to a writer in *Harper's*. "In England it is deemed servile."[19] When Silas boasts, "It's the best paint in God's universe," Tom responds with more restraint: "It's the best in the market" (p. 76). Silas's racial epithets—"shif'less kind of Kanuck" (p. 9) and, in the serial, "nigger" (*Century* 29:26) show him less cultivated than the Coreys, who do not expose their prejudices in this way.

Occasionally, characters of different social classes miss the sense of each other's words. Mrs. Lapham does not understand Sewell's question: "If some one had come to you...in just this perplexity, what would you have thought?" He phrases it more simply: "What do you think someone else ought to do in your place?" (p. 240). When Tom says to Silas, "I want you to take me into the mineral paint business," Silas replies in words he uses in speaking to hands seeking employment—"How do you think I am going to take you on?"—but Tom Corey is "ignorant of the offense" (p. 74). Howells uses quotation marks to indicate Tom's awareness of using colloquialisms characteristic of Silas but not of himself. He says to his father, "I confess that I 'took to' Colonel Lapham from the moment I saw him. He looked as if he 'meant business,' and I mean business too." The absence of quotation marks in the second clause suggests that Tom adopts Silas's sense of purpose as well as his words.

As narrator, Howells maintains distance from Silas Lapham, as he did from Bartley Hubbard, by disclaiming responsibility for the character's words. Silas looks upon the architect designing his Beacon Street house as his property: "It seemed to him that he had discovered the fellow (as he always called him)" (p. 43). In talking, the Laphams "liked to have it, give and take, that way, as they would have said, right along" (p. 37). In bringing Tom Corey to the Lapham cottage, Silas "was feeling, as he would have said, about right" (p. 82). He "liked to knock off early, as he phrased it" (p. 110). Trying to raise money, he spent most of the day shinning round, as he would have expressed it" (p. 319). Thus Howells informs the reader that slang and colloquialisms are Silas's, implying that he, Howells, would not use them. Because nothing that any of the Coreys think or say is branded "as he would have said," "as they phrased it," the reader assumes that they and the narrator adhere to the same standard, from which any deviation is a mark of inferiority.

Even more directly Howells calls attention to differences between the speech of the well-educated and the well-bred and the speech of Silas and Persis Lapham. He not only renders the Laphams' dialect forms—"wa'n't, I done," "here we be"—but comments on their lapses. "At times, the Colonel's grammar failed him" (p. 38); "She left her daughter to distribute the pronouns aright" (p. 147). The narrator observes Silas "lapsing more and more into his vernacular" (p. 132) and Persis reverting "to the parlance of her youth in her pathos at her husband's kindness" (p. 33). The narrator notes that Lapham says *cut* for *coat* (p. 10), *rud* for *road* (p. 18), *doos* for *does* (p. 37), and *purr-ox-eyed* (p. 11) with the accent on the last syllable—Bartley Hubbard understands the word only when Silas spells it. By recording Silas's version of the architect's French, "Ongpeer style" (p. 43), the narrator makes Silas's ignorance of the "Empire style" more grossly comic. Forms in Silas's speech like "should'a' been" (p. 79) and "he'd'a' ruined me" (p. 47), which represent what most people speaking rapidly would say but which never appear in the Coreys' conversations, reinforce the impression of Silas as provincial and uncouth.

Dialect is most marked and the narrator's comments on it most frequent in the first half of the novel, where they heighten the reader's awareness of the futility of Silas's social ambitions. When he becomes drunk at the Coreys' dinner, however, where his social inexperience is most evident, the effects of the wine he thirstily drinks are not represented in his pronunciation. The boorish note of his bragging and patronizing is captured in indirect discourse in standard English ("If anyone had said when he first came to Boston that in less than ten years he should be hobnobbing with Jim Bellingham, he should have told that person he lied...and here he was now worth a million, and meeting you gentlemen like one of you" (p. 206). In direct quotation he is spared the shame of slurred words and missing prepositions and articles, which betray the drunken states of Bartley Hubbard and Hicks (*The Lady of the Aroostook*). Silas also gains in comparison with speakers who, unlike himself, manipulate words to deceive others. Bartley Hubbard mockingly inflates the virtues of Silas Lapham in extravagant compliments of his "prompt comprehensiveness" and "never-failing business sagacity," then drops into anticlimax declaring Silas to be "one of nature's noblemen, to the last inch of his five eleven and a half" (p. 20). The bogus Englishmen who, in collusion with Rogers, seek to buy Silas's worthless mills, reveal their fraudulent character when one, faking a Cockney accent, slips and says "We hoped for an answer," then quickly corrects himself: " 'oped for a hanswer" (p. 326). (Howells may have found the model for the English agent three years before in a store in London, where a clerk selling trunks told him: " 'This one has iron handles,' then corrected himself 'hiron 'andles.' "[20])

Silas is also superior in sense, energy, and virtue to all the other vernacular speakers: the feckless devil Milton Rogers, Silas's erstwhile partner, who utters his favorite locution "I some expected" (or "I some think," "I some suspected") in "dry wooden tones" which had "the flat, succinct sound of two pieces of wood clapped together" (p. 45); Mrs. Millon, who carouses with her daughter's worthless husband and shamelessly appeals to Lapham's generosity in long whining monologues punctuated by "s'd I"; Walker, the bookkeeper, whose good humored but tasteless speculations about Lapham's affairs, belabored in metaphors of storm signals, cold waves, and "increased pressure in the region of the private office" (p. 271), offend Tom Corey and are dismissed by the narrator as "slangy and figurative excesses" (p. 272).

Even Bromfield Corey, the most polished, witty, and entertaining of all the speakers, eventually suffers in comparison with Silas Lapham. When Bromfield Corey contemplates a visit to Silas's office, the narrator remarks the "pleasure which men of weak will sometimes take in recognizing their weakness" (p. 138). Like an episode in an allegory, Corey's visit to

Lapham's office produces in Silas "the struggle of stalwart achievement not to feel flattered at the notice of sterile elegance" (p. 145). After the dinner party, when Silas Lapham confronts the fateful choices foreshadowed in Bartley Hubbard's words "Your money or your life" (p. 3), Bromfield Corey begins to seem inconsequential, his words more than ever an escape from the harsh realities Silas grapples with, his role in the novel reduced to declaring that he will go with his wife to call on Penelope, insisting, "This is a thing that can't be done by halves," then cutting his breakfast orange "in the Neapolitan manner" and eating it "in quarters" (p. 346). As Bromfield's accomplishments grow increasingly trivial, the sense of Silas's uncouth ignorance fades.

Nevertheless, Howells's reduction of Bromfield Corey does not alter the relation of the narrator to Silas Lapham. Although Howells grants Silas not only the wisdom and moral strength to recognize and resist a corrupt deal but also the humility to feel that he has done nothing remarkable, Howells's very stress on the virtue of which the "simple, rude soul" (p. 350) was capable suggests the superior position of one praising unexpected merit in another. That Silas says "I done" three times in his last words to Sewell does not diminish Lapham's "heroic virtue" in which Bromfield Corey takes "a delicate, aesthetic pleasure" (p. 359), but the virtue does not efface the differences between Silas and the genteel Bostonians. Mrs. Corey's brother, James Bellingham, tells Bromfield Corey that Lapham in his financial straits "has behaved very well—like a gentleman" (p. 200), implying that Silas (though he may be "one of nature's noblemen") is not by nature a gentleman as they are.

William James praised *Silas Lapham* for its realism, for its fidelity "to the ways of human nature, with the ideal and the unideal inseparably beaten up together so that you never get them 'clear.' " But more sharply than any other work by Howells, *Silas Lapham* reveals, in the moral rise of its protagonist, one potential source of conflict in Howells's realism. As Alan Trachtenberg has noted, Howells's need to affirm faith in a moral order where characters reap what they sow sometimes obliged him to contrive events that seem improbable or inconsistent.[21] *Silas Lapham* has been criticized on the grounds that Lapham's sacrifice of his fortune to his moral scruples is inconsistent with his character and implausible in the business world of the Gilded Age; according to S. Foster, Howells embraces "ethical idealism which risks being destructive of Realism."[22]

Even if one accepts Howells's premise, that a "rude soul" is capable of moral heroism, there remains the conflict between Howells's affirmation of equality and the recognition of ineffaceable differences which induce in the Coreys feelings of superiority, which the narrator shares.[23] The ultimate relation of the two families, united only by the marriage of Penelope and Tom, who soon after depart for Mexico, where Penelope thinks she will not "feel strange," proves Howells's contention: "It is certain that our manners and customs go for more in life than our qualities. The price that we pay for civilization is the fine yet impassable differentiation of these. Perhaps we pay too much; but it will not be possible to persuade those who have the difference in their favor that this is so" (p. 361). As narrator, Howells notes the deficiencies of the Coreys as well as those of the Laphams, but in applying to Silas a standard to which the narrator and the Coreys but not the Laphams conform, the narrator, for all his sympathy with the Laphams, identifies himself as one of those "who have the difference in their favor."

Chapter Nine

Language and Complicity in
The Minister's Charge

Two years after publication of *The Rise of Silas Lapham*, in *The Minister's Charge* (1887), Howells again dramatized relationships between characters of provincial New England and upper-class Boston. The presence of Bromfield Corey and the minister, David Sewell, one of the two central characters in *The Minister's Charge*, connects that novel to the previous novel. But in *The Minister's Charge* Howells portrayed experiences and types different from those in his earlier novels of New England. He regarded this novel as a turning point in his career; he described it to Henry James as "an example of work in the new way—the performance of a man who won't and can't keep on doing what's been done already."[1] What the "new way" includes is an importance attached to language that marks a departure from Howells's early methods of revealing characters through their speech. As a result, the opposing principles of unity and diversity, embraced in Howells's definition of realism, emerge as the central conflict of the novel itself.

The importance of language in *The Minister's Charge* is first evident in a greater range of types differentiated by their speech than appears in any of the earlier novels. When the protagonist, Lemuel Barker, leaves his mother's farm in Willoughby Pastures, Massachusetts, and seeks to establish himself in Boston, he embarks on a career that exposes him to many kinds of people: rustics like himself, tramps, con men, policemen, shopgirls, car conductors, hotel servants, journalists, art students, and upper-class Bostonians, including his mentor, David Sewell, whose well-intentioned but insincere praise of Lemuel's efforts to write poetry inspired the young man to seek his fortune in Boston. After his literary hopes are crushed by Sewell's belated honesty, Lemuel casts himself adrift: he joins the throng on the Common, where he is fleeced by two sharpers who accost him in jargon incomprehensible to him: "Any them beats 'round here been trying to come their games on *you*?" (p. 34).

Falsely accused of assault by a country-bred shopgirl, or "sales-lady" as she calls herself, Lemuel spends a night in prison and the next day appears in court, where a drunken Irish woman begs "your hanor" to "make it aisy" (p. 60). Lemuel spends his third night in a Wayfarer's Lodge for derelicts, where he meets a reputed ex-sailor and confessed thief who mixes his jaunty slang of "mates" and "lays" and "shabbing the measure" with references to his "sea voyages," which Lemuel does not understand to mean prison terms.

Lemuel moves up the social scale when he works as clerk and waiter at Mrs. Harmon's hotel, the St. Alban's. Most of the guests are people of means: the women are stylishly dressed, their husbands have respectable jobs, but their bad grammar and the quality of their voices betray their inferior status. "They nearly all snuffled and whined as they spoke; some had a soft, lazy nasal; others broke abruptly from silence to silence in voices of nervous sharpness, like the cry or the bleat of an animal; one young girl, who was quite pretty, had a high, hoarse voice, like a gander" (p. 144). They are not out of place in a hotel where the proprietor (a friend of Mrs. Hewitt of *A Woman's Reason*), calls the bills of fare "meanyous" (p. 169) and tells Lemuel that "the boarders are all high-class" (p. 143).

When Lemuel is employed to read to the aging Bromfield Corey, he hears the cultivated speech of a man whose linguistic confidence is revealed in his delight in using "a bit of new slang" (p. 320). Distinctions exist among the upper class as well as the lower: when Lemuel breakfasts with the cousin of Mrs. Corey, he notes that a minister "spoke with an accent different from the others." Once again Lemuel fails to realize all that speech conveys: "He did not know [the accent] for that neat utterance which the Anglican Church bestows upon its servants" (p. 279).

The Minister's Charge not only depicts the speech of more different types of characters than hitherto represented. The novel also gives a fuller transcript of the pronunciation and locutions of the nonstandard speakers. Whereas Howells suggests the vernacular flavor of Silas Lapham's speech by noting his pronunciation, in *The Minister's Charge* he gives a word-by-word transcript of dialect, including not only New England localisms but also the grammatical errors characteristic of the common speech in all parts of the country. H.L. Mencken observed that writers of regional dialects in the 1870s and 1880s virtually ignored the "general dialect." He credited Ring Lardner with the first recording in fiction of the speech of the common people,[2] but *The Minister's Charge* is filled with it. From the lips of the shopgirls, conductors, con men, hotel servants, policemen, and landladies come hundreds of locutions: "I don't know as I did" (p. 18); "there ain't no small bills nowhere" (p. 36); "I ruther wait" (p. 73); "Don't you be took in by no new saw" (p. 79); "I never see folks like some them conductors" (p. 110); "if they got to know we girls" (p. 119); "What me and my wife want to do" (p. 138); "I don't know how many tickets he's give me" (p. 147).

The effects of dialect can best be observed in the speech of Statira Dudley and 'Manda Grier, the shopgirls who entertain Lemuel. (These were the characters Henry James cited in his letter praising the novel: "The girls are sublime, their speech and tone a revelation."[3])

The following passage in which Statira describes 'Manda Grier's opposition to Statira's engagement to Lemuel illustrates the fullness with which Howells cites typical errors: confusion in the forms of pronouns, adjectives used in place of adverbs, double negatives, substitution of personal for demonstrative pronouns, *as* used in place of *that*, *some* used in place of *a*, *hain't* for *haven't*, and dropping of the final *g*. Statira also prolongs her vowels in an effort to sound genteel.

I think we're goin' to get along real nice together. I don't know as we shall live all in the same *hou*-ou-se; I guess it'll be the best thing for Lem and I if we can board till we get some little of our health back; I'm more scared for him than what I am for my-*se*-e-elf. I don't presume but what we shall both miss the city some; but he might be out of a job all winter in town; I shouldn't want he should go back on them *ca*-a-rs. Most I hate is leavin' 'Manda Grier; she is the one that I've roomed with ever since I first came to Boston; but Lem and her don't get on very well; they hain't really either of 'em *got* anything against each other, now, but they don't *like* very *we*-e-ll...and so it's just as well we're goin' to be where they won't *cla*-a-sh. [p. 337]

Such passages not only reinforce awareness of class lines separating Statira from the upper-class Bostonians but also make the dialect the salient feature of the speaker. The vernacular of Silas Lapham is so completely an expression of his personal force that the reader is often hardly conscious of his dialect. But whenever Statira Dudley speaks, the reader is aware of her debasement of language. The effect is heightened to grotesqueness in the speech of 'Manda Grier, who has a whopper-jaw and "spoke a language almost purely consonantal, cutting and clipping her words...till there was nothing but the bare bones left of them" (p. 64).

The Minister's Charge differs from earlier novels not only in the greater uncouthness of the common speech and the prominence this speech assumes. In Statira and 'Manda, Howells associates debasement of language with shallowness, vulgarity, and intellectual poverty hitherto absent from his young female provincial characters. Repeatedly Statira is described as "light"; she is characterized by Howells and by Lemuel as passive, narrow-minded, and ignorant, capable of affection and loyalty but without independence of mind or interests beyond her clothes, her job, and Lemuel's attentions. 'Manda Grier with her distorted jaw is physically grotesque; she appears psychologically twisted as she dominates Statira, first gleefully promoting the awkward lovemaking of Lemuel and Statira, then turning upon Lemuel in a jealous rage.[4]

In an enthusiastic letter to Howells about *The Minister's Charge*, John DeForest praised especially the portrayal of 'Manda and Statira. In response, Howells declared himself indebted to DeForest's example of "bold grappling" with the lovemaking of characters like Lemuel and Statira but suspected in himself "a softer heart for the vulgarity of those poor, silly, common girls—especially 'Manda, in whom I think I struck a new streak."[5] Howells's sympathy for his characters, however, did not prevent his unsparing revelation of girls in whom the innate good taste and dignity that characterize such provincial figures as Lydia Blood and Rachel Woodward are absent. According to the reviewer in *Lippincott's Magazine*, Howells maligned "the whole class of working-girls" in "the unutterable specimens given."[6]

Lemuel's mother is not weak, shallow, or vain, but dresssed in her outmoded Bloomer costume, she is unfashionable to the point of grotesqueness. When she worries that Lemuel "ain't lookin' over and above well" (p. 208) and expresses distrust of "them art-student girls you was tellin' about" (p. 213), the reader is as much aware of her speech as of the force of her feelings. If the dialect of such characters as the aunt and the grandfather of Lydia Blood renders them humorous and quaintly comic, in *The Minister's Charge* the dialect of Lemuel's relations deepens the pathos of their impoverished lives. The impression is intensified by the desolation of the farm in Willoughby Pastures which, unlike Lydia's home in South Bradfield, is not only isolated but squalid—a place of rotting paint, sagging doors, and cracked ceilings.

'Manda and Statira, Lemuel's family in Willoughby Pastures, and the residents at Mrs. Harmon's hotel represent parochial worlds which Lemuel must strive to pass beyond. His progress can be measured by his speech and his perception of what the speech of other characters reveals. At the beginning he is awkward and rustic. His rural origins are apparent in his diction and syntax: "She's middling" (p. 12); "I don't know as you got a letter from me a spell back" (p. 12); "I'd just as lives sit there" (p. 128). In the early chapters, his thoughts are also conveyed in uncouth locutions: "He would see what kind of a looking house they did live in, any way" (p. 113); "he must be very good himself to be anyways fit for her" (p. 165). Initially his speech exhibits such features of his mother's dialect as *ye* and *ha'nt*. But, like Lydia

Blood, Lemuel has innate self-respect. To his advantage, he is reserved and taciturn, and Howells spares him the most uncouth violations of the rules of grammar.

For some time, Lemuel remains unaware of the differences in the way people talk. He does not contrast the speech of Statira and 'Manda with that of Miss Vane, a friend of the Sewells, who hires Lemuel as a handyman. If he notes the snuffles, bleats, and whines of Mrs. Harmon's guests, he "did not mind all this; he talked through his nose too" (p. 144). Gradually, however, the reader notices an improvement in Lemuel's speech, a change confirmed by Sewell, who has continued to counsel and befriend Lemuel: "He's not only well dressed, but he's beginning to be well spoken. I believe he's beginning to observe that there is such a thing as not talking through the nose. He still says 'I don't know *as*,' but most of the men they turn out of Harvard say that" (p. 232).

Likewise, Bromfield Corey notes how readily Lemuel adapts to his new conditions. "It isn't our manners alone that he emulates," he tells his cousin, Charles Bellingham. "I can't find that any of us ever dropped an idea or suggestion of value that Barker didn't pick it up, and turn it to much more account than the owner" (p. 287). Although Bromfield Corey "could not repress some twinges at certain characteristics of Lemuel's accent," and corrects his pronunciation "where he found it faulty" (p. 282), Lemuel by this time is sufficiently well spoken to sit with Charles Bellingham's guests without embarrassing himself or the others and to read aloud, with proper restraint, a passage from that master of the vernacular, Bret Harte.

As Lemuel's own speech improves, he becomes increasingly aware of the speech of others. After experiencing the friendship of a refined art student, Jessie Carver, whose situation parallels that of 'Manda Grier in that she, too, faces the loss of her best friend through marriage, Lemuel sees the deficiencies in 'Manda and Statira. "Their talk, after that he was now used to, was flat and foolish, and their pert ease incensed him" (p. 289). A letter from Statira fills him with a "cruel disgust...its illiteracy made him ashamed" (p. 302). By contrast, the Coreys appear in Lemuel's eyes the embodiment of exquisite taste and gracious kindness. So keen is his sense of the difference between them and Statira, whom he had once thought he loved, that he feels her and 'Manda's talk as contamination, making him "unfit to breathe the refined and gentle air to which he returned in Mr. Corey's presence" (pp. 289-90).

By the end, Lemuel faces a seemingly insoluble dilemma. In the days of his country ignorance, he had expressed love for Statira; she not only returned his love but the alarming illness into which she falls when Lemuel begins to draw away from her suggests that her health, perhaps her life, depends upon his faithfulness. But it is clear that she can offer him nothing but a stultifying devotion that will drag him down and probably arrest his intellectual growth. Clearly, his best hopes lie in marriage to a woman like Jessie Carver, whose devotion to Lemuel is as strong as Statira's. As Alonzo Berry, a law student and Lemuel's friend at the hotel, inelegantly puts it, "What you want...is development, and you can't get it where you've been going" (p. 218). The journalist Evans, whose anomalous social position puzzled Helen Harkness in *A Woman's Reason*, defines the irreconcilable alternatives when he asks Sewell whether Lemuel should "remain a servant; cast his lot with these outcasts; or try to separate and distinguish himself from them, as we all do?" (p. 207). Sewell's answer has far-reaching implications: "He's a very complicated problem" (p. 207).

Ultimately Lemuel's "granite soul" (p. 287) forbids his desertion of Statira. In contrast to Dreiser's Clyde Griffiths, who plots to kill a girl his superior in character in hope of marrying the daughter of a rich man, Lemuel Barker sacrifices the chance of marriage to a young woman of refinement and high principle to remain faithful to the intellectually inferior woman to whom he had first bound himself. So that his own ambitions will not separate him from Statira, Lemuel severs his relations with the Coreys and others of the upper-class world that Statira can never enter, resigns himself to leaving Boston and its opportunities, and prepares to return to Willoughby Pastures.

Howells indicates his approval of Lemuel's decision. He refers to the "real cruelty" in the idea that Lemuel to advance his own interests should cast off Statira, a cruelty that Lemuel himself

perceives by the aid of that "one ray...that lights up every laby-
rinth where our feet wander and stumble" (p. 304). Sewell affirms
the rightness of Lemuel's decision, which seems to illustrate the
minister's belief that to serve those dependent upon one is to live
most in harmony with the divine will: "Only those who had had
the care of others laid upon them, lived usefully, fruitfully. Let no
one shrink from such a burden, or seek to rid himself of it. Rather
let him bind it fast upon his neck, and rejoice in it" (p. 341).

When Sewell's commandments are applied to Lemuel and
Statira, however, they collide with Sewell's conviction that a man
or a woman who refuses to break an engagement when either of
them no longer loves the other succumbs to "that crazy and
mischievous principle of false self-sacrifice" (p. 231). Before he
knows of Statira, Sewell counsels Lemuel that a man's engagement to a woman whose influence he fears will be "degrading and
ruinous" should be broken "in the interest of humanity—of morality" (p. 229).

Sewell does not advise Lemuel to break his engagement to
Statira, but he perceives that Lemuel in cleaving to Statira sacrifices his development in a world that Howells presents as superi-
or to that of Willoughby Pastures. Whereas Silas Lapham is
restored to his self-possession by his return to the country,
Lemuel stands to lose more than he gains by returning home.
Unlike Silas, Lemuel, by virtue of his age and temperament, is
capable of social accommodation to the alien standard; Corey
and Bellingham please themselves in imagining Lemuel as an
Ancestor, the founder of a family which will eventually surpass
the Coreys (p. 275). Furthermore, the manners of the Coreys,
which induced in the Laphams a sense of inferiority, produce for
Lemuel an atmosphere of graciousness in which he gains ease
and confidence. As Edwin Cady observes, "The Bostonians are
permitted a warmth and breadth of sympathy previously denied
them." *Silas Lapham* presents a contrast between two social
classes, each with its virtues and defects; *The Minister's Charge*
presents a contrast between country people ignorant and narrow,
if well meaning, and cultivated people who set standards to
which Lemuel rightly aspires. Lemuel's rocklike integrity appears to be the product of his country origins but his encounters

in the novel indicate that his good qualities are enhanced by his urban experiences.[7]

Lemuel is ultimately released from his bonds by the very weakness and passivity in Statira that initially bound him to her. When she yields to the will of 'Manda Grier to remove her to another city, Lemuel is free to live and marry. But in general terms the problem raised by the novel remains unresolved. The central theme, expressed most fully in Howells's idea of Complicity, affirms the unity through which all people are bound to each other, the whole of society affected by the sin or the suffering of any member. The idea is suggested at several points: by the streetcar conductor's observation that "everybody's mixed up with everybody else" (p. 139); by the journalist Evans's belief that in any sinful transaction the purveyor and the consumer are equally guilty. This idea is fully developed in the sermon in which Sewell preaches the divine equality of all men, bound each to the other "by ties that centered in the hand of God" (p. 341).

At the same time, the novel expresses more powerfully than any of Howells's earlier novels the forces that prevent the translation of spiritual unity into social equality. It is noteworthy that *The Minister's Charge*, which makes the fullest and most explicit statement of the idea of Complicity, is also the novel in which the sense of ineffaceable class lines and class differences is strongest. More fully than any other of his novels, *The Minister's Charge* shows that language, by which people convey their feelings and thoughts to each other and affirm their hope in eventual unity and equality, is also a divisive force, exposing differences and creating barriers, which, so long as the differences exist, cannot be completely overcome. When, early in the novel, Sewell confesses his failure to find with Lemuel "any common ground where we could stand together" and declares them to be "as unlike as if we were of two different species," he blames his failure upon his words. "I saw that everything I said bewildered him more and more; he couldn't understand me!...We understand each other a little if our circumstances are similar, but if they are different all our words leave us dumb and unintelligible" (pp. 29-30).[8]

The class structure portrayed in *The Rise of Silas Lapham* and

The Minister's Charge is not based on money alone. As Bromfield Corey observes of the Laphams, even "good sense and right ideas" do not by themselves qualify one for society or produce its "airy, graceful, winning superstructure." But, in Howells's view, social distinctions, reflected in language, are ultimately traceable to economic inequality. In the Utopian society Howells describes in *A Traveller from Altruria,* a society in which "absolute economic equality" exists and physical labor is required of all, no class lines or social ambitions divide the people and the ideal of Complicity is realized (pp. 160-62). But in a country where economic inequality has produced an upper class with refinements that money alone cannot secure, then language, reflective of social differences, highlights the conflict that emerges as the central theme of Howells's fiction—the conflict between the forces that unite and the forces that divide the American people.

Chapter Ten

Language and Equality
in the Late Novels

After *The Minister's Charge*, the conflict of principles in Howells's theory of realism grows more apparent as his increasingly fervent allegiance to the ideal of equality accompanies his ever more emphatic defense of dialect as a means of revealing the conditions and the culture of fictional characters. In a succession of novels—*Annie Kilburn, A Hazard of New Fortunes, The World of Chance,* and the Altrurian romances—Howells dramatized the evils of economic and social injustice: the degradation of the poor, the strife between employers and workers, the ruthless self-interest fostered by the struggle for survival in what Basil March, in *A Hazard of New Fortunes,* calls "this economic chance-world" (p. 436).[1] Other characters, such as the minister, Mr. Peck, in *Annie Kilburn,* the socialist philosopher, David Hughes, in *The World of Chance,* and the Altrurian traveler, Mr. Homos, directly, in sermons, lectures, essays, and conversations, attack the system that perpetuates injustice and preach the ideals of fraternity and equality.

At the same time, Howells continued to dramatize the gulf between the cultivated characters and the crude, the rustic, and the half-educated by rendering the idioms and grammatical errors of the nonstandard speakers. As in *The Minister's Charge*, the well-educated characters in the later novels judge others by their speech and notice the pronunciation and diction of the nonstandard speakers, while the more intelligent and observant of these, such as Lemuel Barker, strive to modify their speech to conform to a standard set for them. The novels following *The Minister's Charge* depict the growth of a class structure different from that of the Boston of the Arbutons and Stanifords and Coreys, a new social order in which improprieties of speech no longer automatically exclude outsiders. But social change induces some characters to cling even more tenaciously to the standard of speech that represents their threatened traditions. As narrator, Howells continues to reinforce the divisive effects of language by commenting on the peculiarities of characters' speech and insisting upon speech as the unfailing sign of one's culture.

In Howells's later novels, the force of the distinctions that keep the Laphams and the Coreys forever separated is weakened by the growing commercialization of American society, in which money *does* buy position—if not at once, within a generation or two. Howells most fully dramatized the evolution of a commercial society in *A Hazard of New Fortunes*, his most comprehensive picture of New York, the city in which the power of money manifested itself on the grandest scale. The evolving class structure of a plutocracy is revealed through the growing awareness of the protagonist, Basil March, who moves his family from Boston to New York. There he becomes editor of a new magazine, *Every Other Week*, managed by the westerner Fulkerson and owned by a speculator, Jacob Dryfoos, whose fortune, made in the natural gas wells of Indiana and augmented on the New York Stock Exchange, pays the salaries of several characters in the novel. The chief contributors to the magazine—the German socialist Lindau; artists Alma Leighton from St. Barnaby, Maine, and Angus Beaton from Syracuse, New York, by way of Paris; and the southern reactionary, Colonel Woodburn—are, like Fulkerson, the Marches, and the Dryfoos family, all outsiders in New York, making their hazard of new fortunes in the city which, as Fulkerson says, alone "belongs to the whole country" (p. 12).

The variegated character of the magazine staff reflects the New York that March comes to know—a polyglot world that draws its millions from all nationalities and all parts of the United States, the "cosmopolitan Babel," where so many are aliens that "everybody belongs more or less" (p. 216). Amidst crowds of strangers March feels the "intense identification of their Boston life" (p. 297) dissolve in the working of "some solvent in New York life that reduces all men to a common level, that touches everybody with its potent magic and brings to the surface the deeply underlying nobody" (p. 243). His sentiments foreshadow those of the Boston correspondent in *Letters Home*, who observes that Bostonians were "immensely, intensely, personal, and the note of New York is impersonality….Here I feel resolved into my elements at times, in a measure which I do not believe would happen to me even in London or Paris" (p. 65).

The difference between New York and Boston society is most tellingly reflected in the different fates of the Lapham and Dryfoos families. Like Silas Lapham, Jacob Dryfoos, after making his fortune, uproots his family (his wife, son, and two daughters) and installs them in a lavishly furnished house in the city, where they live in isolated splendor, their place in upper-class society still to be secured. Like the Laphams, the Dryfooses betray their ignorance of the manners and traditions of the polite world in their speech—in their double negatives, dropped *g*'s, and rustic idioms. Even more than the Laphams, they reveal their social unfitness and cultural impoverishment whenever they open their mouths. Lacking the vigor of Silas Lapham's hearty colloquialisms, Jacob Dryfoos's speech, like his nature, is stiff and dry, barren of everything but solecisms (*didn't hardly know, I been, you was, I'd a went, I've took, I'll learn him*). His invalid wife, without Persis Lapham's robust vitality and self-reliance, speaks in a rustic vernacular more primitive than that of the Laphams, which in itself confesses her incapacity, as when she complains of her servant, "It seems like a body couldn't git shet of him, nohow" (p. 156).

The Dryfoos sisters mutilate language and violate convention as Irene and Penelope Lapham never do. The younger, Mela, who expresses her simple good nature by "letting out" her large coarse laugh, gurgles, babbles, and yells her way through every social occasion. In her perpetually hoarse voice she mixes slang, gush, and bad grammar, asking "Ain't that rulable?" (p. 266), describing a visit to the opera when "us girls wanted to go 'low neck' " (p. 155), and exclaiming over Margaret Vance, the socialite-social worker who calls on them, "Ain't she just as lovely as she can live?" (p. 258). At the end of a reception, she assures her fashionable hostess: "I've had the best kind of time....I hain't laughed so much, I don't know when" (p. 274). Her sister, Christine, is saved from a multitude of errors only because her proud suspicious nature forbids her to give more than the briefest answers to questions. But the narrator observes that in her conversations with Beaton "she was too ignorant of her ignorance to recognize the mistakes she made then" (p. 313).

Fulkerson has obtained for the Dryfooses the services of a genteel widow, Mrs. Mandel, to chaperone the sisters, polish their manners, and improve their grammar. But although she can teach Mela to correct herself when she says *knowed* and *rulable*, she cannot impart to them her "very ladylike accent" (p. 152) or transform them into cultivated speakers. Conversations at the Dryfoos dinner table are dominated by Mela's "hoarse babble" and Christine's "high-pitched, thin, sharp forays of assertion and denial" (pp. 261-62). To observers, the sisters' comportment suggests the behavior of wild animals. Fulkerson tells the Marches that Mela is "a pretty wild colt now, but you ought to have seen her before she was broken to harness" (p. 165). Christine in her ferocity reminds Fulkerson of "that black leopard they got up there in the Central Park" (p. 165). To Beaton, being with Christine is like "holding a leopardess in leash" (p. 466). Far more than Irene and Penelope Lapham, the Dryfoos sisters illustrate Bromfield Corey's description of "young girls who were so brutally, insolently, willfully indifferent to the arts which make civilization that they ought to have been clothed in the skins of wild beasts and gone about barefoot with clubs over their shoulders" (*Silas Lapham*, p. 117).

Unlike the Laphams, however, the Dryfooses suffer no sense of social inferiority. If anything, they feel superior to the

Marches and Margaret Vance because the Dryfooses have more money. Awareness of social differences oppresses Penelope Lapham, but the Dryfoos girls, "blinded" by their father's wealth "to any difference against them," enjoy "the peace which money gives to ignorance" (p. 273) and never doubt "their equality with the wisest and the finest" (p. 260). At Mrs. Horn's musicale, March notes the perfect confidence of the sisters. "Those girls had no more doubt of their right to be there than if they had been duchesses...they were perfectly natural—like born aristocrats' " (p. 278).

The Laphams and their children will never become part of the old Boston society of the Coreys and Bellinghams. But people of greater crudity like the Dryfooses will not forever be barred from fashionable New York society. Margaret's aunt, Mrs. Horn, witnesses the sisters' capacity for rudeness at her musicale (they come too late, talk too loud, and stay too long), but afterwards she acknowledges to her niece that "such people...people with their money, must of course be received sooner or later. You can't keep them out" (p. 275). In more refined and analytical terms Basil March makes the same point: "Such people as the Dryfooses are the raw material of good society," he tells his wife after Mrs. Horn's musicale. "All the fashionable people there to-night were like the Dryfooses a generation or two ago" (p. 278).

Social acceptance of any member of the Dryfoos family, however, lies in the future, beyond the novel. Mela and Christine are never again invited to Mrs. Horn's. Margaret Vance's call on the sisters proves the truth of Beaton's observation: "You wouldn't know what to do with each other" (p. 248). Margaret Vance does not call a second time. At Saratoga, where Mrs. Mandel takes the Dryfoos sisters, they remain isolated from fashionable guests, who are apparently repelled by Mela's "too instant and hilarious good-fellowship, which expressed itself in hoarse laughter and in a flow of talk full of topical and syntactical freedom" (p. 313). Not only in society do her expensive clothes and her physical beauty fail to mitigate the effects of her speech; her "slang and brag" (p. 270), her hoarse laugh, dropped *g*'s, *ain't*'s, and *haint*'s are far more powerful than the narrator's references to her beauty in creating the reader's impression of her.

The dialect of another character, Madison Woodburn of "Charlottesboag, Virginia," is more obtrusive than the solecisims of the Dryfoos sisters. Reviewers objected to the "uncouth sounds" uttered by Miss Woodburn, found her "tiresome with her dialect," and wished that Howells had given her conversation "boiled" instead of raw."[2] But when the regional speaker makes no grammatical errors, never says *folks* and *don't know as* and departs from standard English only in pronunciation, he or more often she (for such a speaker is usually a woman) suffers little or none of the social stigma that attaches to speakers like the Dryfooses. Nor does her dialect force Madison Woodburn into the stereotype of the languid fluttery southern belle or prevent her from seeming the energetic, capable, resourceful "girl of good sense and right mind" (p. 381) that the narrator claims her to be.

In *April Hopes* (1887), Howells notes the differing styles of American cities: "Boston speaks one language, and New York another, and Washington a third, and though the several dialects have only slight differences of inflection, their moral accents render each a little difficult for the others" (p. 63). In New York, at the turn of the century, Howells was struck particularly by the gulf between the "exclusive society" (the rich) and the "best company" (artists, writers, scientists, etc.). "New York is above all a commercial capital, and its good society must be thoroughly commercial, and can take account only of pecuniary values in its membership." Between the rich and the intelligentsia "there can be no genuine reciprocity."[3] In *A Hazard of New Fortunes*, Beaton asserts that the French *salon*, which "descended from above, out of the great world, and included the aesthetic world in it," is impossible in New York where authors and artists are virtually excluded from the society of the wealthy (p. 244). The narrator portrays Margaret Vance as the one character who unites in her "catholic sympathies" the interests of the two groups; her aunt's is "almost the only house in New York" where the "fashionable people" and the "aesthetic people" meet "on common ground" (p. 243).

Likewise, the Boston society of Coreys, Bellinghams, and Sewells is mercantile, based on wealth inherited by descendants of merchants like Giles Corey and Clara Kingsbury's father. But those of Bromfield Corey's generation require prospective members of their society to pay the price of admission in qualities of breeding and intellect that can't be cultivated without money but can't be measured by it. At dinner parties like the Coreys' in *Silas Lapham*, architects like Seymour, ministers like Sewell, and lawyers like Atherton, blessed by intelligence, social ease, and fashionable patronage, are as welcome as the financial powers of State Street. A professor's wife in *April Hopes*, who endorses her husband's opinion that "Harvard is just like the world," describes Boston society when she says of the college men of "good family" that "a merely rich man couldn't rise in their set any more than a merely gifted man" (p. 42).

Signs of decline appear in Howells's early novels of Boston: the dilettantism of Phillips in *The Undiscovered Country;* the bankruptcy of Helen Harkness's father; the incapacity of the Halleck family, symbolized by Ben Halleck's crippled leg; the shrinking of Bromfield Corey's fortune, which obliges him to sell the summer house in Nahant and reduce their number of servants. In *April Hopes*, Bromfield Corey, the keenest and wittiest analyst of Boston society, exhibits signs of senility. Boston culture in *Letters Home* (1901) is represented by a fussy middle-aged bachelor, who in New York gets his taste of life by speculating, in letters to his invalid sister-in-law in Boston, about the romance of two young westerners and, after begging her to "forgive the aoristic preterit," laments the extinction of what "we once were" in their now "obsolete Boston" (p. 65). In an unpublished fragment of narrative, "Love-Match," Howells describes the sense of alienation suffered by a Boston woman who returns to her native city after twenty years to find her younger relatives in a set of "insincere fastness" with pretensions to immorality, whose men make the club their home and whose women, like the men, are "of a resolute and cynical gayety of conversation," "indifferent to all aesthetic interests that could not be put in evidence."[4]

Howells gives his most graphic picture of Boston's decline in *The Landlord at Lion's Head*, among his later novels second only to *A Hazard of New Fortunes* in interest and power. With male figures like Sewell, Corey, and Atherton in abeyance, society is dominated by women who chaperone young girls at dances and give receptions and teas for Harvard students, whom they seek to interest in their philanthropic projects. The effects of such a social gynarchy are embodied in the chief female character, Bessie Lynde, a fashionable young woman of sophisticated tastes, whose high-strung nerves crave excitement, whose wit and combative spirit demand engagement, but whose sense of decorum weds her to genteel society, which bores her. The other members of her family are a deaf maiden aunt and an alcoholic brother periodically sent to the country for a "cure."

Into her narrow and deadening world the protagonist of the novel, Jeff Durgin, the son of a hotel keeper in rural Vermont and a student at Harvard, brings his rude energy and will to satisfy his ambitions and appetites as directly as possible. Because he remains a "jay" in manners and attitude, he repels the conventional Boston girls. But in Bessie Lynde, described by one critic as a "sexual headhunter," titillated by intimacy with a social inferior,[5] Jeff awakens the desire to master and be mastered, desire which excites his own will to dominate her.

In their struggle, fueled by their commingled contempt and respect for each other, he has the advantage of a man's freedom and physical strength, while she has the consciousness of a superior social position and knows how to use it to make him feel himself inferior by her standard. Because their contest must be carried on by verbal sparring matches (marked by Jeff's cries of *touché* when he is hit), her chief weapon is her power to manipulate words to wound him with the irrefutable sign of their difference. Early in their acquaintance, when she tells him, "You don't talk like a country person," he replies, "Not in Cambridge. I do in the country" (p. 210). In the country, as she knows, his family are his *folks*. "Yes, they would be *folks;* and *what* folks!" she exclaims to a Boston friend when she imagines meeting Jeff's people at his Class Day (p. 325). Soon afterwards, she taunts him with the word. When Jeff suggests that Bessie come to Class Day, she replies:

> "That would be delightful. But what would become of your—folks?"
> She caught a corner of her mouth with her teeth, as if the word had slipped out.
> "Do you call them folks?" asked Jeff quietly.
> "I—supposed—Don't you?"
> "Not in Boston. I do at Lion's Head."
> "Oh! Well—people."
> "I don't know as they're coming." [p. 332]

When she asks if she has offended him, he replies "I know I'm a jay, and in the country I've got folks" (p. 333).

In this exchange, Jeff, who with country people speaks as they do, comes off better than Bessie, who willfully violates a rule of good breeding in calling attention to another's lapses. Like Colonel Ellison in *A Chance Acquaintance,* who, amused by a driver's pride in his English, goodheartedly follows his example by saying *link* for the plural of *lynx* (p. 28), Jeff exhibits courtesy that elevates him above sophisticated critics like the Lyndes. Bessie says that Jeff is "no more like one of us than a—bear is" (p. 320), but the difference is not all in her favor.

In other ways Howells shows how language creates or exposes barriers between characters. The vernacular of the rural New Englanders Mrs. Durgin and Whitwell, her neighbor, who says *pooty, as far forth, all is, I done, you was, over and above,* at once separates them from the hotel guests they serve. Phonetic rendering of their mispronunciations—e.g. *meanyous* (menus), *colyums, ammyture,* and *theaytre*—implies their inability to spell as well as pronounce the words correctly. Jeff is most acutely aware of the difference between Boston and his country world when, forced to be "very elemental," he vainly struggles for words to convey to his mother Bessie Lynde's "purely *chic* nature....In the end she seemed to conceive of her simply as a hussy" (p. 361).

The painter Westover, the cultivated, self-conscious Howellsian observer, who philosophizes the action and characters, links Boston and Lion's Head. A recurrent visitor to the hotel, he aids the Durgins, befriends Jeff in Boston, where Westover lives and works, attends teas and receptions at which Bessie Lynde appears, and eventually marries Whitwell's daughter Cynthia, to whom Jeff is briefly engaged. Westover's early life, which makes him sympathetic to Jeff's struggles, resembles Howells's. The son of emigrants, Westover lived in the Wisconsin woods until at sixteen, as he tells Cynthia, "I began to paint my way out" (p. 300). But Westover, with his creator's keen sense of social nuances and class differences revealed by language, accentuates the differences between genteel characters like himself, who have shed their provincialism, and the Durgins and Whitwells.

Perhaps because he suffers from the contrast between his physical weakness and recurrent illness and Jeff Durgin's robust health and vigor, Westover is patronizing in his acknowledgment of Jeff's intellectual growth at Harvard: "He had phrases and could handle them" (p. 282). Although Westover never loses his sense of "something rarely pure and fine" in Cynthia (p. 287), he notes her "rustic silence" (p. 311), hears her say "don't know as" and "don't want you should," and on the eve of his proposal of marriage, reflects that between them "there were many disparities, and that there would be certain disadvantages which could never be quite overcome" (p. 456). Whether Westover strikes readers as snobbish or simply realistic, he clearly holds himself superior to Cynthia and her family.[6]

Howells does not fail to look with irony upon a character who, like Westover, reflects on "the easy play of the life, which [he] was rather proud to find so charming" (p. 74). But in recording conversations, Howells identifies himself with Westover's superior breeding by making the vernacular seem uncouth and comic. When Whitwell asks Westover, "Ever been in the Place de la Concorde?" Howells notes that he "gave it the full English pronunciation" (p. 67). "Place Vendôme" represents Westover's correct pronunciation of the name; "Plass Vonndome" represents Whitwell's version. Whitwell has one moment of penetrating insight, when his dialect all but disappears and he startles Westover by asking in reference to Jeff, "How do you know that a strong-willed man a'n't a weak one?...A'n't what we call a strong will just a kind of bull-dog clinch that the dog himself can't unloose. I take it a man that has a *good* will is a strong man" (p. 297). But when Howells reproduces Whitwell's praise of Jeff's new hotel at Lion's Head, done in the "runnaysonce" style with "colyums" and rooms "done off into soots" (p. 448), he invites the reader to laugh at Whitwell and to feel Westover's judgment of Whitwell as "irreparably rustic" (p. 456) to be both true and damning.

To Westover, it is a limitation in Whitwell that "he was and always must be practically Yankee" (p. 456). Westover in his analysis is more restricted than Howells, who in his fiction portrayed scores of New England provincials of different ages and degrees of refinement. But in observing that "Westover was not a Yankee, and he did not love or honor the type, though its struggles against itself touched and amused him" (p. 456), Howells, who was not a Yankee either, reflected his own attitude. At best, his rural Yankees whose grammatical errors and idioms signal their provinciality are like the Laphams—generous, forthright, and energetic, but socially inept. (Country people who are keen-minded critics of the social order, such as the Camps in *A Traveller from Altruria*, speak flawless English.) At worst, Yankees in Howells's novels are mean-spirited, callous, grasping protectors of their own interests like the rustics in *The Undiscovered Country* and the landlady, Mrs. Burwell, of the "hard mouth and hard eyes" in *The Son of Royal Langbrith* (p. 74).

The Yankee girls, Rachel Woodward, Lydia Blood, and Cynthia Whitwell, have a stiff charm and freshness that years of toil and privation have extinguished in women like Mrs. Woodward and Mrs. Durgin. But with few exceptions, Howells's New England women, young and old, exhibit the primary traits of the Yankee type as Howells conceived it—stubborn independence and rigid adherence to principles or prejudices, as seen in Rachel's refusal to take money for her painting and Lydia's refusal in Venice to do as the Venetians do. With one important exception, Howells's New England speakers of nonstandard English bear a stigma they must either lose or never show, if, like Lydia and Penelope, they are to cross the barriers of social class.

The exception is the protagonist of one of Howells's least discussed novels, *Ragged Lady*, serialized in *Harper's Bazar* in 1898. In Clementina Claxon, Howells created a young New England woman whose provincial speech never stigmatizes her in her creator's eyes because she has none of the negative qualities associated with nonstandard Yankee speakers. Her leading traits are not stiff pride, reserve, or shyness, but cheerful good nature, optimism, kindness, and obliging readiness to serve others and accommodate herself to their needs. Unlike Lydia, Cynthia, and Rachel, she is flexible and adaptable, quick to assume the manners, including the habits of speech, of those around her. Even as a ragged barefoot girl on her father's impoverished farm, she displays an instinctive sense of courtesy and decorum that lifts her above the squalor of her surroundings. Not surprisingly, Howells's model for her was not a New England girl but a carpetwoman's daughter growing up in a little Ohio town among "the lowest of the low," as Howells recalled, but graced by a lady's refinement and "the most wonderful instinct in manner and dress."[7] His association of the Ohio girl with the flower "ragged lady" is reflected in his description of Clementina, who has a face "as glad as a flower's" and who on one occasion appears in a pale green dress "like the light seen in a thin wood" (pp. 3, 177).[8] A neighbor tells her she is "as pretty as a pink"; a Russian baron turned socialist calls her "a daughter of the fields and woods" (p. 190); a woman of fashion who introduces her to society in Florence concludes that she "was not rustic, but was sylvan in a way of her own, and not so much ignorant as innocent" (p. 175). Like the Ohio girl who Howells said "overturned so many of my rooted social dogmas,"[9] Clementina surprises others by her unconscious dignity and social grace. The clerk at the hotel where she works marvels that she "knew just the right thing to do, every time" (p. 47). Her sponsor in Florence and her most discriminating critic and friend discovers that when she most feels Clementina "an untried wilderness in the conventional things," she most feels "her equality to any social fortune that might befall her" (p. 175).

What most strongly roots Clementina in her rural New England culture is her speech. Like her family, neighbors, and employers at the Middlemount Inn, where she works, she says *I guess, I presume,* and *had ought,* and drops *r*'s before consonants, saying *winta time, summa time, ga'den, sistas, brothas, eva, fust,* and *youa folks.* The one thing she has in common with Mrs. Lander, the elderly widow, "as rich as she was vulgar," who takes Clementina to Europe as her nurse and companion, is their pronunciation. "The girl and the woman in their parlance replaced the letter *r* by vowel sounds almost too obscure to be represented, except where it came last in a word before a word beginning with a vowel; there it was annexed to the vowel by a strong *liaison,* according to the custom universal in rural New England" (p. 4).

Dialect, which does not blight Clementina's charm, fixes Mr. and Mrs. Lander in the inferior station from which the fortune he has made in the boys' clothing business cannot lift them. "She could not help talking, and her accent and her diction gave her away for a middle-class New England person of village birth and unfashionable sojourn in Boston" (p. 17). This unenviable history is less evident in her husband's speech only because he lurks in his wife's shadow in silence "so dignified that when his verbs and nominatives seemed not to agree, you accused your own hearing" (p. 17).

In a generally favorable review of *Ragged Lady,* John Kendrick Bangs criticized as "not convincing" the use of the "r-less dialect" by both the heroine and the Landers: "the ingenuousness of the one is made to appear the same thing as the vulgarity of the other."[10] But Mrs. Lander's vulgarity is revealed not only in her speech but in behavior utterly lacking in the grace and dignity native to Clementina. When she first meets the girl, she bombards her with personal questions, then in "a quiver of intolerable curiosity" pumps a neighbor for more information (p. 9). With strangers she talks about her ailments, her husband's ailments, her troubles with their servants, her intention to leave money to Clementina. Clementina is complimented by one of the hotel guests for her "very agreeable voice" (p. 72); Mrs. Landers speaks with "a snuffle expressive of deep-seated affliction" (p. 27). Her dialect seems vulgar because she herself is vulgar in her domineering self-pity, foolish pride, and selfishness. A minister whom the Claxons ask to meet Mrs. Lander before she takes Clementina to Europe, although not called upon to judge her by "her syntax, or her social quality" (p. 111), perceives her "intense and inexpugnable vulgarity" (pp. 116-17).

Although Clementina speaks the vernacular of the country people, her speech is never so uncouth as theirs. She does not say *doos, pooty, goin', them kind, I suspicioned,* as do her parents, neighbors, the Landers, and the Atwells who run the hotel where she works. She never utters such a substandard sentence as Mrs. Atwell's "them red-complected kind is liable to freckle" (p. 54). Mrs. Lander, who in one short scene says *she done, I've give, ain't, Where was you,* and *them cold brooks,* is the helpless captive of habits of speech far more debased than Clementina's at her most vernacular.

Clementina differs from other rural speakers not only in her instinctive courtesy and refinement, but in her responsiveness to new conditions as mirrored in the changes in her speech. Her education begins when at the Atwells' hotel she encounters Gregory, a divinity school student working there as head waiter. A militant champion of equality who chafes at his status as servant, he vents some of his anger in attacking crudities and ignorance in the waitresses: "He was as apt to correct a girl in her grammar as in her table service" (p. 50). He frowns when Clementina says *so do* (p. 51), corrects her when she says *you was,* and bitterly reproves her for servility in saying "No'm" and "yes'm." "Just say Yes and No, and let your voice do the rest" (p. 52). Obediently she trains herself to say "yes, indeed," responding to his instructions as equably as she receives the gracious corrections of a guest at the hotel, who, when she reads to him, assures her that she "pronounced admirably, but he would like now and then to differ with her about a word if she did not mind" (p. 74).

After her husband's death, Mrs. Lander takes Clementina to Florence, where at first the girl lives in isolation at their expensive hotel, seeing only "mothers as shy and ungrammatical as Mrs. Lander herself" (p. 165). When she enters Florentine society as the protégée of Miss Milray, the sister of the man at the Middlemount Inn who had so tactfully corrected Clementina's pronunciation, the girl "put on the world" and with English people unconsciously assumes an English manner and intonation. Because even "in the region of harsh nasals," she had "never spoken through her nose" (p. 193), she never emits the flat wooden tones by which so many Americans in Europe reveal their nationality. But months later, in Venice, where Clementina nurses Mrs. Lander in her last illness and sees only her middle-western suitor, George Hinkle, whom she later marries, she loses the "English rhythm" and "alien inflections" and reverts to "her clipped Yankee accent" (p. 262).

Her "reyankeefied English" (p. 279) pains Gregory, whom she sees in Venice, but Hinkle delights in it. When she says "I presume," he exclaims "Ah, that's a regular Yankee word" (p. 243). She says *fatha* and *sista;* he says *fatherr* and *sisterr,* the double *r* representing the "burr which the Scotch-Irish settlers have imparted to the whole middle West" (p. 329). But the letter *r* is no barrier to their love. When she says *eva*, he tells her, "I like your Eastern way of saying *everr.. ..*I like New England folks" (p. 243). While married to Hinkle and living with his people in Ohio she speaks with "their Western burr" (p. 339). After her husband's death, she returns to her native New England village, regains her "Yankee accent," and lapses into the ungrammatical parlance of her neighbors. Miss Milray, who visits her, reflects that "she had never heard Clementina say had ought so much, if ever" (p. 350). But Clementina's marriage to Gregory at the end of the novel promises to restore her to proper use of verbs.

Clementina in her natural grace and dignity confounds the

assumptions of class-conscious observers and is as great a
social success at a Florentine prince's ball as at the Middlemount Inn's summer dance. But the class-consciousness of
those around her hardly belies the conviction of the Russian
baron that the American "doctrine of liberty and equality was
a shameless hypocrisy" (p. 187). To the English Lord Lioncourt,
as to Lord Rainford, the social distinctions among Americans
are meaningless—one American is no more plebian or patrician than another (p. 140). But Americans feel the distinctions
keenly, whether they judge from below in ignorance, like the
Atwells, who admire the Landers for being "away up" in society, or whether they judge from above, like the Milrays, who
oppose the marriage of one of their family to a "little Western
hoyden" with a "Pike county accent" (p. 71). At the hotel,
Gregory affronts convention by treating the waitresses and
guests in the same way, while Clementina is learning from the
Swedish maid, engaged by Mrs. Lander, to imagine for the first
time "the impassable gulf between mistress and maid" (p. 121).

As usual, Howells as narrator underscores class differences
by calling attention to the way characters speak. In portraying
the Landers he not only insists upon "the commonness of their
origin" (p. 17) but tags as theirs expressions that more cultivated people would not use: Mrs. Lander "had been doctored
(as she called it) for all her organs" (p. 19); in Boston, "they
resided (as they would have said) on Pinckney Street" (p. 18).
Fane, the clerk at the Middlemount Inn, shows the results of an
education that "had ended at a commercial college" (p. 45)
when he says *ain't* and *don't know as*, asks Gregory whether
apology is spelled with one *p* or two, and after groping in vain
for *ascetic* says that the austere Gregory is "so aesthetic" (p.
123). In charming everyone she meets, Clementina seems to
transcend class barriers, but the fact that refinement and
social grace in a girl of her conditions are made to seem
remarkable in itself attests to the strength of the class structure and the assumptions it fosters.

Did Howells find this strength and these assumptions deplorable or implicitly reassuring? He never asserted that a
class-based society had virtue in itself, but he valued the cul-

ture represented by the Sewells, the Coreys, and the Marches of his fictonal world. Although he does not let Clementina's provincial speech diminish her charm, he shows that, like Lemuel Barker, she is fortunate in her association with cultivated people and in the ability to profit by their best example. He would not have exchanged the American social order, with all its inequalities and inequities, for a classless society in which culture should be lost. If the price of civilization—of righteousness, refinement, gracious manners, and good taste—was the perpetuation of the class structure, Howells's fiction indicates that he was prepared to pay the price. By creating characters like Lemuel, Clementina, Lydia Blood and Staniford, Penelope Lapham and Tom Corey, he represented the grounds of his hope that a new society might be created in which the price need not be paid, in which neither civilization nor social equality need be sacrificed.

Most of Howells's later novels dramatize the gulf between provincial speakers and educated genteel observers such as Westover, March, and Miss Milray, who are sensitive to language as an indicator of social class and who note deviations from the standard of polite society. Several of the characters most disturbed by social inequality are those most alert to class differences as revealed by syntax and diction. In *Their Silver Wedding Journey*, Basil March, who is pained by the barriers separating him from second- and third-class passengers on shipboard (1:91, 2:450), exhibits the class-consciousness that erects these barriers when he talks to a man "with a strong Lancashire accent" and "understood him to mean his wife" when he refers to his "Missus" (2:451). Annie Kilburn returns from Europe to her native New England village of Hatboro, longing to serve those less fortunate than herself, yet she regards as "uncouth" the way a laborer's wife expresses her grief at her baby's death *(Annie Kilburn,* p. 163); once, to show her fellow feeling with her caretaker's wife, Annie consciously adopts her idiom "don't know as," but the very act of "mimicking [her] accent and syntax" marks the distance between them (p. 234).

Sometimes correctness of characters' speech recommends them to the person who might otherwise find them socially unacceptable. Mrs. Hilary, a Bostonian with the social traditions of Mrs. Corey, reconciles herself to her son's engagement to Suzette Northwick, the daughter of a defalcator, in these terms: "I've been afraid that he would end by marrying some farmer's daughter, and bringing somebody into the family who would say 'Want to know,' and 'How?' and 'What-say?' through her nose. Suzette is indefinitely better than that, no matter what her father is" (*The Quality of Mercy*, p. 296). She can better tolerate her daughter's marriage to Brice Maxwell, an impoverished journalist and aspiring playwright whose mother keeps a boarding house, because the young man has refined features and the "neat accent and quiet tone" of a gentleman (p. 103). Mrs. Hilary finds it a merit in his mother, a "country person," that "she did not chant, in a vain attempt to be genteel in her speech" (*The Story of a Play*, p. 39).

Well-bred characters who are offended or injured by the actions or attitudes of social inferiors distance themselves and register their sense of superiority in noting evidences of the uncouth or vulgar in the offender's speech. The novelist Verrian, in *Fennel and Rue*, expresses his contempt of Jerusha Brown, who has falsely confessed herself doomed to die before his magazine serial ends and begs to know the conclusion, by mocking the language of her letter confessing the hoax: "She will 'get together,' as she calls it, with that other girl and have 'a *real* good time' over it. You know the village type and the village conditions, where the vulgar ignorance of any larger world is so thick you could cut it with a knife" (p. 17). Ann Powell, who abhors the "social squalor" surrounding her family at New Leaf Mills, where her husband dreams of creating a communal society, disdains the illiterate speech of the miller's wife as well as her suspicions and accusations. When the miller's wife challenges Ann: "It 'pears like, from his tell, that your man wanted to do him a mischief," Ann "recalled the backwoods use of pronouns by which wives and husbands shunned explicit mention of each other" (*New Leaf Mills*, p. 40).

"A country confidence in her pronouns" is noted by the

narrator of *The Vacation of the Kelwyns* when a farm woman gives Parthenope Brook a novel of James Fenimore Cooper that "his [her husband's] uncle give him" (p. 245). Parthenope's cousins, the Kelwyns, suffer not only from the terrible cooking of their tenant's wife, Mrs. Kite (whom her husband calls "the Woman"), but from the readiness of their two sons to emulate the Kites' bad grammar. When the Kelwyn boys announce that the Kites' son Arthur "has give us the white horse" (p. 201), their father corrects them, adding to his wife, "If we stayed here much longer they would not have a grammatical principle uncorrupted" (p. 202).

Speech in Howells's novels is the surest index of a character's breeding. It is sometimes but not always reflective of moral character. Locutions such as *you was* and *I seen* relegate the speaker to an inferior social status in the eyes (or ears) of the better-educated, but there is no necessary correspondence between the management of verb tenses and moral virtue. The speech of some of Howells's least admirable characters, such as Alan and Bessie Lynde, makes them secure in their upper-class status. The socially impeccable Mrs. Corey harbors a meaner spirit than Mrs. Lapham, whom she patronizes. The minister Breckon, an easterner, who marries Ellen Kenton, recognizes that that she "was undoubtedly a lady in every instinct," although he compiles a rather formidable list of her defects in speaking: "She had certain provincialisms which he could not ignore. She did not know the right use of will and shall, and would and should, and she pronounced the letter *r* with a hard mid-Western twist. Her voice was weak and thin, and she could not govern it from being at times a gasp and at times a drawl" (*The Kentons*, p. 111).

Only a few of Howells's provincial New Englanders—Lemuel Barker, Clementina, and Lydia Blood—seem capable of acquiring the speech and manners of those above them and moving up the social ladder. Much more easily crossed is the barrier separating easterners from westerners, for whom Howells shows a certain partiality. Protagonists from the West to whom Howells gave not only his moral and social principles but also his urbane and witty style include Kitty Ellison,

March, and Colville *(Indian Summer)*. His exemplary young men of Brahmin families, such as Tom Corey, Matthew Hilary, and the minister Caryl Wade *(The Quality of Mercy)*, are no more refined and gentlemanly than young westerners such as Wallace Ardith *(Letters Home)*, Percy Ray *(The World of Chance* and *The Story of a Play)*, and Burnamy *(Their Silver Wedding Journey)*—aspiring writers, like Howells, who go east to make their name in journalism and the arts.

On the other hand, some of Howells's most aggressively boorish characters are westerners. In *Their Silver Wedding Journey* the Marches encounter Stoller, a middlewestern businessman, who in making his fortune has acquired even less dignity and polish than Dryfoos. He not only says *I done, I seen, you was, some of them turns, I've let it lay,* but chews a toothpick while talking, pares his nails with a knife in public, and says on being introduced to the Marches at Carlsbad, "You see Jews enough here to make you feel at home?" (1:250). His two daughters, bold and boisterous, "without respect or reverence for anyone," engage in "foolish babble" about the "cuteness" of the German officers and brag about America in "Illinois English" with a "strong contortion of the Western *r*" (2:150). Eye dialect (laff, goun', talkun) reinforces the reader's impression of their rude ignorance.

Not all daughters of western businessmen who amass fortunes and move east are barbarians. America Ralson, the daughter of the Cheese and Churn Trust magnate, who in *Letters Home* begins the social climb in New York with her father, is, as her name indicates, the personification of a national ideal. Built on a grand scale ("on the sky-scraping plan of the new girl"), she is patriotically beautiful (with dark red hair, white skin, and blue eyes), is feminine but businesslike, intelligent, and "inexhaustively good natured" (p. 71). Her lover describes her as "whole-souled." Her critical secretary-companion, Frances Dennam, has to admit her virtues: "She was so large-minded, noble, and good" (p. 210). As March prophesies that the Dryfooses will eventually rise to the top of the commercial aristocracy in New York, so Frances predicts that the Ralsons will be the *fine fleur* of the patriciate in a few generations (p. 90) But unlike Mela and Christine Dryfoos, America Ralson writes and speaks English without a syntactical flaw, requiring the services of her secretary only to correct her spelling. She shines even more brightly by the side of her rival, Essie Baysley, a timid clinging country girl whose "grammar was terrible," according to Frances, and whose father, one of Ralson's employees, "resides" in New York in a dingy apartment and is physically broken by a terrible case of the flu (America and her father are never sick). After Ardith has chosen America over Essie, he writes to his brother in Iowa: "That is about the way the land lays, and it don't seem to mother and I that it looks well for young A" (p. 243).

An idealized figure, America is spared the errors and vulgar striving for gentility that betray the pretensions of certain other social climbers in New York. The narrator of *Fennel and Rue* notes that a Long Island hostess *sujjests* instead of *suggests* a plan to her guests, "but no one felt that it mattered" (p. 52). In *Through the Eye of the Needle*, the Altrurian traveler observes that the imperfectly fashionable Mrs. Makely, knowing that the upper classes do not have *parlors*, catches herself when showing him her apartment: "now we'll go back to the pa— drawing room" (*Altrurian Romances*, p. 287). Because Fulkerson is not a snob like Mrs. Makely, he does not seem vulgar in the same way when at the Dryfoos dinner he catches himself in addressing the men: "You fel—you gentlemen" (p. 339).

The characters of Howells's novels whose speech conforms to the genteel standard, as well as those who fall short of it, may be morally exemplary or deficient, easterners or westerners, rich or poor, fashionable or unfashionable. In Howells's plays, language divides the characters into only two groups. The main characters, representing the upper middle class, speak standard English. (As a member of this group, the Californian Willis Campbell, who speaks as much slang as Fulkerson, makes none of Fulkerson's grammatical errors.) Nonstandard speech identifies servants and others who work with their hands—porters, chorewomen, elevator boys, chambermaids, a German florist ("Bride Roses"), an Irish cook ("The Albany Depot"), a French waiter ("The Impossible: A Mystery

Play"). In "Saved: An Emotional Drama," a little child who surprises a burglar in the house one night corrects him three times when he says "them boys." "You must say *those* boys," she instructs him, to no avail (*Complete Plays*, p. 585). Because the young mother from Bangor whom Campbell's friend Roberts encounters in "The Smoking Car" says *my husband's folks*, *ain't*, and a *perfect fidge*, Roberts concludes that she is not a lady "in the society sense," but is a "nice village person" who might be "the wife of a prosperous mechanic" (*Complete Plays*, p. 522).

In one of his *American Letters*, Howells cited with apparent agreement the observation of the Russian revolutionary Stepniak, who after a tour of the United States told Howells that "nowhere in Europe had he seen such absolute division between rich and poor, such utter absence of all kindness between the upper and the lower classes."[11] Howells himself was keenly aware of the contradiction within American society, which affirmed the principles of equality and justice for all, yet perpetuated an economic system and a class structure that divided rich from poor, employers from laborers. He never ceased to believe that "more distinctively than anything else we can call Americanism" is "our faith in humanity, our love of equality." Yet the evolution of a democratic to a plutocratic society convinced him that "inequality is as dear to the American heart as liberty itself."[11] In later years, he dwelt repeatedly upon the inequities and inequalities that led him to reflect how "far we have drifted from our once fast anchorage in right and humanity," and to mourn America as "the land of broken promises." He called his country "the most ridiculous in the world" for its war between our "fundamental principles and sacred ideals" and "our facts." "We pretend to be a democracy, but it is money that rules us indoors and out."[12] Even in pre–Civil War western cities such as Columbus, "where there was as much social as pecuniary equality," the exclusion from society of those who worked with their hands, which "forever belies our democracy," was unquestioned (*Years of My Youth*, p. 149).

The central insight of *Letters of an Altrurian Traveller* is the

Traveller's perception that a "ridiculous contradiction" exists at the "heart of America" (p. 302). Americans profess the Altrurian belief that "all men are born equal, with the right to life, liberty, and the pursuit of happiness" (p. 21), yet most Americans "regard the idea of human brotherhood with distrust and dislike" (p. 193) and support a system that perpetuates "economic inequality among men" (pp. 193-94), relegates servants to the status of slaves and "social outcasts" (p. 302), and widens the gulf between the classes of a society in which already the "division into classes...is made as sharply as in any country of Europe" (p. 195). The other side of Mr. Twelvemough's erroneous belief that Americans are "equal in opportunities" (p. 18) is his more accurate perception that America is "based upon the great principle of self-seeking" (p. 71). In fact, the myth of equality reinforces rather than removes class barriers and the resultant feelings of inferiority and superiority. If one's station is presumably determined not by one's birth into a particular class but by one's capacity to profit by the equality of opportunity, that station is therefore a source of justifiable pride or shame.

Those characters, such as Peck, Lindau, and David Hughes, who commit themselves totally to the ideal of equality, preach it, and attempt to live by it do not survive. (Peck dies in a railroad accident—the fate of Stepniak; Lindau dies of wounds suffered in a strike; Hughes, of illness.) Their deaths imply that the world, so at variance with their ideal, has no place for them. Other characters who champion the ideals of equality and brotherhood but remain in some way bound to the world of privilege and power survive as embodiments of the contradiction Howells documented. The contradiction is represented not only by Mr. Twelvemough, the popular novelist with humanitarian sympathies who entertains Mr. Homos, but, as Gregory Crider points out, by the Traveller himself, who extols the Altrurian doctrine of equality but frequents the company not of the poor and lowly but of the rich Makeleys and who marries a woman socially their equal and intellectually their superior.[13] Annie Kilburn, a "gentlewoman born and bred" (p. 329), champions Mr. Peck's ideal of social equality, but keeps her social position in Hatboro, becoming "the fiercest apostle of labour that never did a stroke of work," as her friend, the lawyer Putney, describes her (p. 329). Basil March teaches his children his hatred of social cruelty and snobbery, yet values the "inner elegance of his life" as much as his "democratic instincts," and prides himself on being a person of superior taste and refinement, "rather distinguished, even in the simplification of his desires" (*A Hazard of New Fortunes*, p. 27). His wife is inevitably divided: "As a woman she was naturally an aristocrat, but as an American she was theoretically a democrat" (p. 292).

One readily sees in such characters as March, Annie Kilburn, Sewell, and Mr. Twelvemough the reflection of Howells's own divided nature and conflicting sympathies. His reading of Tolstoy in the mid-1880s, which he compared to a religious conversion, and his growing awareness of the inequities in American society, which moved him in 1887 to public defense of the anarchists arrested in the Haymarket shootings, did not destroy his patrician tastes and sensibilities cultivated for more than twenty years. Rather, his social conscience committed him to an ideal of equality which he knew he would not and could not realize in his own life. The contradictions he dramatized through the characters of his novels became the burden of some of the most memorable passages in his letters. He wrote to Henry James (October 10, 1888) that he despaired of American civilization "unless it bases itself anew on a real equality," and added: "Meantime, I wear a fur-lined overcoat, and live in all the luxury my money can buy." Writing to his father from Boston (June 14, 1891), he confessed: "Elinor and I live along like our neighbors; only, we have a bad conscience." Earlier he had characterized themselves and Samuel and Olivia Clemens as "theoretical socialists, and practical aristocrats. But it is a comfort to be right theoretically, and to be ashamed of one's self practically" (Feb. 2, 1890). There was comfort, too, in the irony with which, in another letter to his father (Oct. 25, 1891), he viewed himself at a club dinner, "where a lot of fat comfortable people sat gorged with good cheer, and listened to speeches about the tenement house horrors, and how to abate them."[14] As Howells knew, when one substitutes self-mockery for corrective action, one never reaches the irony that is not self-indulgence.

Howells's divided sympathies reveal themselves in the conflicting meanings he attached to the words *common* and *commonplace*, key terms in his philosophy of realism. The Marches share his liking to "divine the poetry of the commonplace" (*A Hazard of New Fortunes*, p. 25). In *Silas Lapham*, he expressed through Charles Bellingham, a guest at the Coreys' dinner party, his belief that fiction should shun the improbable and melodramatic and capture "the light, impalpable aerial essence" of the commonplace (p. 202). In his own voice, he urged writers to seek the "delicate and elusive charm of the average."[15] He complained to Brander Matthews that in America *The Kentons* "has been fairly killed by the stupid and stupefying cry of 'commonplace people'....I had hoped I was helping my people know themselves in the delicate beauty of their everyday lives, and to find cause for pride in the loveliness of an apparently homely *average*, but they don't want it. They bray of my flowers picked from the fruitful fields of our common life, and turn aside among the thistles with keen appetites for the false and impossible."[16]

In Howells's fiction, however, *common* and *commonplace* often signify the undistinguished, mean, vulgar, and inferior. Howells does not compliment the Landers in referring to their "common origins." In Boston, Westover receives a negative impression of Whitwell, reinforced by the use of dialect, when in Whitwell's talk he "tasted a quality of the commonplace" (p. 423). Tom Corey has "the smallest amount of inspiration that can save a man from being commonplace" (*Silas Lapham*, p. 127). Maxwell disparages the journalist Kinney as "an awfully common nature" (*Quality of Mercy*, p. 261). Neither Mrs. Hilary nor Howells finds "the poetry of the commonplace" in the "pervading commonness of things" in the house of Brice Maxwell's mother (*Story of a Play*, p. 38).

But Howells was not a snob who desired inferiors to patronize and superiors to flatter and emulate. His ideal, set forth in "Equality as the Basis of Good Society," was a society of equals comprehending all peoples, in which equality, essential to the "spirit of good society," should be "imparted to the whole of life," to become "the rule and fashion of the whole race."[17] He made distinctions between the well bred and the ill bred; he insisted upon the importance of manners, believing that one "cannot behave rudely without ultimately becoming at heart a savage"; but he wished all to possess the manners and "social instincts" qualifying them for "good society," that "good society" should become a "whole civility, a universal condition." He based his faith in the possibility of such an ideal state upon his conviction, expressed repeatedly, that people are better than their conditions, that inequality and injustice are not the inevitable results of human nature but the product of conditions that can be changed.[18] In *April Hopes* he celebrated the democratic character of Washington as represented by a diplomatic reception at which all Americans, "rich and poor, plain and fashionable, urbane and rustic," mingled "upon a perfect equality" (p. 319). In this free society, "so much opener and therefore so much wiser than any other," Dan Mavering, the young Harvard graduate, feels a "sense of liberation, of expansion" (p. 320).

To create characters who champion equality and to approve the communities that approach nearest to social equality was not, however, to embody in the work itself the egalitarian ideal that to Howells was a fundamental principle of literary realism. It is true, as E.H. Cady observes, that the realist asserts the importance of the "simple separate person" who is "ultimately valuable for personhood alone," and that the techniques of realism, such as dialect, that render the individuality of characters affirm their literary importance. It is also true, as Leo Marx points out, that the vernacular style itself is "a vehicle for the affirmation of an egalitarian faith" that "sweeps aside received notions of class and status."[19] But in the works Marx cites, "Song of Myself" and *Adventures of Huckleberry Finn*, the presence of the first-person narrator or speaker makes the language of the "I"—whether vernacular or not—the standard. In Howells's novels the vernacular is always the nonstandard. In both his first-person and his third-person narratives, the diction and syntax of the narrator are always those of standard English. More often than not the protagonist speaks standard English, as do important characters such as Atherton, Sewell, March, Westover, and Peck, who present Howells's ideas about literature and society. Inevitably the character whose ungrammatical speech is noted by the genteel speakers will seem inferior when judged by their standard.

Howells repeatedly insisted that the likenesses among people were immeasurably more important than the differences. But in separating the standard from the nonstandard speakers he opened rather than closed what Shaw in *Pygmalion* called "the deepest gulf that separates class from class and soul from soul" (Act III). Howells not only represented nonstandard speech; through punctuation and narrative comment he repeatedly called attention to its deviation from the standard. In so doing he exposed the contradictions not only within American society and within his own mind but also at the heart of his philosophy of realism. To render the identity of certain characters he used dialect representative of a particular region, race, or social class. Often the effect was to stereotype rather than individualize characters and to make them seem inferior to others. At the same time, use of dialect helped him to achieve a realistic picture of American society, in which the barriers of race and class did in fact belie the ideal of equality that his realism affirmed.

Conclusion

Both Howells and Henry James wrote essays about the speech of American women for *Harper's Bazar* in 1906. Both insisted upon the importance of propriety in speaking as an index of moral character and culture. "There is no isolated question of speech," James wrote; "the interest of tone is the interest of manners, and the interest of manners is the interest of morals, and the interest of morals is the interest of civilization." Howells was equally emphatic: "The average must be first taught that it is worth while to speak beautifully, that it is even a duty to speak beautifully." Manners comprehend speech, and a person's manners, "if they are bad or null, end in vitiating or vacating his morals. He cannot behave rudely without becoming at heart a savage."[1]

Both Howells and James stressed the failure of Americans, men and women alike, to "speak beautifully." According to James, Americans not only lacked any standard of speech; they did not even recognize the need for a standard and were content to exhibit in their speech "an inimitable union of looseness and flatness." Instead of speaking, James complained, Americans yelled and shrieked or grunted and mumbled. Howells listened as Americans twanged and whiffled, snuffled, whined, and whinnied—college men along with "the fairest and dearest of our women." Like James, Howells considered the existence of a standard of cultivated speech, such as European societies preserved, to be more desirable than the absence of a standard. A "conventional enunciation, a conventional manner" were to be preferred to "the personal manner" and "the personal enunciation," he believed; "in this the English ideal is right, and the American ideal is wrong."[2]

The most important difference between James and Howells lies in their views of democracy and its effects. James repeatedly expressed his antipathy to "our great scheme of social equality," which, he believed, worked to the detriment of superior achievement and to the reduction of all enterprise to a gray level of mediocrity. The speech of American women caused him to marvel at the "universal non-existence of any criticism, worthy of the name,...to which we mainly owe (though with democracy aiding) the unlighted chaos of our manners."[3] He viewed a group of shouting school girls and a surly-speaking car conductor as "flowers of the same democratic garden." He accepted class divisions and social inequality as necessary to insure the highest development of the few: "common lives" are "required always and everywhere to fertilize the ground for the single type of the gentleman."[4]

Howells, for all his patrician instincts and habits of discrimination, never repudiated the ideals of democracy and social equality. In fact, his adherence to democratic ideals of equality became more fervent as his censure of vulgarity and impropriety became more pointed. As we have seen, he desired the destruction of class barriers so that the virtues of "good society" might be "imparted to the whole of life." As if to counter James's view, Howells declared: "I do not believe one lovely or amiable thing would be lost if equality were to become the rule and fashion of the whole race, as it is now the rule and fashion of the best and wisest of the race in society."[5]

Howells equated the aims of realism with the ideals of democracy: "Democracy in literature...wishes to know and to tell the truth, confident that consolation and delight are there."[6] He identified romanticism with the aristocratic spirit, which takes pride in caste and rejects the ideal of social equality. In one respect, however, fiction partaking of romance, informed by the aristocratic spirit, may be more democratic in effect than fiction that exemplifies every tenet of Howells's realism.

The point may be made by a comparison of *The Minister's Charge* and James's novel *The Princess Casamassima*. Both novels, published in 1886, portray societies in which class lines, powerfully drawn, affect action at every point. Both novels center on the fortunes of a protagonist who seeks to rise above lowly origins and whose attachments to women of his own and of a higher class symbolize his inner conflict—conflict which James's Hyacinth Robinson can surmount only by suicide, and from which Howells rescues Lemuel Barker by manipulation of the plot. What is of concern here is the rendering by the two novelists of the speech of characters of the lower classes. As we have seen, Howells sought a representation of the speech of 'Manda and Statira faithful to the last error and vulgarity. The effect of their vernacular is not to reveal the "inner loveliness" of deprived lives, such as Howells praised in Mary Murfree's stories of the Tennessee mountains.[7] The effect is to prove Statira's eternal unfitness for genteel Boston society, which has recognized in Lemuel the capacity of an Ancestor. Lemuel himself realizes that Statira can never join him in the world of the Coreys (p. 327).

James, in portraying the shop-girl Millicent Henning, does not gloss over her ignorance and vulgarity. She seems as little capable of intellectual development as 'Manda and Statira. But James does not record every error she may be assumed to make in speaking. A few dropped *h*'s and an occasional word like *plice* indicate her Cockney origins but are not so degrading as to make it implausible that Hyacinth should see her as "magnificently plebian," as "a daughter of London," vulgar but "elementally free," the incarnation of the city's vitality, elevated to the status of an allegorical figure, the "muse of Cockneyism."[8]

By departing from strict realism in representing Millicent's speech, James presents Millicent as a plebian princess, a foil to the Princess Casamassima, not simply her social inferior. So far as beauty and vitality can make women equal, they are equal in the world of the novel, as Statira and Jessie Carver are not equal. Hyacinth even notes that "the distinguished personage exhibited certain coincidences with the shop-girl" (6:176). Another character of the working class, Paul Muniment, is said to speak in a "north-country accent" (6:231), but James does not reproduce the accent except to let the Princess note that Muniment says *emiable* instead of *amiable* (6:293), and pronounces *weary* as *weery* (6:414). But these words do not make Muniment seem comic or any less compelling in her eyes. Indeed, his few provincialisms enhance the power of his personality precisely because they cannot diminish it.

In viewing Millicent Henning and Muniment through the eyes of characters capable, like the Princess, of seeing others "in the spirit of imaginative transfiguration" (6:293), James to a certain extent romanticized his characters as they romanticized themselves and each other. Hyacinth feels that with the appearance of Muniment "the whole complexion of his life seemed changed; it was pervaded by an element of romance" (5:161). The cup of experience he drinks at the Princess's country house, Medley, is "purple with the wine of romance, of reality, of civilisation" (6:41). Even Millicent perceives in Hyacinth something "romantic, almost theatrical, in his whole little person" (5:79). In *The Minister's Charge, romance* and *romantic* have negative connotations as Sybil Vane torments Lemuel with her expressions of "romantic beneficence" (p. 131) and Sewell preaches against the kind of false sacrifice idealized in romantic novels.

The romance of *The Princess Casamassima*, of course, was to Howells very different from the romance of the "pernicious fiction" he attacked in the "Editor's Study" and in his novels. Howells had only praise for *The Princess Casamassima*, which he considered "incomparably the greatest novel of the year in our language."[9] Apparently the romantic character of James's novel did not diminish its reality in Howells's eyes. One can go even further and argue that the characters in Howells's novel, which preaches spiritual unity and presents experience without the light of romance, seem to exhibit less equality than do the characters in *The Princess Casamassima*. Paradoxically, it is in James's novel, in which romance has positive values and the protagonist defends the inequality on which he believes civilization to be based, that the kind of artistic equality that Howells identified with realism is more fully realized.

In representing speech that departs from standard English, James followed the principle he introduced in the first chapter of *The Bostonians*. Rather than reproducing the "charming dialect" of the Mississippian Basil Ransom, he encouraged the reader who "likes a complete image, who desires to read with the senses as well as with the reason," to imagine Ransom's speech, to remember that "he prolonged his consonants and swallowed his vowels, that he was guilty of elisions and interpolations which were equally unexpected."[10] After this, nothing more is said of Ransom's pronunciation. If the standard English that Ransom speaks along with Olive, Verena, Miss Birdseye, and the others does not move the reader to imagine a speech different from theirs, his culture will seem equal to theirs. If the reader does imagine his Mississippi dialect, the act of imagination that Ransom inspires may impart to him a kind of vitality beyond that of the other characters. In either case, Ransom escapes the stigma of dialect reproduced on the printed page.

Howells in his novels of the 1880s and 1890s took the opposite path. As he strove for greater realism, he relied not upon the reader's imagination but upon the reproduction of certain characters' pronunciation and syntax to create the illusion of actual speech. This method is not necessarily an artistic weakness. By presenting the speech of characters like 'Manda and Statira and the Dryfoos sisters as if he were recording it word for word, Howells creates an impression of ignorance and crudity beyond the reach of description alone. But the effect of their uncouth speech is to do the opposite of what Howells believed realism should do; the effect is to emphasize the forces that sever rather than unite humanity.

Howells wrote nothing to suggest that he was aware of any conflict between his conception of realism and the effect produced by the speech of his characters. But he was keenly aware of the power of language to divide people of different cultures and circumstances. No novelist was more sensitive than he was to the way people place themselves by their speech. More than any other American novelist he made characters' awareness of habits of speech a determining force of action in fiction. As powerfully as any force in the fictional worlds Howells created, the speech of his characters creates barriers and exposes gulfs—sometimes bridged, more often not—between races and social classes.

Although Howells repudiated no part of his philosophy of realism, his definition of the artist's position in America exposes the source of the conflict between the realist's ideals of unity and equality and of truth to reality. According to Howells's essay "The Man of Letters as a Man of Business," the artist is homeless, belonging neither to "the masses," i.e., the wage-earners, nor to "the classes," who pay the wages and buy the artist's work. As the creator of something new, the artist belongs with his "fellow working-men," but neither he nor they, Howells believed, recognize the "mystic bond" uniting them. Some members of the classes may appreciate the art they buy, but the artist does not belong with them. "He knows that he is not of their kind." As a result, he is at home nowhere. So long as people are divided into the masses and the classes, Howells believed, the artist's position will remain anomalous. Howells did not foresee a time when the realists' ideals of unity and equality would be realized in the world they sought to represent, but he did not lose faith in the possibility: "The prospect is not brilliant for any artist now living, but perhaps the artist of the future will see in the flesh the accomplishment of that human equality of which the instinct has been divinely planted in the human soul."[11]

We have yet to see the accomplishment of the human equality that Howells imagined. All that his fiction reveals of the forces that still divide the American people is as timely as it was when he wrote. William James prophesied that Howells's work would "grow in importance year by year and stand, as the great chronicle of the manners and morals of people as they really were during the 50 years we have lived through."[12] Since James wrote these words in 1910, those fifty years have more than doubled, but the conditions Howells portrayed still exist, as we see in the controversies in the 1980s about language—about the status of Black English, the validity of standardized tests, the effects of proposed bilingual instruction in the schools, and legislation of English as the official language. So long as Americans gain or lose by the way they speak, so long as language reinforces barriers of race and social class in America, the chronicle that Howells sustained for half a century will continue to reflect realities of both the past and the present.

Notes

Abbreviations Used in the Notes

AM	*Atlantic Monthly*
Appl.	*Appleton's Journal*
EEC	William Dean Howells, "Editor's Easy Chair"
ES	William Dean Howells, "Editor's Study"
GLB	*Godey's Lady's Book*
HJ	Henry James
HM	*Harper's Magazine*
HW	*Harper's Weekly*
JRL	James Russell Lowell
Lipp.	*Lippincott's Magazine*
NAR	*North American Review*
Scrib. Mag.	*Scribner's Magazine*
Scrib. Mon.	*Scribner's Monthly*
WDH	William Dean Howells

Introduction

1. HJ to WDH, Feb. 19,1912, *The Letters of Henry James,* ed. Percy Lubbock (New York: Scribner's, 1920), 2: 225.

2. Thomas Wentworth Higginson in *Literary World,* 10 (Aug. 2, 1879): 249-50, quoted in *Critics on William Dean Howells, Readings in Literary Criticism,* ed. Paul A. Eschholz (Coral Gables, Fla.: Univ. of Miami Press, 1975), p. 17; *Saturday Review* quoted in *Critic,* n.s. 4 (Nov. 7, 1885): 224; James Fullarton Muirhead, *America, The Land of Contrasts: A Briton's View of His American Kin* (London: John Lane, 1898), p. 172.

3. *Public Meeting of the American Academy and the National Institute of Arts and Letters, in Honor of William Dean Howells* (New York: American Academy of Arts and Letters, 1922), pp. 27, 39; *The Responsibilities of the Critic: Essays and Reviews by F.O. Matthiessen* (New York: Oxford Univ. Press, 1952), pp. 99-100.

4. WDH, Travel Diaries: Ohio, n.d.; Journal of W.D. Howells in Cambridge, Aug. 1, 1869; Venice, April 19, 1883; Capri, 1864; Ronda, Spain, Nov. 11, 1911; at sea, Nov. 2, 1894; London, Sept. 7, 1882; all in Houghton Library, Harvard University.

WDH to Elinor M. Howells, Nov. 6, 1899, *Selected Letters* 4: 223; T.S. Perry, "William Dean Howells," *Century* 23 (March 1882): 682; WDH to William Cooper Howells, Feb. 9, 1890, *Selected Letters* 3: 274.

5. Alice Meynall, "The Trick of Education," *HM* 108 (Feb. 1904): 379; WDH to William Cooper Howells, Jan. 15, 1872. Houghton Library, Harvard Univ. H.L. Mencken, *The American Language: An Inquiry into the Development of English in the United States* (New York: Knopf, 1921), p. 20.

6. WDH to T.W. Higginson, May 6, 1909, Houghton Library, Harvard Univ. EEC, *HM* 113 (Sept. 1906): 634, 635; WDH to E.C. Stedman, Dec. 8, 1874, *Selected Letters* 2: 80-81.

7. *AM* 22 (Nov. 1868): 635; WDH to Frederick A. Duneka, Feb. 14, 1912, American Antiquarian Society; Oscar Firkins, *William Dean Howells: A Study* (Cambridge: Harvard Univ. Press, 1924), p. 308; Robert Frost to Hamlin Garland, Feb. 4, 1921, *Selected Letters of Robert Frost*, ed. Lawrance Thompson (New York: Holt, Rinehart, Winston, 1964), p. 265. Howells's interest in language was not limited to human speech. He wrote to his father of a call from Richard Lynch Garner, author of *The Speech of Monkeys* (1892), "a very interesting man" who "is recording his curious philological researches with the phonograph. He is able to exchange some few elemental ideas with the simians in their own language; and he believes that we shall yet converse with all the animals." WDH to William Cooper Howells, Jan. 29, 1892, Houghton Library, Harvard Univ.

8. Alexis de Toqueville, *Democracy in America*, trans. Henry Reeve, ed. with an intro. by Henry Steele Commager (New York: Oxford Univ. Press, 1947), pp. 3, 287, 288.

Chapter One. Language in Howells's America

1. Muirhead, *America, the Land of Contrasts*, p. 186.
2. Richard Grant White, "Americanisms," AM 42 (Nov. 1878): 619.

3. WDH, *AM* 27 (March 1872): 395; idem, "Literary and Philological Manuals," *AM* 45 (March 1880): 359, 360; JRL to WDH, May 2, 1879, Houghton Library, Harvard Univ.

4. "Contributor's Club," *AM* 43 (Jan. 1879): 114; 42 (Nov. 1878): 639; 42 (Dec. 1878): 773; 43 (Feb. 1879): 258. The item on *hesh, hizer, himer* is identified as Horace E. Scudder's by Philip B. Eppard and George Monteiro, *A Guide to the Atlantic Monthly Contributor's Club* (Boston: G.K. Hall, 1983), p. 16.

5. John Fiske, "What We Learn from Old Aryan Words," *AM* 47 (April 1881): 489.

6. Adam S. Hill, "English in the Schools," *HM* 71 (June 1883): 123; Alfred Ayres, "A Plea for Cultivating the English Language," *HM* 103 (July 1901): 266-67; T.W. Higginson, "The Test of Talk," *Book and Heart: Essays on Literature* (New York: Harper, 1897), p. 219; James Fenimore Cooper, "On Language," *The American Democrat,* in *James Fenimore Cooper: Representative Selections,* intro., bibliography, and notes by Robert E. Spiller (New York: American Book Co., 1936), p. 205.

7. Dennis E. Baron, *Grammar and Good Taste: Reforming the American Language* (New Haven: Yale Univ. Press, 1982), pp. 167, 187. Intentional slovenliness of speech—its causes and its prevalence in the United States—is discussed by J.M. Steadman, Jr., "Affected and Effeminate Words," *American Speech* 13 (Feb. 1938): 13; and by James Truslow Adams, "The Mucker Pose," *HM* 157 (Nov. 1928): 661-71.

8. EEC, *HM* 114 (April 1907): 803; *The Laws of Etiquette, or, Short Rules and Reflections for Conduct in Society* (Philadelphia: Carey, Lea & Blanchard, 1839), p. 19. Arthur M. Schlesinger, in *Learning How to Behave* (New York: Macmillan, 1946), pp. 31-37, documents the importance of magazines, newspapers, and books of etiquette in defining proper behavior, including correct speech.

9. Reviews of George P. Marsh, *Lectures on the English Language, HM* 20:(April 1860): 694; of John S. Hart, *Composition and Rhetoric, HM* 42 (Dec. 1870): 141; of William Swinton, *Progressive Grammar of the English Tongue, HM* 45 (Nov. 1872): 943; and of *English Synonyms,* ed. Archbishop Whately, *HM* 5 (June 1852): 137.

10. "Editor's Table," *HM* 14 (May 1857): 842; EEC, *HM* 76 (May 1888): 962; "Editor's Table," *HM* 14 (May 1857): 843, 845; 14 (May 1857): 845.

11. HJ, "The Speech of American Women," *French Writers and American Women: Essays,* ed. with an intro. by Peter Buitenhuis (Branford, Ct.: Compass, 1960), p. 47; Meynall, "Trick of Education,"

p. 277; *Scrib. Mon.* 11 (April 1876): Higginson, "Test of Talk," p. 220.

12. Richard Grant White, "Words and Their Uses," *Galaxy* 4 (May 1, 1867): 103; 6 (Dec. 1868): 824-25.

13. *GLB* 84 (1872): 94, 572, 92; 82 (1871): 571; 83 (1871): 472.

14. EEC, *HM* 76 (May 1888): 964; White, *Words and Their Uses* (New York: Sheldon, 1872), pp. 222-26; *GLB* 82 (1871): 475; Adam S. Hill, "English in Newspapers and Novels," *Scrib. Mag.* 2 (Sept. 1887): 375; Brander Matthews, "New Words and Old," *HM* 97 (July 1898): 308.

15. White, "Words and Their Uses," *Galaxy* 7 (June 1869): 894; Fitzedward Hall, "Shall We Say 'Is Being Built'?" *Scrib. Mon.* 3 (April 1872): 702, 703; *GLB* 83 (1871): 471; EEC, *HM* 134 (March 1917): 594; T.R. Lounsbury, "The Story of an Idiom," *HM* 109 (June 1904): 30.

16. See Baron, *Grammar and Good Taste,* ch. 7; Greene's statement is quoted on p. 157. T.E. Blakely, "Macaulay's English," *HM* 105 (Sept. 1902): 529-33, is typical in its praise of Macaulay.

17. Julia Collier Harris, *The Life and Letters of Joel Chandler Harris* (Boston: Houghton, Mifflin, 1918), p. 395; Brander Matthews, "Questions of Usage in Words," *HM* 102 (Feb. 1901): 432; Lounsbury, "Story of an Idiom," p. 28; idem, "The Standard of Usage," *HM* 111 (June 1905): 36.

18. T.R. Lounsbury, "Is English Becoming Corrupt?" *HM* 108 (Jan. 1904): 198; idem, "Standard of Usage," p. 39; idem, "Uncertainties of Usage," *HM* 111 (Aug. 1905): 434. See also Matthews, "Questions of Usage in Words," p. 431; Hill, "English in the Schools," p. 127; Mark H. Liddell, "On the Teaching of English," *AM* 81 (April 1898): 471.

19. Brander Matthews, "The Function of Slang," *HM* 87 (July 1893): 311; T.R. Lounsbury, " 'To' and the Infinitive," *HM* 108 (April 1904): 73; Brander Matthews, "Foreign Words in English Speech," *HM* 107 (Aug. 1903): 477; idem, "Questions of Usage in Words," pp. 433, 434, 435; Lounsbury, "Schoolmastering the Speech," *HM* 112 (Feb. 1906): 461; idem, "The Linguistic Authority of the Great Writers," *HM* 112 (Dec. 1905): 110-11.

20. T.R. Lounsbury, "The Standard of Pronunciation," *HM* 107 (Sept. 1903): 579; C.W. Ernst, "Wit and Diplomacy in Dictionaries," *Lipp.* 34 (Oct. 1884): 411-14; Richard Grant White, "Words and Their Uses," *Galaxy* 6 (Dec. 1868): 820; 7 (May 1869): 656-57.

21. Richard Grant White, "Words and Their Uses," *Galaxy* 7 (Feb. 1869): 267; 7 (Jan. 1869): 101; 6 (Sept. 1868): 373; Lounsbury, "Schoolmastering the Speech," 459; White, "Words and Their Uses," *Galaxy* 6 (Sept. 1868): 373.

22. Richard Grant White, "Words and Their Uses," *Galaxy* 7

(March 1869): 333. See also Ayres, "Plea for Cultivating the English Language," p. 265; Frederic M. Bird, "Paralyzers of Style," *Lipp.* 57 (March 1896): 280; Henry S. Pancoast, "Young America at the Gates of Literature," *Lipp.* 66 (Sept. 1900): 434-43; Alice A. Stevens, "The Question of English," *HM* 104 (Jan. 1902): 287.

23. Brander Matthews, "Briticisms of All Sorts," *HM* 106 (April 1902): 712; T.R. Lounsbury, "Is English Becoming Corrupt?" *HM* 108 (Dec. 1903): 108-13; (Jan. 1904): 193-98; Richard Grant White, "Americanisms," *AM* 42 (Nov. 1878): 619. See also S.S. Cox, "American Humor," pt. 2, *HM* 50 (May 1875): 847-59; Fitzedward Hall, "Retrogressive English," *NAR* 119 (Oct. 1874): 324.

24. W.D. Whitney, "Steinthal on the Origin of Language," *NAR* 114 (April 1872): 275; George L. Kittredge, "The Coinage of Words," *HM* 106 (Jan. 1903): 301. See also Hall, "Retrogressive English," p. 326; Mark H. Liddell, "English Literature and the Vernacular," *AM* 81 (May 1898): 621; Richard Grant White, "Words and Their Uses," *Galaxy* 3 (Feb. 15, 1869): 394.

25. Matthews, "Foreign Words in English Speech," p. 477; review of T.R. Lounsbury's *The Standard Usage in English, NAR* 188 (Aug. 1908): 301 Matthews, "Questions of Usage in Words," p. 431; W.D. Whitney, "Darwinism and Language," *NAR* 119 (July 1874): 63; Hall, "Retrogressive English," pp. 309-10; Matthews, "Questions of Usage in Words," p. 436; idem, "Foreign Words in English Speech," p. 477.

26. Richard Grant White, "Words and Their Uses," *Galaxy* 6 (Nov. 1868): 689, 691; Matthews, "Briticisms of All Sorts," p. 711; Kittredge, "Coinage of Words," p. 303; EEC, *HM* 76 (May 1888): 963, 964; T.R. Lounsbury, "On the Hostility to Certain Words," *HM* 113 (Aug. 1906): 364; Matthews, "New Words and Old," p. 305; HJ., "Speech of American Women," pp. 47-48.

27. Matthews, "Foreign Words in English Speech," p. 477; Cox, "American Humor," p. 854; Joseph Fitzgerald, "Anarchism in Language," *HM* 104 (March 1902): 597; *GLB* 82 (1871): 475.

28. Matthews, "New Words and Old," p. 307; George L. Kittredge, "Ways of Words in English Speech," *HM* 105 (July 1902): 272; Muirhead, *America, the Land of Contrasts*, p. 89; Mrs. Burton Kingsland, *Correct Social Usage* (New York: New York Society of Self-Culture, 1908), p. 50; Theodore Roosevelt, "Citizenship in a Republic," *History as Literature and Other Essays* (New York: Scribner's, 1913), p. 152.

29. W.W. Story, "The Origin of the Italian Language," *NAR* 126 (Feb. 1878): 103; Matthews, "Briticisms of All Sorts," p. 712; *Portrait of America: Letters of Henry Sienkiewicz*, ed. and trans. by Charles Morley

(New York: Columbia Univ. Press, 1959), p. 289; Frank E. Bryant, "Language in a New Country," *Modern Language Association Publications* 22 (1907): 279; "Editor's Table," *HM* 17 (Aug. 1858): 411; Richard Grant White, "Words and Their Uses," *Galaxy* 6 (Sept. 1868): 373; "Editor's Drawer," *HM* 8 (Dec. 1853): 134; Agnes Repplier, "Modern Word-Parsimony," *Lipp.* 41 (Feb. 1888): 274; Gilbert M. Tucker, *Our Common Speech: Six Papers* (New York: Dodd, Mead, 1895), p. 10.

30. "Atalanta in Calydon," l. 1204, *The Poems of Charles Algernon Swinburne*, 6 vols. (New York: Harper, 1904), 4: 316; ES, *HM* 80 (March 1890): 643; John Hay to WDH, 28, 1890, *John Hay-Howells Letters: The Correspondence of John Milton Hay and William Dean Howells, 1861-1905*, ed. with intro. by George Monteiro and Brenda Murphy (Boston: Twayne, 1980), p. 98.

31. Kittredge "Ways of Words in English Speech," p. 271.

32. Joseph Conrad, *Under Western Eyes* (Edinburgh: John Grant, 1925), p. 3; William Faulkner, *Mosquitoes* (New York: Liveright, 1927), p. 186; Lounsbury, "Is English Becoming Corrupt?" p. 194.

Chapter Two. "Good Natural English"

1. WDH to Mark Twain, Jan. 19, 1876: "I'd have that swearing out in an instant." *Mark Twain-Howells Letters: The Correspondence of Samuel L. Clemens and Willliam D. Howells, 1872-1910.* 2 vols., ed. Henry Nash Smith and William M. Gibson (Cambridge: Harvard Univ. Press, 1960), 1:124. The most provocative criticism was made by Van Wyck Brooks, who presented Howells as the spokesman for Puritan repression and genteel prudery that crippled Twain's genius. (*The Ordeal of Mark Twain* [New York: Dutton, 1920], pp. 68-69, 123). Responses to Brooks's thesis are collected in *A Casebook on Mark Twain's Wound*, ed. Lewis Leary (New York: Crowell, 1962). The value of Howells's editing of Mark Twain's manuscripts is stressed by Edwin H. Cady, *The Road to Realism: The Early Years, 1837-1885, of William Dean Howells* (Syracuse: Syracuse Univ. Press, 1956), pp. 165-67; Kenneth E. Eble, *Old Clemens and W.D.H.: The Story of a Remarkable Friendship* (Baton Rouge: Louisiana State Univ. Press, 1985), p. 82; and Kenneth Lynn, *William Dean Howells: An American Life* (New York: Harcourt, Brace, Jovanovitch, 1970), pp. 159-60.

2. ES, *HM* 72 (Jan. 1886): 325; WDH, review of Richard Grant White's *Words and Their Uses, Past and Present, AM* 27 (March 1871): 394. JRL, introduction to "The Biglow Papers," Second Series, *The*

Poetical Works of James Russell Lowell (Boston: n.p., n.d.), p. 214; WDH, review of White's *Words and Their Uses*, p. 395.

3. WDH to T.W. Higginson, May 20, 1894, *Selected Letters* 4: 66-67; interview by Clifton Johnson, *Outlook* 49 (1894): 580-82, reprinted in *Interviews with William Dean Howells*, ed. Ulrich Halfmann, *American Literary Realism* 6 (Fall 1973): 318.

4. JRL, *Among My Books* (Boston: Houghton, Mifflin, 1898), p. 155; Mark H. Liddell, *AM* 81 (May 1898):614; T.R. Lounsbury, "Expletives and Non Expletives," *HM* 115 (Oct. 1907):716; Brander Matthews, "New Words and Old," *HM* 97 (July 1898): 307; George L. Kittredge, "The Coinage of Words," *HM* 106 (Jan. 1903): 301. See also A.S. Hill, "Colloquial English," *HM* 78 (Feb. 1889): 272-79.

5. Richard Bridgman, *The Development of the Colloquial Style in America* (New York: Oxford Univ. Press, 1966), pp. 3-12 and *passim*.

6. A. Schade van Westrum, "Mr. Howells on Love and Literature," *American Literary Realism* 6 (Fall 1973): 355; ES, *HM* 78 (Feb. 1889): 492; WDH, *My Literary Passions* (New York: Greenwood, 1969), p. 172; ES, *HM* 75 (Sept. 1887): 640.

7. (New York: Scribner's, 1918), pp. xii-xiii.

8. ES, *HM* 76 (Feb. 1888): 479; 79 (Aug. 1889): 477; 77 (Oct. 1888): 580.

9. WDH, "Life and Letters," *HW* 39 (June 22, 1895): 580; EEC, *HM* 134 (March 1917):596.

10. Interview by Clifton Johnson (1894) in *American Literary Realism* 6 (Fall 1973):318; WDH to Lee Foster Hartman, Feb. 1, 1914, *Selected Letters* 6:48; EEC, *HM* 134 (March 1917): 596; WDH to Higginson, Nov. 5, 1891, *Selected Letters* 3:325.

11. EEC, *HM* 134 (March 1917): 594-96.

12. WDH to William Cooper Howells; April 7, 1867, and Feb. 21, 1869, Houghton Library, Harvard Univ.; WDH to Joseph Howells, Sept. 29, 1905, *Selected Letters* 5:137; WDH to Joseph Howells, Oct. 30, 1906, Houghton Library, Harvard Univ.

13. JRL to WDH, Dec. 17, 1875, Houghton Library, Harvard Univ.

14. James L. Woodress, Jr., "The Lowell-Howells Friendship: Some Unpublished Letters," *New England Quarterly* 26 (Dec. 1953): 526.

15. WDH to JRL, Dec. 19, 1875, Houghton Library, Harvard Univ.

16. WDH to JRL, June 22, 1879, *Selected Letters* 2:231; JRL to WDH, Feb. 2, 1886, Houghton Library, Harvard Univ.; WDH to JRL, Feb. 3, 1886, *Selected Letters* 3:153.

17. Firkins, *William Dean Howells*, p. 310.

18. WDH, *Literary Friends and Acquaintance* (New York: Harper, 1901), pp. 234-35.

19. See William T. Stafford, "Lowell 'Edits' James: Some Revisions in *French Poets and Novelists,*" *New England Quarterly* 32 (March 1959): 92-98.

20. WDH, "Charles Eliot Norton: A Reminiscence," *NAR* 198 (Dec. 1913): 846.

21. Lounsbury, "Expletives and Non Expletives," *HM* 115 (Oct. 1907): 713.

22. Agnes Repplier, "Words," *AM* 71 (March 1893): 370. For representative statements see also Alfred Ayres, "A Plea for Cultivating the English Language," *HM* 103 (July 1901): 267; Frederic M. Bird, "Paralyzers of Style," *Lipp.* 57 (March 1896): 282; Price Collier, "Gentle Speech," *NAR* 188 (Nov. 1908): 719; Eliza Cook, "Exaggeration," *HM* 5 (Nov. 1852): 780; James Fenimore Cooper, *Gleanings in Europe: England,* ed. Robert E. Spiller (New York: Oxford Univ. Press, 1930), p. 347.

23. Richard Grant "Words and Their Uses," *Galaxy* 3 (April 15, 1867): 906-07; Cooper, "On Language," p. 209; Henry James, *Notes and Reviews,* preface by Pierre de Chaignon (Cambridge, Mass.: Dunster House, 1921), p. 31; HJ, "The Madonna of the Future," *AM* 31 (March 1873): 283.

24. T.W. Higginson, "Americanism in Literature," *AM* 25 (Jan. 1870): 61, 58; S.S. Cox, "American Humor," *HM* 50 (May 1875): 855, 858; Higginson, "Americanism in Literature," p. 61; Cox, "American Humor," pp. 854, 859.

25. WDH, "Minor Topics," *Nation* 2 (March 8, 1866): 293.

26. WDH, "Minor Topics," *Nation* 2 (March 15, 1866): 325.

27. Frederick Marryat, *A Diary in America with Remarks on Its Institutions,* ed. with notes and intro. by Sydney Jackman (New York: Knopf, 1962), p. 273; White, "Words and Their Uses," *Galaxy* 6 (Oct. 1868): 521; Cooper, "On Language," p. 209; Kittredge, "Ways of Words in English Speech," *HM* 105 (July 1902): 270.

28. WDH, "Minor Topics," *Nation* 2 (Feb. 22, 1866): 229; (March 15, 1866): 325.

29. WDH, "Some Unpalatable Suggestions," *NAR* 188 (Aug. 1908): 255.

30. Amelia E. Barr, "The Decline of Politeness," *Lipp.* 49 (Jan. 1892): 87. See also EEC, *HM* 34 (May 1867): 792; James J. Belcher, "A Talk about Talking," *HM* 34 (Feb. 1867): 322; Anna C. Brackett, "Can We Speak English?" *HM* 51 (Sept. 1875): 592.

31. "Live Metaphors," *Galaxy* 2 (Oct. 1, 1866): 272; Walt Whitman, "Slang in America," *Complete Prose Works: Specimen Days and Collect, November Boughs and Good Bye My Fancy* (Boston: Small, Maynard, 1901), pp. 410, 406, 409.

32. Brander Matthews, "The Function of Slang," *HM* 87 (July 1893): 306; Kittredge, "Ways of Words in English Speech," p. 270.

33. Matthews, "Function of Slang," pp. 307, 309; Muirhead, *America, the Land of Contrasts*, p. 158.

34. *AM* 71 (March 1893): 425.

35. WDH, "American Letter: Chicago in Fiction," *Literature* 2 (July 2, 1898): 758; WDH, "Certain of the Chicago School of Fiction," *NAR* 176 (May 1903): 740; WDH, "Recent Literature," *AM* 29 (April 1872): 500; JRL, *Poetical Works*, p. 232; ES, *HM* 72 (Jan. 1886): 325.

36. EEC, *HM* 131 (Sept. 1915): 635, 637; "Recent Literature," *AM* 29 (May 1872): 624; ES, *HM* 80 (May 1890): 969; 83 (Nov. 1891): 963; 81 (Oct. 1890): 801; 83 (Sept. 1891): 641; 81 (Sept. 1890): 640; 78 (Feb. 1889): 490; 90 (March 1890): 644, 646-47.

37. Bridgman, *Colloquial Style in America*, p. 23; Alfred Habegger, *Gender, Fantasy, and Realism in American Literature* (New York: Columbia Univ. Press, 1982), p. 81; Matthews, Function of Slang," pp. 310-11.

38. EEC, *HM* 134 (March 1917): 595; WDH, "A Sennight of the Centennial," *AM* 38 (July 1876): 103; WDH, "Professor Barrett Wendell's Notions of American Literature," *NAR* 117 (April 1901): 627-28; WDH, "Some Unpalatable Suggestions," p. 255; WDH, *Literature and Life* (New York: Harper, 1911), p. 268.

39. ES, *HM* 72 (April 1886): 805; 80 (Feb. 1890): 482; WDH, *New Leaf Mills*, p. 51; *A Fearful Responsibility and Other Stories*, p. 135; *April Hopes*, p. 303; *The World of Chance*, pp. 340, 12. Oscar Firkins, who has analyzed Howells's style most fully, gives many examples of his coinages; see *William Dean Howells*, pp. 305-06.

40. WDH to Frederick A. Duneka, Sept. 30, 1917, *Selected Letters* 6: 124, n. 3; WDH to Joseph A. Howells, March 24, 1908, Houghton Library, Harvard Univ.

41. JRL to WDH, May 2, 1879, and Higginson to WDH, Sept. 24, 1881, Aug. 7, 1888, Houghton Library, Harvard Univ.; WDH to Higginson, Aug. 9, 1888, *Selected Letters* 3:227; *Critic*, n.s. 4 (Aug. 22, 1885): 84; (Sept. 5, 1885): 108. Edward Wagenknecht cites a number of misspellings and errors of fact and usage in *William Dean Howells: The Friendly Eye* (New York: Oxford Univ. Press, 1969), pp. 289-90.

42. *Nation* 13 (July 13, 1871): 30; "Editor's Literary Record," *HM*

44 (April 1872): 781; "Literature of the Day," *Lipp.* 9 (June 1872): 726; Whipple, *HM* 52 (March 1876): 527; Twain, *HM* 113 (July 1906): 221.

43. Hamlin Garland, *Roadside Meetings* (New York: Macmillan, 1930), pp. 60, 62; JRL, *NAR* 112 (Jan. 1871): 236-37.

44. ES, *HM* 83 (Nov. 1891): 964.

Chapter Three. American and British English

1. WDH, "Our Real Grievance with England," *Literature*, n.s. 1 (Oct. 6, 1899): 297.

2. Marryat, *A Diary in America*, pp. 259, 268, 259, 260.

3. Muirhead, *America, the Land of Contrasts*, p. 169.

4. Brander Matthews, "Briticisms and Americanisms," *HM* 83 (July 1891): 215.

5. Brander Matthews, "As to American Spelling," *HM* 85 (July 1892): 277.

6. See for instance, "Editor's Literary Record," *HM* 59 (Nov. 1879): 949; EEC, *HM* 68 (Feb. 1884): 478-79.

7. JRL, introduction to *The Biglow Papers*, p. 217; Henry Cabot Lodge, "Shakespeare's Americanisms," *HM* 90 (Jan. 1895): 253; Matthews, "Briticisms and Americanisms," p. 270; George Wakeman, "Live Metaphors," *Galaxy* 2 (Oct. 1, 1866): 277; idem, "The Confusion of Tongues," *Galaxy* 2 (Nov. 1, 1866): 449; Richard Grant White, "Assorted Americanisms," *AM* 44 (Nov. 1879): 654-60; idem, "Americanisms," *AM* 41 (April 1878): 499-502; 42 (July 1878): 98, 104-06; 42 (Nov. 1878): 627-30; 43 (Jan. 1879): 88-89.

8. "Contributor's Club," *AM* 41 (May 1878): 668; Matthews, "Briticisms and Americanisms," pp. 215-16.

9. Richard Grant White, "Words and Their Uses," *Galaxy* 6 (Aug. 1868): 238; 6 (Oct. 1868): 516; Matthews, "Briticisms of All Sorts," *HM* 106 (April 1902): 711; idem, "Briticisms and Americanisms," pp. 217-19; White, "Words and Their Uses," *Galaxy* 4 (July 1867): 269; idem, "The Quest for English," *Galaxy* 3 (Jan. 1, 1867): 62-70; *AM* 39 (April 1877): 485; 42 (Sept. 1878): 376; 42 (Aug. 1878): 250; White, "Words and Their Uses," *Galaxy* 6 (Oct. 1868): 515; Henry Cabot Lodge, "Shakespeare's Americanisms," p. 90; Matthews, "Briticisms and Americanisms," p. 220.

10. Brander Matthews, "As to American Spelling," *HM* 85 (July 1892): 278-82; T.R. Lounsbury, "The Question of 'Honor,' " *HM* 110 (Jan. 1905): 190, 194.

11. Charles Dudley Warner, "Editor's Drawer," *HM* 90 (Jan. 1895): 320.

12. See for instance Howells's Travel Diaries, Carlsbad, July 20, 1897, Rome, 1908, Stratford, 1913, in Houghton Library, Harvard Univ,; *An Open-Eyed Conspiracy*, p. 45; *Their Silver Wedding Journey*, 1: 247; "Our Daily Speech," *Harper's Bazar* 40 (Oct. 1906): 933; HJ, "Question of Our Speech," pp. 11, 12, 16.

13. Richard Grant White, "English in England," *AM* 45 (March 1880): 382; idem, "Words and Their Uses," *Galaxy* 4 (May 1, 1867): 100; *GLB* 4 (April 1872): 381.

14. George William Curtis, "Editor's Easy Chair," *HM* 55 (July 1877): 303; Charles Dudley Warner, "Editor's Drawer," *HM* 78 (May 1889): 989.

15. For detailed discussion of the promoters of Federal English, see Baron, *Grammar and Good Taste*, pp. 13-15, 41-47.

16. *AM* 40 (Aug. 1877): 234; "Americanisms in England," *Lipp.* 19 (April 1877): 514; Mark H. Liddell, "On the Teaching of English," *AM* 81 (April 1898): 465-73; White, "English in England," p. 374.

17. Matthews, "Briticisms of All Sorts," p. 709; idem, "Briticisms and Americanisms," p. 222; Lodge, "Shakespeare's Americanisms," pp. 252, 253.

18. The definition follows the entry dated July 23, Wells Beach, "Savings Bank" notebook, Houghton Library, Harvard Univ.

19. ES, *HM* 72 (Jan. 1886): 323; "Recent Literature," *AM* 36 (Aug. 1875): 244.

20. "Life and Letters," *HW* 39 (Nov. 2, 1895): 1037; "An Anxious Inquiry," 46 (May 24, 1902): 651.

21. "Recent Literature," *AM* 33 (May 1874): 617; "Diversions of the Higher Journalist," *HW* 47 (Nov. 28, 1903): 1896; ES, *HM* 72 (Feb. 1886): 485; WDH to E.C. Stedman, Dec. 27, 1904, *Selected Letters* 5:115.

22. *Complete Plays*, pp. 403-05.

23. ES, *HM* 78 (Feb. 1889): 492.

24. ES, *HM* 72 (Jan. 1886): 344; 78 (Feb. 1889): 492; 81 (Oct. 1890): 804. JRL, intro. to *The Biglow Papers*, p. 216; ES, *HM* 72 (Jan. 1886): 325.

25. Brander Matthews, "The English Lanuage: Its Debt to King Alfred," *HM* 103 (June 1901): 141; idem, "Briticisms and Americanisms," p. 222; Henry S. Pancoast, *An Introduction to American Literature* (New York: Holt, 1898), p. 2. Defenses of the view supported by Pancoast and Matthews, which prevailed at the turn of the century, continue to appear in the leading scholarly journals. See, for instance, William C. Spengemann, "American Writers and English Literature," *ELH* 5 (Spring 1985): 209-38. Spengemann asserts that English liter-

ature (including American) must be seen as a "single literary subject," that Americans' writings are part of "English literary history" (pp. 225, 227). In "The Extra," *American Literature* 57 (Oct. 1985): 456-81, he declares: "The history of what we call American Literature...is inseparable from the history of literature in English as a whole" (p. 477).

26. According to their President's Reports, Cornell University offered its first course in American literature in 1897; the University of California in 1898; the University of Chicago in 1897-98. In 1902, one course in American literature joined eighteen courses in English literature at Yale University. Brown University, which introduced American literature in 1890, by 1897 had an Associate Professor of American literature.

27. Charles W. Kent, "A Study of Lanier's Poems," in vol. 7 (1892); Wm. M. Baskerville, "Southern Literature," vol. 7 (1892); Gustav Gruener, "Notes on the Influence of E.T.A. Hoffmann upon Edgar Allan Poe," vol. 19 (1903).

28. Frank Egbert Bryant, "Language in a New Country," *Modern Language Association Publications* 22 (1907): 276-90.

29. Richard Grant White, "Americanisms," *AM* 41 (April 1878): 495.

30. Charles Dudley Warner, "Editor's Study," *HM* 86 (Dec. 1892): 150; 107 (Sept. 1903): 647.

31. Richard Grant White, "Words and Their Uses," *Galaxy* 4 (May 1, 1867): 101; Brander Matthews, "Questions of Usage in Words," *HM* 102 (Feb. 1901): 432; idem, *Parts of Speech* (New York: Scribner's, 1901), p. 31;; William Dwight Whitney, "Steinthal on the Origin of Language," *NAR* 114 (April 1872): 280, 303. On the relation of language and race in nineteenth-century German literature and scholarship, see Frank H. Hankins, *The Racial Basis of Civilization: A Critique of the Nordic Doctrine* (New York: Knopf, 1931), pp. 60-62; Reginald Horsman, *Race and Manifest Destiny: The Origins of American Racial Anglo-Saxonism* (Cambridge: Harvard Univ. Press, 1981), pp. 27-29, 32-36.

32. T.W. Higginson, "Americanisms in Literature," *AM* 25 (Jan. 1870): 59; Barrett Wendell, *A Literary History of America* (New York: Scribner's, 1931), p. 521. For further discussion of the teaching of American literature in the universities, see Thomas F. Gossett, *Race: The History of an Idea in America* (Dallas: Southern Methodist Univ. Press, 1963), pp. 140-42; Howard Mumford Jones, *The Theory of American Literature* (Ithaca, N.Y.: Cornell Univ. Press, 1948), pp. 94 ff.

Ferner Nuhn, in "Teaching American Literature in American Colleges," *American Mercury* 13 (March 1928): 328-31, notes that in 1928 universities and colleges on an average offered ten times as many courses in English literature as in American and that only Pennsylvania State College had a separate department of American literature (p. 331).

33. George William Curtis, "Editor's Easy Chair," *HM* 80 (April 1890): 804; 26 (March 1863): 566; Matthews, "Briticisms and Americanisms," p. 222. For detailed treatment of the Teutonic origins theory in America, see Gossett, *Race*, pp. 84-122.

34. Hay, *Addresses of John Hay* (New York: Century, 1906), pp. 85, 78; T.W. Higginson, as quoted in *Century Magazine* 72 (May 1906): 474.

35. John Dos Passos, *The Anglo-Saxon Century and the Unification of the English-Speaking People*, 2nd ed. (New York: Putnam, 1903), p. 234. Of American literature, Dos Passos wrote: "In all that is best, it shows the common origin" (p. 122).

36. Fitzedward Hall, "Retrogressive English," *NAR* 119 (Oct. 1874): 308; Lodge, "Shakespeare's Americanisms," p. 252; Brander Matthews, "Foreign Words in English Speech," *HM* 107 (Aug. 1903): 476; John Fiske, "Who Are the Aryans?" *AM* 47 (Feb. 1881): 229; Lafcadio Hearn, "English, the Universal Tongue of the Future," Oct. 23, 1881, in *Editorials* (Boston: Houghton, Mifflin, 1926), p. 167.

37. Furness's letter appears in "English in the High School," *Modern Language Notes* 1 (Nov. 1886): 218. Willis D. Jacobs surveys seven of Barnes's philological works in *William Barnes, Linguist* (Albuquerque: Univ. of New Mexico Press, 1952); Dennis Baron treats the work of Elias Molee in *Grammar and Good Taste*, pp. 182-86.

38. *President's Report, University of Chicago, July 1897-July 1898*, pp. 57-59; James M. Garnett, "The Position of Old English in a General Education," *Academy* 5 (Feb. 1890): 122. Further evidence of the importance of Anglo-Saxon in the universities is presented by Gossett, *Race*, pp. 126-33; Jones, *Theory of American Literature*, pp. 87-95.

39. T.L.K. Oliphant quoted in *GLB* 89 (July 1874): 90; Charles Dudley Warner, "Editor's Study," *HM* 108 (Dec. 1903): 162; "Editor's Table," *HM* 14 (Dec. 1856): 125; "Editor's Table," *HM* 14 (May 1857): 845; "Samples of Fine English," *HM* 22 (March 1861): 545; "Editor's Literary Record," *HM* 41 (Aug. 1870): 463; 14 (Dec. 1856): 125.

40. For instance, Hall, "Retrogressive English," p. 327; Edgar Fawcett, "Certain Points of Style in Writing," *Lipp.* 52 (July 1893): 126.

41. For Howells's attacks on England and English criticism, see his "Editor's Study," *HM* 75 (June 1887): 157; 79 (Nov. 1889): 966; 80 (Jan.

1890) 320-21; WDH to Bayard Taylor, Nov. 24, 1868, *Selected Letters* 1:308; to John W. DeForest, Sept. 2, 1887, ibid., 3:195; to T. W. Higginson, Aug. 14, 1881, ibid., 2:292.

42. WDH, *Tuscan Cities* (Boston: Ticknor, 1886), p. 14; "The Militant Muse," *HW* 46 (Jan. 18, 1902): 69; "Life and Letters," *HW* 40 (Jan. 4, 1896): 7; *Their Silver Wedding Journey* 2:370; "Life and Letters," *HW* 40 (March 28, 1896): 294; "American Literature in Exile," *Literature*, n.s. 1 (March 3, 1899): 170.

43. ES, *HM* 72 (May 1886): 975; 83 (Nov. 1891): 963; "Some Books of Short Stories," *Literature* 3 (Dec. 31, 1898): 628.

44. WDH, "Suggestions of a Patriotic Play," *Literature* 4 (March 11, 1899): 264; "Race-Patriotism," *HW* 46 (May 10, 1902): 585; EEC, *HW* 113 (Sept. 1906): 636-37. A different argument against the promotion of English as the international language was advanced by Albert Sching, who asserted that to become universal a language must suffer "disfigurement and flattening." "Will English Be the International Language?" *NAR* 189 (May 1909): 770.

45. WDH's "Our Italian Assimilators," *HW* 53 (April 10, 1909): 28.

46. EEC, *HM* 113 (Oct. 1906): 798; ES, *HM* 75 (Oct. 1887): 803; 78 (March 1889): 660.

47. WDH, *Certain Delightful English Towns* (New York: Harper, 1906), p. 1; WDH to S. Weir Mitchell, Dec. 12, 1904, *Selected Letters* 5:113. He praised Hardy in 53 (April 10, 1909): 28.

48. "Suggestions of a Patriotic Play," p. 265; EEC, *HM* 102 (Feb. 1901): 478.

49. *AM* 29 (Feb. 1872): 241; *Impressions and Experiences* (New York: Harper, 1896), p. 238; *AM* 22 (Sept. 1868): 374; "An Italian View of Humor," *NAR* 173 (Nov. 1901): 709, 710; WDH to William Cooper Howells, Nov. 12, 1882, *Life in Letters* 1:326.

50. ES, *HM* 74 (Dec. 1886): 161; 73 (June 1886): 156.

51. "Professor Barrett Wendell's Notions," p. 631; ES, *HM* 74 (Dec. 1886): 161.

52. Jones, *Theory of American Literature*, p. 79.

53. Pancoast, *Introduction to American Literature*, p. 6.

Chapter Four. Realism and Dialect

1. ES, *HM* 75 (Oct. 1887): 803 (Howells slightly misquotes the passage from Emerson); 76 (Feb. 1888): 479; 79 (July 1889): 315 (see also Howells's letter to William Archer, Sept. 17, 1890, in C. Archer,

William Archer, Life, Work and Friendships [London: Allen and Unwin, 1931], p. 188). WDH, "Some Books of Short Stories," *Literature* 3 (Dec. 31, 1898): 628.

2. *Public Ledger* (Philadelphia), Nov. 29, 1914; ES, *HM* 81 (July 1890): 317: 76 (Dec. 1887): 154.

3. ES, *HM* 73 (Aug. 1886): 478; 74 (Feb. 1887): 483; 83 (July 1891): 317; 74 (May 1887): 987; "Life and Letters," *HW* 39 (June 1, 1895): 508.

4. "Life and Letters," *HW* 40 (March 7, 1896): 223; 39 (May 11, 1895): 436.

5. ES, *HM* 72 (Jan. 1886): 324; "Life and Letters," *HW* 39 (June 22, 1895): 581.

6. *AM* 21 (June 1868): 761: 34 (Sept. 1874): 363; 19 (Jan. 1867): 125.

7. Lynn, *William Dean Howells*, pp. 167-68.

8. ES, *HM* 72 (Jan. 1886): 324-25; 75 (Sept. 1887): 640; "Certain of the Chicago School of Fiction," *NAR* 176 (May 1903): 738; "Life and Letters," *HW* 39 (Oct. 26, 1895): 1013.

9. John Hay to WDH, Dec. 29, 1870, *John Hay-Howells Letters*, p. 14; Hamlin Garland, *Roadside Meetings* (New York: Macmillan, 1930), p. 104; ES, *HM* 85 (June 1892): 156.

10. Warner, "Editor's Study," *HM* 92 (May 1896): 961; John Kendrick Bangs, "Literary Notes," *HM* 98 (April 1899): 1; Frederic Bird, "Bad Story-Telling," *Lipp.* 60 (Oct. 1897): 539; T.C. DeLeon, "The Day of Dialect," *Lipp.* 60 (Nov. 1897): 680-82; James Whitcomb Riley, "Dialect in Literature," *Forum* 14 (Dec. 1892): 466, 467; "The Novel of Dialect," *The American Essays of Henry James*, edited with an introduction by Leon Edel (New York: Vintage, 1956), pp. 253-54. See also DeLeon, "Day of Dialect," p. 681; James W. Gerard, "Some American Changes," *Lipp.* 48 (July 1891): 109; and George Wakeman, "The Confusion of Tongues," *Galaxy* 2 (Nov. 1, 1866): 446-47.

11. EEC, *HM* 134 (Feb. 1917): 442; *AM* 22 (Oct. 1868): 511; "Life and Letters," *HW* 39 (June 22, 1895): 581; *AM* 33 (June 1874): 745; 19 (Jan. 1867): 124.

12. WDH, "A Psychological Counter-Current in Recent Fiction," *NAR* 173 (Dec. 1901): 880; *AM* 41 (Jan. 1878): 140; EEC, *HM* 112 (May 1906): 959; ES, *HM* 75 (Sept. 1887): 640.

13. ES, *HM* 72 (May 1886): 973; 75 (Sept. 1887): 639; 77 (July 1888): 317; *My Literary Passions*, pp. 211, 232; ES, *HM* 75 (Sept. 1887): 641.

14. WDH, "Concerning a Counsel of Imperfection," *Literature*, n.s. 1 (April 7, 1899): 290.

15. EEC, *HM* 134 (March 1917): 595.

16. See, for instance, *HM* 22 (Dec. 1860): 131; 22 (Jan. 1861): 262; 24 (May 1862): 840; 26 (Feb. 1863): 413; 31 (Aug. 1865): 393; 32 (Dec. 1865): 121.

17. Charles C. Abbott, "The Unlettered Learned," *Lipp.* 62 (July 1898): 125; Charles Dudley Warner, "Editor's Study," *HM* 95 (Nov. 1897): 962.

18. Baron, *Grammar and Good Taste*, p. 21; Spiller, *James Fenimore Cooper*, pp. 32, 31; Baron, *Grammar and Good Taste*, p. 35; Price Collier, "Gentle Speech," *NAR* 188 (Nov. 1908): 717; A.S. Hill, "Colloquial English," *HM* 78 (Jan. 1889): 273; Mrs. Burton Kingsland, *Correct Social Usage*, p. 47.

Chapter Five. The Problem of "Negro Dialect" in Literature

1. Brander Matthews, "The English Language: Its Debt to King Alfred," *HM* 103 (June 1901): 143; Charles Nordhoff, "Prodigious Talkers," *HM* 23 (July 1861): 197; Charles Dudley Warner, "Editor's Study," *HM* 91 (July 1895): 313.

2. Quotations are from *Scrib. Mon.* "Mahsr John," 14 (May 1877): 127; "Novern People," 13 (Jan. 1877): 430; "Precepts at Parting," 12 (Sept. 1876): 767; "Uncle Gabe's White Folks," 13 (April 1877): 882; "Kree," 12 (Oct. 1876): 916.

3. *Scrib. Mon.* 15 (Jan. 1878): 446.

4. Joel Chandler Harris, Intro. to *Poems by Irwin Russell* (New York: Century, 1888), x, xi; Louis Rubin, "Southern Local Color and the Black Man," *Southern Review*, n.s. 6 (Oct. 1970): 1011-30; Joel Chandler Harris, introduction to *Uncle Remus: His Songs and His Sayings*, in *The Complete Tales of Uncle Remus*, comp. Richard Chase (Boston: Houghton, Mifflin, 1955), xxvi-xxvii.

5. Irwin Russell, "The Mississippi Witness," *Scrib. Mon.* 13 (Dec. 1876): 286; *Century* 30 (Oct. 1885): 975; *HM* 76 (Jan. 1888): 325; 14 (Dec. 1856): 142. For more examples of cartoons, poems, and stories that caricature blacks in the popular magazines, see Rayford W. Logan, *The Negro in American Life and Thought: The Nadir, 1877-1901* (New York: Dial Press, 1954), esp. ch. 13, pp. 239-74.

6. *HM* 77 (Aug. 1888): 319-20.

7. Jean Wagner, *Black Poets of the United States: From Paul Laurence Dunbar to Langston Hughes*, tr. Kenneth Douglas (Urbana: Univ. of Illinois Press, 1973), pp. 205, 106; Sterling Brown, *The Negro in American Fiction* (New York: Argosy, 1969), pp. 53-54; Rubin,

"Southern Local Color," p. 1016. The stereotypes are identified by Sterling Brown, "Negro Character as Seen by White Authors," *Journal of Negro Education* 2 (April 1933): 180-200. See also William L. Andrews, *The Literary Career of Charles W. Chesnutt* (Baton Rouge: Louisiana State Univ. Press, 1980), p. 47; Benjamin Brawley, *The Negro in Literature and Art in the United States* (New York: Duffield, 1930), p. 197; Logan, *Negro in American Life and Thought,* p. 162; William H. Robinson, ed., *Early Black American Poets* (Dubuque, Iowa: Wm. C. Brown, 1969), p. 229. For defense of the white southerners' rendering of dialect of blacks, see John Herbert Nelson, *The Negro Character in American Literature* (College Park, Md.: McGrath, 1926).

8. Thomas Nelson Page, letter in *Critic,* n.s. 4 (July 4, 1885): 6; Stella Brewer Brookes, *Joel Chandler Harris: Folklorist* (Athens: Univ. of Georgia Press, 1950), p. 119; Harris, *Life and Letters of Joel Chandler Harris,* pp. 403-404; *Complete Tales of Uncle Remus,* p. xxi; *Atlanta Constitution,* editorial, April 9, 1880, quoted by Paul M. Cousins, *Joel Chander Harris: A Biography* (Baton Rouge: Louisiana State Univ. Press, 1968), pp. 111, 108-09.

9. Charles Foster Smith, *Southern Bivouac* 4 (Nov. 1885): 350-51 Charles Coleman, "The Recent Movement in Southern Literature," *HM* 74 (May 1887): 848.

10. *New York Evening Post,* Dec. 6, 1880, quoted by Cousins, *Joel Chandler Harris,* p. 115; Winston, *Lipp.* 62 (Aug. 1898): 296.

11. George Philip Krapp, "Literary Dialects," *The English Language in America,* 2 vols. (New York: Ungar, 1960 [1925], esp. 1:246-51; Sumner Ives, "Dialect Differentiation in the Stories of Joel Chandler Harris," *American Literature* 27 (Nov. 1955): 92; William Cecil Elam, "Lingo in Literature," *Lipp.* 55 (Feb. 1895): 286.

12. Quoted in Logan, *Negro in American Life and Thought,* p. 241. For evidence of Chesnutt's desire to turn away from the story in dialect, see Andrews, *Literary Career of Charles W. Chesnutt,* pp. 21, 22; Frances Richardson Keller, *An American Crusade: The Life of Charles Waddell Chesnutt* (Provo, Utah: Brigham Young Univ. Press, 1978), p. 121.

13. Thomas Nelson Page, letter in *Critic,* n.s. 4 (July 4, 1885): 6; (Aug. 1, 1885): 53; (Sept. 5, 1885): 114.

14. Thomas Nelson Page, *The Negro: The Southerner's Problem* (New York: Scribner's, 1904), pp. 259, 292; WDH, "American Letter: The Southern States in Recent American Literature," *Literature* 3 (Sept. 17, 1898): 258; ES, *HM.* 83 (Sept. 1891): 641.

15. WDH, "Life and Letters," *HW* 40 (June 27, 1896): 630. For

discussion of the importance of Howells's recognition of Dunbar, see Cady, *Realist at War*, pp. 161-63; Clare R. Goldfarb, "The Question of William Dean Howells' Racism," *Ball State University Forum* 12 (1971): 22-25; James B. Stronks, "Paul Laurence Dunbar and William Dean Howells," *Ohio Historical Quarterly* 67 (April 1958): 95-108.

16. WDH, "Life and Letters," *HW* 40 (June 27, 1896): 630.

17. WDH, intro. to *Lyrics of Lowly Life* (New York: Dodd, Mead, 1896), p. xvii.

18. Paul Laurence Dunbar to WDH, July 13, 1896, in *The Paul Laurence Dunbar Reader*, ed. Jay Martin and Gossie H. Hudson (New York: Dodd, Mead, 1975), p. 435; WDH to Ripley Hitchcock, July 29, 1896, Columbia Univ.

19. Dunbar to WDH, Sept. 19, 1896, in *Paul Laurence Dunbar Reader*, p. 436; Stronks, "Paul Laurence Dunbar and William Dean Howells," 104.

20. Dunbar to James Newton Matthews, August 12, 1893, in *Paul Laurence Dunbar Reader*, p. 423; Lida Keck Wiggins, *The Life and Works of Paul Laurence Dunbar* (New York: Kraus Reprint, 1971), p. 109; *Paul Laurence Dunbar Reader*, p. 262. For Dunbar's interest in dialect and his debt to Riley, see Benjamin Brawley, *Paul Laurence Dunbar: Poet of His People* (Chapel Hill: Univ. of North Carolina Press, 1936), pp. 74-75; Virginia Cunningham, *Paul Laurence Dunbar and His Song* (New York: Biblo and Tanner, 1969), p. 57; James Weldon Johnson, preface to first edition of *The Book of American Negro Poetry*, reprinted in the revised edition (New York: Harcourt, Brace & World, 1931), p. 50; *Paul Laurence Dunbar Reader*, pp. 18, 261-62, 410; Peter Revell, *Paul Laurence Dunbar* (Boston: Twayne, 1979), pp. 80-84, 91-92; Myron Simon, "Dunbar and Dialect Poetry," in *A Singer in the Dawn: Reinterpretations of Paul Laurence Dunbar*, ed. Jay Martin (New York: Dodd, Mead, 1975), p. 126; Wagner, *Black Poets of the United States*, pp. 76, 108.

21. Johnson, preface to first edition of *Book of Negro Poetry*, pp. 40, 41; idem, preface to revised edition of *Book of Negro Poetry*, p. 5; J. Saunders Redding, *To Make a Poet Black* (Chapel Hill: Univ. of North Carolina Press, 1931), pp. 62-63.

22. Sarah Webster Fabio, "Who Speaks Negro?" in *Black Expression: Essays By and About Black Americans in the Creative Arts*, ed. Addison Gayle, Jr. (New York: Weybright and Talley, 1969), p. 117; Wagner, *Black Poets of the United States*, p. 111. See also Bert Bender, "The Lyrical Short Fiction of Dunbar and Chesnutt," in *A Singer in the Dawn*, pp. 211-12; Robert Farnsworth, "Testing the Color Line—Dun-

bar and Chesnutt," in *The Black American Writer*, vol. 1: *Fiction*, ed. C.W.E. Bigsby (Deland, Fla.: Everett/Edwards, 1969), p. 111; Addison Gayle, Jr., "Literature as Catharsis," in *A Singer in the Dawn*, p. 142; Revell, *Paul Laurence Dunbar*, pp. 45, 164-65; Robinson, *Early Black American Poets*, p. 230; Kenny J. Williams, "The Masking of the Novelist," in *A Singer in the Dawn*, pp. 161, 201.

23. Dickson Bruce, Jr., "On Dunbar's 'Jingles in a Broken Tongue': Dunbar's Dialect Poetry and the Afro-American Folk Tradition," *A Singer in the Dawn*, pp. 95-99; Chidi Ikonné, *From DuBois to Van-Vechten: The Early New Negro Literature, 1903-1926* (Westport, Ct.: Greenwood, 1981), p. 54; Darwin Turner, "Paul Laurence Dunbar: The Poet and the Myths," in *A Singer in the Dawn*, p. 72; Brawley, *Negro in Literature and Art*, pp. 198, 68, 72, 74; Stronks, "Paul Laurence Dunbar and William Dean Howells," p. 108.

24. WDH, "The New Poetry," *NAR* 168 (May 1899): 590; *HW* 40 (June 27, 1896): 630.

25. WDH, "Mr. Charles W. Chesnutt's Stories," *AM* 85 (May 1900): 700, 701; "A Psychological Counter-Current in Recent Fiction," *NAR* 173 (Dec. 1901): 882; WDH to Henry B. Fuller, Nov. 10, 1901, *Selected Letters* 4:274; "An Exemplary Citizen," *NAR* 173 (Aug. 1901): 280; intro. to *Lyrics of Lowly Life*, p. xvii.

26. Chesnutt to his publishers at Houghton, Mifflin, Dec. 28, 1901, in Helen M. Chesnutt, *Charles Waddell Chesnutt: Pioneer of the Color Line* (Chapel Hill: Univ. of North Carolina Press, 1952), p. 178; Houston A. Baker, *The Journey Back: Issues in Black Literature and Criticism* (Chicago: Univ. of Chicago Press, 1980), p. 158; Bender, "Lyrical Short Fiction of Dunbar and Chesnutt," p. 218; Gayle, "Literature as Catharsis," p. 142; idem, *Oak and Ivy: A Biography of Paul Laurence Dunbar* (Garden City: Doubleday, 1971), pp. 75-77. The fullest analysis of Howells's view of black writers as expressed in his criticism is William L. Andrews, "William Dean Howells and Charles W. Chesnutt: Criticism and Race Fiction in the Age of Booker T. Washington," *American Literature* 48 (Nov. 1976): 327-39.

Chapter Six. Language, Race, and Nationality
in Howells's Fiction

1. WDH, *AM* 49 (Jan. 1882): 11.

2. See Howells's essay on Washington, "An Exemplary Citizen," *NAR* 73 (Aug. 1901): 280-88.

3. *Paul Laurence Dunbar Reader*, p. 78.

4. WDH, Cambridge Journal, "Memo for Copying the Tragedy of Don Ippolito," Houghton Library, Harvard Univ.

5. HJ, *Literary Reviews and Essays on American, English, and French Literature*, ed. Albert Mordell (New York: Grove, 1957), p. 211.

6. WDH, *Venetian Life*, 2nd ed. (New York: Hurd and Houghton, 1867), pp. 350-53.

7. EEC, *HM* 80 (Jan. 1890): 314.

8. WDH to Annie T. and Aurelia H. Howells, Nov. 13, 1859, *Selected Letters* 1:50; *Years of My Youth*, p. 135.

9. ES, *HM* 72 (May 1886): 973.

10. WDH, "At the Sign of the Savage," *A Fearful Responsibility and Other Stories*, p. 205.

11. For detailed discussion of attitudes towards Jews in Howells's fiction and nonfiction, see George Arms and William M. Gibson, "*Silas Lapham, Daisy Miller* and the Jews," *New England Quarterly* 16 (March 1943): 118-22; Sanford E. Marovitz, "Howells and the Ghetto: 'The Mystery of Misery,' " *Modern Fiction Studies* 16 (Autumn 1970): 345-62; Kermit Vanderbilt, *The Achievement of William Dean Howells: A Reinterpretation* (Princeton: Princeton Univ. Press, 1968), pp. 123-26, 188-89.

12. WDH, *My Literary Passions*, p. 141; EEC, *HM* 130 (May 1915): 959; *Literature*, n.s. 1 (Feb. 10, 1899): 98.

13. Rudolf and Clara M. Kirk, "Abraham Cahan and William Dean Howells: The Story of a Friendship," *American Jewish Historical Quarterly* 52 (Sept. 1962): 37, 40. See also Jules Chametsky, *From the Ghetto: The Fiction of Abraham Cahan* (Amherst: Univ. of Massachusetts Press, 1977), pp. 66-68; idem, "Regional Literature and Ethnic Realities," *Antioch Review* 31 (1971): 387; Louis Harap, *The Image of the Jew in American Literature: From Early Republic to Mass Immigration* (Philadelphia: Jewish Publication Society of America, 1974), p. 495; Marowitz, "Howells and the Ghetto," pp. 354-55.

14. WDH, "New York Low Life in Fiction," *New York World*, July 26, 1896, II: 18. In *The American Scene*, describing the East Side cafés in New York, James prophesied: "The accent of the very ultimate future, in the States, may be destined to become the most beautiful on the globe and the very music of humanity (here the 'ethnic' synthesis shrouds itself thicker than ever); but whatever we shall know it for, certainly, we shall not know it for English—in any sense for which there is an existing literary measure." *The American Scene*, ed. with an intro. by W.H. Auden (New York: Scribner's, 1946), p. 139.

15. Abraham Cahan, *Yekl: A Tale of the New York Ghetto* (New York:

D. Appleton, 1896), p. 36. Subsequent references to this edition will be given in parentheses in the text. The language of Cahan's characters in *Yekl* and other works is analyzed by Chametsky in *From the Ghetto*, pp. 49-63. Cahan recounts his own experiences in learning English in his autobiography, *The Education of Abraham Cahan*, trans. Leon Stein, Abraham P. Conan, and Lynn Davison, from the Yiddish autobiography, *Bleter fun mein Leben* (Philadelphia: Jewish Publication Society of America, 1969), pp. 238-41.

16. See Harap, *Image of the Jew in American Literature*, pp. 495-96.

17. WDH, "American Letter: Some Books of Short Stories," *Literature* 3 (Dec. 31, 1898): 629.

18. EEC, *HM* 102 (Feb. 1901): 480.

19. EEC, *HM* 117 (Oct. 1908): 798; WDH, Travel Diary, Rockaway Beach, July 25, 1896, Houghton Library, Harvard Univ.

20. WDH to William Cooper Howells, April 25, 1896, Houghton Library, Harvard Univ. For discussion of Howells's dislike of the Irish, see Vanderbilt, *Achievement of William Dean Howells*, pp. 111-16. The attitudes of Howells's New England contemporaries are analyzed in detail in Barbara Miller Solomon. *Ancestors and Immigrants: A Changing New England Tradition* (Cambridge: Harvard Univ. Press, 1956).

21. EEC, *HM* 114 (Dec. 1906): 156.

22. Gregory L. Crider, "Howells' Altruria: The Ambivalent Utopia," *Old Northwest* 1 (1975): 410.

23. See for instance his letter to William Cooper Howells, June 3, 1883: "Elinor and I have quite changed our minds about the Italians; we now think them not only very sympathetic and brilliant, but really and thoroughly good hearted." *Selected Letters* 3:67. WDH to T.S. Perry, Jan. 9, 1905: "I'm mentally and morally a Russophile, and I wish the Russian people all good." *Life in Letters* 2: 204. WDH to Joseph A. Howells, Christmas, 1908: "In every generous and enlightened political and religious move [France] has led the world.... There is now more democracy and equality in France than with us." Houghton Library, Harvard Univ.

24. WDH to Hjalmar Boyesen, Dec. 29, 1872, Sept. 27, 1880, March 27, 1873, William Dean Howells Collection (Accession No. 5651), Clifton Waller Barrett Library, Manuscripts Department, Univ. of Virginia Library; quoted by permission. "New York Low Life in Fiction," p. 18.

25. WDH, "Mr. Harben's Georgia Fiction," *NAR* 191 (March 1910): 357.

26. WDH, "Concerning a Counsel of Imperfection," *Literature*, n.s. 1 (April 7, 1899): 290.

Chapter Seven. Language and Class in the Early Novels

1. WDH, *The English Language in America*, 2 vols. (New York: Century, 1925), 1:228.

2. WDH to William Cooper Howells, March 12, 1871, Houghton Library, Harvard Univ. WDH to J.M. Comly, March 31, 1871, quoted by Olov Fryckstedt, *In Quest of America: A Study of Howells' Early Development as a Novelist* (Cambridge: Harvard Univ. Press, 1958), p. 102.

3. John K. Reeves, "The Limited Realism of Howells' *Their Wedding Journey*, *PMLA* 72 (Dec. 1962): 621.

4. The Marches' sense of superiority to and detachment from those they observe has been analyzed by George C. Carrington, Jr., *The Immense Complex Drama: The World and Art of the Howells Novel* (Columbus: Ohio State Univ. Press, 1966), pp. 129-30, 148; Clayton L. Eichelberger, "William Dean Howells: Perception and Ambivalence," *The Chief Glory of Every People: Essays on Classic American Writers*, ed. Matthew J. Bruccoli (Carbondale: Southern Illinois Univ. Press, 1973), pp. 125-27; David L. Frazier, *"Their Wedding Journey:* Howells' Fictional Craft," *New England Quarterly* 42 (Sept. 1969): 323-49; Habegger, *Gender, Fantasy, and Realism*, pp. 81-82; Gary A. Hunt, "A Reality that Can't Be Quite Definitely Spoken: Sexuality in *Their Wedding Journey*," *Studies in the Novel* 9 (Spring 1977): 117-32; Henry Nash Smith, "Fiction and American Ideology: The Genesis of Howells' Early Realism," *The American Self: Myth, Ideology, and Popular Culture*, ed. Sam B. Girgus (Albuquerque: Univ. of New Mexico Press, 1981), pp. 43-57.

5. "Literature of the Day," *Lipp*. 9 (June 1872): 726.

6. Quoted by T.W. Higginson, "The Test of Talk," *Book and Heart: Essays on Literature* (New York: Harper, 1897), pp. 218-19.

7. T.S. Perry, "William Dean Howells," *Century* 23 (March 1882): 684; WDH to Bayard Taylor, Sept. 5, 1871, Cornell Univ.

8. The satiric effects of this and other passages are analyzed by Carrington, *Immense Complex Drama*, pp. 55-56, 221-22.

9. *Letters of Theodore Dreiser: A Selection*, 3 vols., ed. with preface and notes by Robert H. Elias (Philadelphia: Univ. of Pennsylvania Press, 1959), 1:121; Dorothy Dudley, *Forgotten Frontiers: Dreiser and the Land of the Free* (New York: Harrison Smith and Robert Haas,

1932), p. 142; Fryckstedt, *In Quest of America*, p. 268; Dreiser to George Ade, *Lettters of Theodore Dreiser* 3:949.

10. Fryckstedt, *In Quest of America*, p. 106.

11. See, for instance, Carrington, *Immense Complex Drama*, pp. 150-51; Marion W. Cumpiano, "The Dark Side of *Their Wedding Journey*," *American Literature* 44 (Jan. 1969): 472-86; Frazier, *"Their Wedding Journey,"* pp. 326-31, 337-42; Hunt, "A Reality," pp. 19-23; Habegger, *Gender, Fantasy, and Realism*, pp. 82-84; Kenneth Seib, "Uneasiness at Niagara: Howells' *Their Wedding Journey*," *Studies in American Fiction* 4 (Spring 1976): 15-25.

12. Fryckstedt, *In Quest of America*, pp. 104-111; Reeves, "Limited Realism," p. 617; Henry Adams, "Their Wedding Journey," *NAR* 114 (April 1872): 444.

13. HJ to WDH, Sept. 9, 1873, *Henry James Letters* 1:401-02.

14. *The Novels and Tales of Henry James* (New York: Scribner's, 1901), 18:15,51.

15. James Tuttleton, "Howells and the Manners of the Good Heart," *Modern Fiction Studies* 16 (Autumn 1970): 286.

16. WDH to William Cooper Howells, Feb. 5, 1873, *Selected Letters* 2:13. See also William M. Gibson, "Materials and Forms in Howells's First Novels," *American Literature* 19 (1947): 158-59.

17. WDH to HJ, March 10, 1873, *Selected Letters* 2:17.

18. Ibid.

19. Ibid.

20. WDH, *Heroines of Fiction*, 2 vols. (New York: Harper, 1901), 1:47. WDH, intro. to *Pride and Prejudice* (New York: Scribner's, 1918), xi. The resemblances between Jane Austen and Howells were stressed by J.M. Robertson, "Mr. Howells' Novels," *Westminster Review* 122 (Oct. 1884): 349. See also William M. Gibson, *William Dean Howells* (Minneapolis: Univ. of Minnesota Press, 1967), p. 18.

21. *HM* 47 (Aug. 1873): 461; WDH, *Literary Friends and Acquaintance: A Personal Retrospect of American Authorship* (New York: Harper, 1901), p. 149; HJ to WDH, Sept. 9, June 22, 1873, *Henry James Letters* 1:401, 396; T.S. Perry, "William Dean Howells," *Century* 23 (1882): 684.

22. *Complete Plays*, p. 50.

23. Quoted from Cahan's lecture on "Realism" (1889) by Rudolf and Clara Kirk, "Abraham Cahan and William Dean Howells," p. 29.

24. WDH to William Cooper Howells, April 20, 1873, *Selected Letters* 2:24.

25. *Sarah Orne Jewett Letters*, edited with an introduction and

notes by Richard Cary (Waterville, Maine: Colby College Press, 1956), pp. 19-20; *The Best Short Stories of Sarah Orne Jewett*, intro. by Willa Cather (Gloucester, Mass.: Peter Smith, 1965), p. 73.

26. John Hay to WDH, April 4, 1879, *John Hay-Howells Letters*, p. 37.

27. WDH to John Hay, May 2, 1879, *John Hay-Howells Letters*, p. 38. George N. Bennett, in *William Dean Howells: The Development of a Novelist* (Norman: Univ. of Oklahoma Press, 1959), p. 69, stresses the effectiveness of the "varying accents" in characterizing the speakers in the novel.

28. *Lipp.* 23 (June 1879): 776.

29. John W. Crowley, "An Interoceanic Episode: *The Lady of the 'Aroostook,'* " *American Literature* 49 (May 1977): 180, 190.

30. Edwin Cady, *The Gentleman in America: A Literary Study in American Culture* (Syracuse: Syracuse Univ. Press, 1949), p. 190.

31. Bridgman, *Colloquial Style in America*, pp. 73-76, 17.

Chapter Eight. Language and Class in Novels
of Country and City

1. HJ to WDH, April 7, 1879, *Henry James Letters* 2:226-27; HJ to WDH, July 22, 1879, and January 3, 1880, Houghton Library, Harvard Univ.

2. For discussion of Hawthorne's influence in *The Undiscovered Country,* see Richard H. Brodhead, "Hawthorne among the Realists: The Case of Howells," in *American Realism: New Essays* (Baltimore: Johns Hopkins Univ. Press, 1982), pp. 29-32; Paul John Eakin, *The New England Girl: Cultural Ideals in Hawthorne, Stowe, Howells, and James* (Athens: Univ. of Georgia Press, 1976), pp. 92-95; Robert Emmet Long, *The Great Succession: Henry James and the Legacy of Hawthorne* (Pittsburgh: Univ. of Pittsburgh Press, 1979), pp. 141-46; Kermit Vanderbilt, *Achievement of William Dean Howells*, pp. 46-47.

3. *AM* 37 (June 1876): 708-09.

4. Ibid., p. 704.

5. *The Complete Tales of Henry James*, 12 vols., ed. Leon Edel (Philadelphia: Lippincott, 1961-64), 3:271, 285.

6. HJ to WDH, July 20, 1880, *Henry James Letters* 2:299, 300.

7. William Lyon Phelps in *New Haven Journal-Courier*, May 14, 1920, p. 8; "A Dialogue between William Dean Howells and Hjalmar

Hjorth Boyesen" (1893), in "Interviews with William Dean Howells," ed. Ulrich Halfmann, *American Literary Realism* 6 (Fall 1973): 309. John Hay to WDH, Nov. 30, 1881; *John Hay-Howells Letters* p. 54.

8. Baron, *Grammar and Good Taste*, p. 29.

9. Bartley's parody of sentimental fiction is most fully analyzed by Fred G. See, "The Demystification of Style: Metaphoric and Metonymic Language in *A Modern Instance*," *Nineteenth-Century Fiction* 28 (March 1974): 392-95.

10. *Century Magazine* 23 (Dec. 1881): 252. For discussion of Howells's attitude of superiority to the colloquialisms of his characters in *A Modern Instance* and *The Rise of Silas Lapham*, see William C. Fischer, Jr., "William Dean Howells: Reverie and the Nonsymbolic Aesthetic," *Nineteenth-Century Fiction* 25 (June 1970): 1-30.

11. Horace Scudder, "A Modern Instance," *AM* 50 (Nov. 1882): 711. ES, *HM* 81 (July 1890): 318, 317.

12. Henry Nash Smith, *Democracy and the Novel: Popular Resistance to Classic American Writers* (New York: Oxford Univ. Press, 1978), p. 100. Smith documents Howells's shifting attitude toward Bartley by comparing passages in which Bartley's thoughts, vulgar but plausible, are represented in his own slangy idiom, and those which sacrifice realism to the rhetoric of stage melodrama and Christian theology (pp. 82-93). Other critics who find ambivalence in Howells's portrayal of Bartley include Brodhead, "Hawthorne among the Realists," p. 35; Paul A. Eschholz, "Howells' *A Modern Instance:* A Realist's Moralistic Vision of America," *South Dakota Review* 10 (Spring 1972): 91-102; George M. Spangler, "Moral Anxiety in *A Modern Instance*," *New England Quarterly* 46 (June 1973): 236-49; Jacqueline Tavernier-Courbin, "Towards the City: Howells' Characterization in *A Modern Instance*," *Modern Fiction Studies* 24 (Spring 1978): 111-27. Habegger analyzes Bartley Hubbard as the double of Ben Halleck, the two characters embodying "the two opposed gender ideals that divided Howells." *Gender, Fantasy, and Realism*, p. 96.

13. Brodhead, "Hawthorne among the Realists," p. 36.

14. *A Woman's Reason* has received little critical attention. Its importance as a picture of American society and its class structure is noted by Bennett, *William Dean Howells*, p. 146, and by Fryckstedt, *Quest for America*, pp. 215-16. See also George Arms, "A Novel and Two Letters," *Journal of the Rutgers University Library* 7 (June 1944): 9-13.

15. Janet McKay, *Narration and Discourse in American Realistic Fiction* (Philadelphia: Univ. of Pennsylvania Press, 1982), p. 106. The

chapter on *Silas Lapham* is the most detailed study of the narrator's attitude as revealed through the characters' speech.

16. Firkins, *William Dean Howells*, p. 115. Habegger analyzes Penelope's humor as essentially that of a "vernacular male storyteller" in *Gender, Fantasy, and Realism in American Literature*, pp. 184-95. Elizabeth Stevens Priorleau stresses Penelope's use of humor as a legitimate means of engaging in rivalry with her sister and attracting Tom Corey to herself. *The Circle of Eros: Sexuality in the Works of William Dean Howells* (Durham, N.C.: Duke Univ. Press, 1983), pp. 79-80.

17. Habegger, *Gender, Fantasy, and Realism*, p. 190.

18. McKay, *Narration and Discourse*, pp. 49, 107-14.

19. George C. McWhorter, "Etiquette," *HM* 36 (Feb. 1868): 386.

20. WDH, Travel Diary, London, Aug. 2, 1882, Houghton Library, Harvard Univ.

21. William James to WDH, June 21, 1891, Houghton Library, Harvard Univ. Alan Trachtenberg, *The Incorporation of America: Culture and Society in the Gilded Age* (New York: Hill and Wang, 1982), p. 192.

22. S. Foster, "W.D. Howells: *The Rise of Silas Lapham*," in *The Monster in the Mirror: Studies in Nineteenth-Century Realism*, ed. D.A. Williams (Oxford: Oxford Univ. Press, 1978), p. 176. Other critics have likewise questioned the plausibility of Silas's sacrifices. See, for instance, Elaine R. Hedges, "*Cesar Birotteau* and *The Rise of Silas Lapham*: A Study in Parallels," *Nineteenth-Century Fiction* 17 (Sept. 1962): 171-73; Robie Macauley, " 'Let Me Tell You about the Rich,' " *Kenyon Review* 37 (Autumn 1965): 658; H.E. Scudder, *AM* 56 (Oct. 1885): 554-56. Others accept Silas's sacrifices as essential to the symbolic pattern and ethical theme of the novel. See, for instance, John E. Hart, "The Commonplace as Heroic in *The Rise of Silas Lapham*," *Modern Fiction Studies* 8 (Winter 1962-63): 375-76, 382-83; Donald Pizer, "The Ethical Unity of *The Rise of Silas Lapham*," *American Literature* 32 (Nov. 1960): 326 and *passim;* G. Thomas Tanselle, "The Architecture of *The Rise of Silas Lapham*," *American Literature* 37 (Jan. 1966): 456-57. Cady analyzes the concluding chapters as the vision of a "literary realist" in *The Road to Realism*, p. 239.

23. Critics do not agree on which group of characters, if any, Howells favors. Alfred Kazin has called Howells a "slave of Corey's sterile elegance," in "Howells the Bostonian," *Clio* 3 (Feb. 1974): 231. Others who believe that Howells favors the Coreys over the Laphams include Ralph Behrens, "Howells' Portrait of a Boston Brahmin," *Markham Review* 3 (Oct. 1972): 72; Firkins, *William Dean Howells*, p.

113; McKay, *Narration and Discourse,* pp. 96-97 and *passim.* The opposing view, that the gentility of the Coreys suffers in comparison with the energy and integrity of the Laphams, is argued by Bennett, *William Dean Howells,* p. 155; Cady, *Road to Realism,* p. 231; and Harold Kolb, Jr., *The Illusion of Life: American Realism as a Literary Form* (Charlottesville: Univ. of Virginia Press, 1969), p. 88.

Those who believe that Howells sides with neither family against the other but impartially represents the virtues and deficiencies of both groups include Kenneth Eble, *William Dean Howells,* 2nd ed. (Boston: Twayne, 1982), p. 95; Foster, *"The Rise of Silas Lapham,"* p. 164; Habegger, *Gender, Fantasy, and Realism,* p. 193; and Vanderbilt, *Achievement of William Dean Howells,* p. 136.

Chapter Nine. Language and Complicity in *The Minister's Charge*

1. WDH to HJ, Dec. 25, 1886, *Life in Letters* 1:387.
2. H.L. Mencken, *American Language,* pp. 268-69.
3. HJ to WDH, Dec. 7, 1886, *Henry James Letters* 3:148.
4. For a detailed analysis, see Clare R. Goldfarb, "William Dean Howells' *The Minister's Charge:* A Study of Psychological Perception," *Markham Review* 2 (Sept. 1969).
5. WDH to John DeForest, Dec. 9, 1886, *Selected Letters* 3:170.
6. *Lipp.* 38 (Aug. 1886): 225.
7. Edwin Cady, *The Realist at War: The Mature Years, 1885-1920, of William Dean Howells* (Syracuse: Syracuse Univ. Press, 1958), p. 4. Howells's belief that city life offered more advantages than disadvantages is documented by Gregory L. Crider, "William Dean Howells and the Antiurban Tradition: A Reconsideration," *American Studies* 19 (Spring 1978): 55-64.
8. William Alexander notes that Sewell, in his first conversation with Lemuel in Boston, slips into his "preacher's rhetoric" and in showing his pictures to Lemuel speaks of them in phrases habitual to his class but alien to Lemuel. *William Dean Howells: The Realist as Humanist* (New York: Burt Franklin, 1981), p. 51.

Chapter Ten. Language and Equality in the Late Novels

1. Detailed studies of Howells's social philosophy and its backgrounds include Daniel Aaron, *Men of Good Hope: A Story of American*

Progressives (New York: Oxford Univ. Press, 1961), pp. 172-207; George Arms, "The Literary Background of Howells's Social Criticism," *American Literature* 14 (Nov. 1942): 260-76; Louis J. Budd, "Altruism Arrives in America," *American Quarterly* 8 (Spring 1956): 40-52; Richard Foster, "The Contemporaneity of Howells," *New England Quarterly* 32 (March 1959): 54-78; Arnold B. Fox, "Howells' Doctrine of Complicity," *Modern Language Quarterly* 13 (March 1952): 56-60; Peter J. Frederick, *Knights of the Golden Rule: The Intellectual as Christian Social Reformer in the 1890's* (Lexington: Univ. Press of Kentucky, 1976), pp. 37-56; Robert L. Hough, *The Quiet Rebel: William Dean Howells as Social Commentator* (Lincoln: Univ. of Nebraska Press, 1959); Clara M. and Rudolf Kirk, "Howells and the Church of the Carpenter," *New England Quarterly* 32 (June 1959): 185-206; Robert W. Schneider, *Five Novelists of the Progressive Era* (New York: Columbia Univ. Press, 1965), pp. 19-59; Walter F. Taylor, *The Economic Novel in America* (Chapel Hill: Univ. of North Carolina Press, 1942), pp. 214-81.

2. *Nation* 50 (June 5, 1890): 454; *Critic* n.s. 13 (Jan. 11, 1890): 14; "New York in Recent Fiction," *AM* 65 (April 1890): 566.

3. EEC, *HM* 103 (July 1901): 313-14.

4. WDH, "Love-Match," p. 82, Houghton Library, Harvard Univ. On Howells's portrayal of Boston's decline, see Susan Allen Toth, "Character and Focus in *The Landlord at Lion's Head*," *Colby Library Quarterly* ser. 11, no. 2 (June 1975): 116-28; Vanderbilt, *Achievement of William Dean Howells*, pp. 88-95.

5. Gary P. Storhoff, "Ironic Techniques in *The Landlord at Lion's Head*," *North Dakota Quarterly* 46 (Spring 1978): 60.

6. Several critics perceive Westover as snobbish, self-righteous, repressed, and imperceptive. See, for instance, Paul A. Eschholz, "*The Landlord at Lion's Head:* William Dean Howells' Use of the Vermont Scene," *Vermont History* 42 (Winter 1974): 44-47; Storhoff, "Ironic Techniques," pp. 58-62; Toth, Character and Focus," pp. 118-22. Others share Cady's view of Westover as representative of the values of civilization and a "natural gentleman" superior to Jeff Durgin (*Realist at War*, p. 226). See, for instance, William McMurray, "Point of View in Howells's *The Landlord at Lion's Head*," *American Literature* 34 (May 1962): 207-14; Sister Mary Petrus Sullivan, "The Function of Setting in Howells's *The Landlord at Lion's Head*," *American Literature* 35 (March 1963): 38-52.

7. Interview with Stephen Crane, *New York Times*, Oct. 28, 1894, *American Literary Realism* 6 (Fall 1973): 324.

8. George N. Bennett's analysis of *Ragged Lady* as a reworking of the Cinderalla story is the only detailed discussion of the novel. *The Realism of William Dean Howells, 1889-1920* (Nashville: Vanderbilt Univ. Press, 1973), pp. 153-62.

9. *Interviews with William Dean Howells*, p. 324.

10. John Kendrick Bangs, "Literary Notes," *HM* 98 (April 1899): 1.

11. WDH, "The Latest Avatar of American Girlhood," *Literature* 5 (Aug. 12, 1899): 156; ES, *HM* 78 (March 1889): 660; *Impressions and Experiences* (New York: Harper, 1896), p. 274. Subsequent references to this edition will be given in parentheses in the text.

12. WDH to Mr. Garrison, Feb. 7, 1901, Univ. of Virginia; WDH to C.E. Norton, Aug. 6, 1899, Houghton Librtary, Harvard Univ. *Harper's Weekly* 47 (Aug. 1, 1903): 1256.

13. Gregory Crider, "William Dean Howells and the Gilded Age: Socialist in a Fur-lined Overcoat," *Ohio History* 88 (Autum 1979): 416. Other critics who note conflicting sympathies within Howells and his characters include Arthur Boardman, "Social Point of View in the Novels of William Dean Howells," *American Literature* 39 (March 1967): 42-59; William F. Ekstrom, "The Equalitarian Principle in the Fiction of William Dean Howells," *American Literature* 24 (March 1952): 40-50; Lynn, *William Dean Howells*, pp. 300-302 and *passim;* Vanderbilt, *Achievement of William Dean Howells*, pp. 138-43.

14. WDH to HJ, *Selected Letters* 3:231; WDH to William Cooper Howells, ibid., pp. 314, 271, 325.

15. *Literature* 2 (July 2, 1898): 759.

16. WDH to Brander Matthews, Aug. 3, 1902, *Life in Letters* 2:161.

17. "Equality as the Basis of Good Society," *Century* 51 (Nov. 1895): 65.

18. EEC, *HM* 102 (Jan. 1901): 317; "Equality as the Basis of Good Society," pp. 66, 67; *Through the Eye of the Needle*, in *Altrurian Romances*, p. 275.

19. Edwin H. Cady, *The Light of Common Day: Realism in American Fiction* (Bloomington: Indiana Univ. Press, 1971), p. 33; Leo Marx, "The Vernacular Tradition in American Literature," in *Studies in American Culture: Dominant Images and Ideas*, ed. Joseph J. Kwiat and Mary C. Turpie (Minneapolis: Univ. of Minnesota Press, 1960), pp. 113-14.

Notes concluded on next page

Conclusion

1. HJ, "Speech of American Women," p. 50; WDH, "Our Daily Speech," *Harper's Bazar* 15 (Oct. 1906): 933; EEC, *HM* 102 (Jan. 1901): 317.

2. HJ, "Speech of American Women," p. 40; idem, "Our Daily Speech," 933.

3. HJ, "Speech of American Women," pp. 33, 20.

4. HJ, "The Manners of American Women," *Harper's Bazar* 41 (April 1904): 358; idem, "Speech of American Women," p. 35.

5. WDH, "Equality as the Basis of Good Society," p. 65.

6. ES, *HM* 75 (Sept. 1887): 639.

7. Ibid.

8. *Novels and Tales of Henry James*, 163, 164. Subsequent references to *The Princess Casamassima* in this edition will be given in parentheses in the text.

9. ES, *HM* 74 (April 1887): 829.

10. HJ, *The Bostonians* (New York: Random House, 1956), p. 5.

11. WDH, *Literature and Life: Studies* (New York: Harper, 1902), pp. 34-35.

12. William James to WDH, May 26, 1910, Houghton Library, Harvard Univ.

Works of William Dean Howells

Parenthetical references in the text (by page number) are to the following editions.

The Altrurian Romances. Intro. and notes by Clara Kirk and Rudolf Kirk, Bloomington: Indiana Univ. Press, 1968.

Annie Kilburn. New York: Harper, 1889.

April Hopes. Intro. and notes by Kermit Vanderbilt. Bloomington; Indiana Univ. Press, 1974.

A Chance Acquaintance. Ed. Jonathan Thomas and David J. Nordloh. Bloomington: Indiana Univ. Press, 1971.

The Complete Plays of W.D. Howells. Ed. with intro. by Walter J. Meserve. New York: New York Univ. Press, 1960.

Dr. Breen's Practice. Boston: James R. Osgood, 1881.

A Fearful Responsibility and Other Stories. Westport, Conn.: Greenwood, 1970.

Fennel and Rue. New York: Harper, 1908.

A Foregone Conclusion. Boston: James R. Osgood, 1875.

A Hazard of New Fortunes. Intro. by Everett Carter; notes by David J. Nordloh et al. Bloomington: Indiana Univ. Press, 1976.

An Imperative Duty. Intro. and notes by Martha Banta. Bloomington; Indiana Univ. Press, 1970.

Indian Summer. Intro. and notes by Scott Bennett. Bloomington: Indiana Univ. Press, 1971.

The Kentons. Intro. by George C. Carrington, Jr. Bloomington: Indiana Univ. Press, 1971.

The Lady of the Aroostook. Boston: Houghton, James R. Osgood, 1879.

The Landlord at Lion's Head. New York: Harper, 1897.

Letters Home. New York: Harper, 1903.

The Minister's Charge, or The Apprenticeship of Lemuel Barker. Intro. and notes by Howard M. Munford. Bloomington: Indiana Univ. Press, 1978.

Miss Bellard's Inspiration. New York: Harper, 1905.

A Modern Instance. Ed. George N. Bennett. Blooomington: Indiana Univ. Press, 1977.

Mrs. Farrell. Intro. by Mildred Howells. New York: Harper, 1921.

New Leaf Mills: A Chronicle. New York: Harper, 1913.

An Open-Eyed Conspiracy: An Idyl of Saratoga. New York: Harper, 1897.

The Quality of Mercy. Intro. and notes by James P. Elliott. Bloomington: Indiana Univ. Press, 1979.

Ragged Lady. New York: Harper, 1899.

The Rise of Silas Lapham. Intro. and notes by Walter J. Meserve. Bloomington: Indiana Univ. Press, 1971.

Selected Letters. Ed. George Arms et al. 6 vols. Boston: Twayne, 1979-1981.

The Son of Royal Langbrith. Intro. and notes by David Burrows. Bloomington: Indiana Univ. Press, 1969.

The Story of a Play. New York: Harper, 1898.

Suburban Sketches. New York: Hurd and Houghton, 1870.

Their Silver Wedding Journey. New York: Harper, 1899.

Their Wedding Journey. Ed. John K. Reeves. Bloomington: Indiana Univ. Press, 1968.

Through the Eye of the Needle: A Romance. New York: Harper, 1907 (quoted from *Altrurian Romances*).

The Undiscovered Country. Boston: Houghton, Mifflin, 1880.

The Vacation of the Kelwyns: An Idyl of the Middle Eighteen-seventies. New York: Harper, 1920.

A Woman's Reason. Boston: James R. Osgood, 1883.

The World of Chance. New York: Harper, 1893.

Years of My Youth and Three Essays. Intro. and notes by David J. Nordloh, Bloomington: Indiana Univ. Press, 1975.

Index